The JEWS of Prime Time

Murray Friedman and Albert D. Chernin, editors, 1999
  A Second Exodus: The American Movement to Free Soviet Jews

Stephen J. Whitfield, 1999
  In Search of American Jewish Culture

Naomi W. Cohen, 1999
  Jacob H. Schiff: A Study in American Jewish Leadership

Barbara Kessel, 2000
  Suddenly Jewish: Jews Raised as Gentiles

Jonathan N. Barron and Eric Murphy Selinger, editors, 2000
  Jewish American Poetry: Poems, Commentary, and Reflections

Steven T. Rosenthal, 2001
  Irreconcilable Differences: The Waning of the American Jewish Love Affair with Israel

Pamela S. Nadell and Jonathan D. Sarna, editors, 2001
  Women and American Judaism: Historical Perspectives

Annelise Orleck, with photographs by Elizabeth Cooke, 2001
  The Soviet Jewish Americans

Ilana Abramovitch and Seán Galvin, editors, 2001
  Jews of Brooklyn

Ranen Omer-Sherman, 2002
  Diaspora and Zionism in American Jewish Literature: Lazarus, Syrkin, Reznikoff, and Roth

Ori Z. Sotles, 2002
  Fixing the World: Jewish American Painters in the Twentieth Century

David Zurawik, 2003
  The Jews of Prime Time

The Jews of Prime Time

DAVID ZURAWIK

BRANDEIS UNIVERSITY PRESS

Published by University Press of New England

Hanover & London

BRANDEIS UNIVERSITY PRESS

Published by University Press of New England,

37 Lafayette St., Lebanon, NH 03766

© 2003 by David Zurawik

Printed in the United States of America

5 4 3 2 1

Library of Congress Cataloging-in-Publication Data

Zurawik, David.

The Jews of prime time / David Zurawik.

p.   cm.—(Brandeis series in American Jewish history, culture,

and life)

Includes bibliographical references and index.

ISBN 1–58465–234–9 (cloth : alk. paper)

1. Jews on television.   I. Title.   II. Series.

PN1992.8.J48 z87 2003

791.45'6520924—dc21   2002155476

FOR CHRIS STOEHR

writer, critic, and teacher

CONTENTS

ACKNOWLEDGMENTS

This book would not have been possible without the many men and women in the television industry who talked to me about their work. I am grateful to each of them.

I especially want to thank Meredith Baxter, Henry Bromell, Charlotte Brown, Allan Burns, Al Franken, Gary David Goldberg, Zalman King, Barry Levinson, Sidney Lumet, Peter Mehlman, Ken Olin, David Poltrack, Richard Rosenstock, Lynn Roth, and Fred Silverman. The conversations with Brown, Burns, Franken, Goldberg, Lumet, Mehlman, Olin, Rosenstock, and Roth were more than interviews. They were moments of inspiration that reminded me why I started and had to complete this ten-year journey. They shared their great intelligence and vast experience. They spoke candidly about a topic that it has never been easy for any of us to discuss.

I am also grateful to the archives and libraries that provided videotapes or opened their doors to me: The Gertude Berg Papers and the Oral History of Television Project at the E. S. Bird Library, Syracuse University; The National Jewish Archive of Broadcasting of the Jewish Museum, New York; the Motion Picture, Broadcasting, and Recorded Sound Division of the Library of Congress, Washington, D.C.; the University of Maryland Library and Broadcast Pioneers Library of American Broadcasting, College Park, Maryland; YIVO Institute for Jewish Research, New York; Julia Rogers Library at Goucher College, Baltimore, Maryland; and the University of California Los Angeles Film and Television Archive. Special thanks to Stacey May, Michael Henry, and Randy Smith.

Thanks to friends and colleagues at the *Baltimore Sun*, particularly Steve Sullivan and Amy Davis, and to the other critics who have helped me wrestle with this history over the years: David Bianculli, Michael Davis,

Mark Dawidziak, David Eden, Michael Elkin, R. D. Heldenfels, and Gail Shister. Elkin was the first to explore some of the history told in this book in his work at the *Jewish Exponent*, and I am grateful for the ground he broke.

I am also grateful to the Baltimore Jewish Community Center for providing forums to discuss my findings. Specifically, I thank Claudine Davison and those members of the Jewish Film Festival Committee who have been especially involved with me in this discussion: Norman La Cholter, Howard A. Davidov, Joseph Greenblum, and Suzanne S. Lapides. Thanks also to Richard B. Milner.

No group has been more supportive than my academic colleagues, particularly those in the American Studies Department at the University of Maryland, which also offered me many forums in which to refine my thesis, as did the Department of Communication and Media Studies at Goucher College. I am further grateful to the Johns Hopkins University for providing me with a weekly show on its public radio station for four years in which to explore such matters of popular culture. Thanks to Neil Alperstein, Peter Bardaglio, Maurine Beasley, Michael Brody, John Caughey, Donna Flayhan, Douglas Gomery, Myron Lounsbury, Lawrence E. Mintz, David Marc, Lisa Morgan, Sheri Parks, Shirley Peroutka, and Robert J. Thompson. I especially want to thank Mintz and Thompson, two senior scholars who generously walked virtually every mile of this journey with me both intellectually and emotionally. The seed from which this book began was an interview Mintz did with Cherney Berg for the Jewish Museum. Thompson and his Center for the Study of Popular Television at Syracuse University helped open several doors to me in Hollywood along the way. I can never repay their kindness.

In addition to Mintz and Thompson, who also read virtually every word of this book in several drafts, I want to thank Jonathan D. Sarna and Sylvia Barack Fishman of the Department of Near Eastern and Judaic Studies at Brandeis University. As editor and associate editor of the Brandeis series in which this book appears, they also read an early version of the study and offered valuable comments and suggestions.

Of the hundreds of decisions involved in a work like this, perhaps none is as important as where to publish. My deepest thanks to Phyllis Deutsch and Richard Abel at the University Press of New England for their enthusiasm in acquiring *The Jews of Prime Time* and their continued commitment to it. I cannot imagine an editor being more engaged in improving a manuscript that Phyllis Deutsch has been with mine.

I might not have had the pleasure of working with the University Press of New England if not for Meghan Devine, my agent and friend. My heartfelt thanks to her and Gregg Wilhelm at Bookwise Associates in Baltimore.

And I am sure I would have never written this book if not for Chris Stoehr, one of the first television critics in daily newspapers to prepare for that job with specialized graduate study. She is also one of those rare critics who believes we have a moral obligation to write the truth about the television industry no matter what the price. This book is written in admiration and emulation of the example she set.

D.Z.

The JEWS of Prime Time

INTRODUCTION

On Being "Too Jewish" in "This Weird Loop"

You have to understand how much of the creative community through the years has been Jewish. It's complicated to think about Jews writing about Jews—desiring, if you're too realistic, not to seem anti-Semitic. Or, because they're Jewish [desiring] not to be too self-serving. I think a lot of the answers to your question about the history of Jewish characters on television are in that area.

Norman Lear, creator of *All in the Family*[1]

I think one of the things we should talk about is the level of self-censorship that has gone into the depiction of Jews by Jews over the years.

Marshall Herskovitz, co-creator of *thirtysomething*[2]

A riddle: what is "too Jewish" yet not Jewish enough?

An answer: the strange history of Jewish characters on prime-time network television starting in 1949 with *The Goldbergs*, a remarkable CBS sitcom about a multigeneration Jewish family living in a six-room apartment in the Bronx.

I set out in 1991 to explore this landscape of television characters with names like Rhoda and Bernie and the Jewish identity that they came to represent for millions of Americans thinking the study would take two years at most. It was 1998 before I was able to even start making sense of the land on which I stood.

The fog started to lift during an interview in a California hotel room with Al Franken, the Emmy Award–winning writer from *Saturday Night Live* who had gone on to become a bestselling author, actor, and television producer. I was interviewing him in connection with a 1998 NBC midseason series, *Lateline*, in which Franken played a television newsman named Al Freundlich. When Franken, creator of the series, described Freundlich during a press conference earlier in the day as "the foolish Jew," I knew we had to talk.

I opened the interview by asking Franken about a story Brandon Tartikoff, the late president of NBC Entertainment, had told me about *Saturday Night Live* and his own self-consciousness and ambivalence when it came to Jewish images.

No program tested what he called his "skill with the censors" more than *Saturday Night Live*, Tartikoff had said. And the *SNL* sketch that gave him "the most grief" was the "Jew/Not-a-Jew game show." The sketch featured *SNL* guest host Tom Hanks as the emcee of a game show in which a photograph of a famous person would appear on the screen, and panelists then tried to guess if the celebrity was Jewish.

"Our first famous personality," Hanks says in the sketch, "is Penny Marshall, the star of television's *Laverne & Shirley*. Okay, panelists, Jew or not a Jew?"

After the panelists gave their answers, the sketch cut to a mock-commercial, which was a parody of a series of IBM commercials titled "You Make the Call." The parody featured baseball pitcher Sandy Koufax, with a narrator's voice saying, "Sandy Koufax is on the mound for the Los Angeles Dodgers. It's Game Seven of the World Series against the Minnesota Twins. The stylish left-hander is involved in a tense battle . . . Okay, IBM invites you to make the call: Sandy Koufax—Jew, not a Jew?"

The sketch ends with Hanks telling the audience that Penny Marshall was really Italian—and then awarding prizes to those contestants who guessed "not a Jew."

"I thought it was funny," Tartikoff said, "but was it anti-Semitic? All week long, I agonized over that question. Since I'm Jewish, I wondered if I was being too sensitive—or maybe I wasn't being sensitive enough. If this was about Italians, would I think it should be kept off the air? Finally, a few hours before airtime, I took a deep breath, conferred with the standards people [Broadcast and Standards—the network censors], and we decided to air the sketch."

According to Tartikoff, the morning after controversial material airs is usually taken up with phone calls—most of them negative. The phone rang off the hook the Sunday morning after the Jew/Not-a-Jew sketch aired, with calls from colleagues, many of whom were Jewish. The call Tartikoff said he remembered best, though, was from his mother.

"I cannot believe it," Tartikoff quoted his mother as saying, "I'm embarrassed to call you my son. This Jew/Not-a-Jew sketch was the most anti-Semitic thing I've ever seen." Tartikoff said there was silence between them for a few moments as his mother paused and he tried to think of an appropriate reply. It was his mother who spoke first.

"Besides," she said, "I always thought Penny Marshall *was* Jewish."[3]

I had barely started recounting the anecdote, which I often used at the start of interviews because the punch line seemed to get Jewish producers and writers talking about their own self-consciousness in depictions of Jewish identity, when Franken stopped me.

"Yes, I'm familiar with 'Jew/Not-a-Jew.' I wrote it," Franken said. "Yeah, I wrote the sketch. I wrote it with Jim Downey and Tom Davis. And I have a follow-up to Tartikoff's story about his mother chastising him the morning after for airing it," he added excitedly.

"Day Two after the sketch airs, Monday, and we get a phone call from the Jewish Anti-Defamation League. So, I call the guy back, and he says they got all kinds of calls of complaint. He wants to know what was the sketch, because he heard all these terrible things about it.

"So, I explain the sketch to him, and he starts laughing. He says he totally understands it. He did the same thing in his house, he says—tried to figure out which of the performers on TV was Jewish."

Franken said he ended the call thinking the matter closed, only to find out that NBC received a formal letter of complaint several days later from the Anti-Defamation League about the sketch. "So, I call the guy back again and say, 'Hey, what's the deal? You know, I told you what the sketch was, you laughed, we both discussed how funny it was. Why the letter?'"

According to Franken, the League official said, "Yeah, I know, but I had to write the letter. That's my job."

"And then, he asked me for tickets for his son for the show," Franken said, delivering it like a punch line, raising his eyebrows and shaking his head with incredulity.

Franken barely stopped to take a breath and he was on to another anecdote involving Jews and *Saturday Night Live*. This story was about a sketch scheduled to air during the Congressional elections of 1994. It featured Franken and Norm McDonald at the "News Update" desk, with Franken reporting on fictitious political attack ads running on the Christian Broadcasting Network.

The first fictitious ad features an actress playing California Senate candidate Arianna Huffington, who says of her opponent, Diane Feinstein, "Diane Feinstein is against prayer in the schools. And no wonder: [pause] she's a Jew."

Then Franken introduces videotape with a second ad featuring an actor as Oliver North attacking his opponent in the Virginia Senate race by saying, "Chuck Robb is against prayer in the schools. And no wonder: [pause] he's a Jew."

At which point the none-too-bright anchorman McDonald interrupts, saying, "Hey, wait a minute, Chuck Robb isn't Jewish." And correspondent Franken says, "Norm, you know that, and I know that. But it's a very close election."

Franken said that Lorne Michael, the Jewish executive producer of *SNL*, asked him not to do the segment with the Jew jokes following dress rehearsal. "Didn't you hear the audience kind of go 'ooooooh' [groan] when you did it?" Franken remembered Michaels asking him.

"And I said, 'No, Lorne, I didn't, actually. What I *heard* was them laughing.' "

But the end result was that Franken did *not* do the Jew jokes on air when the "News Update" segment aired live that night. Why did he think Michaels didn't want him to do them?

"I think that Lorne to some extent does it as a defensive reaction," Franken said. "I mean, there's a feeling among some Jews that 'Hey, let's not get too out front in our Jewishness, because people might not like it.' And I think there's a little of that. And, I mean, that's his judgment. I think it's more being protective of Jews. It's a bit of "Hey, let's not get too far out front and draw fire. There's a lot of us in this business, let's not call attention to it, you know.' "

Franken told me yet a third story about an *SNL* sketch involving Jewish identity that he wrote called "The Night Hanukkah Harry Saved Christmas." It featured Jon Lovitz as Hanukkah Harry and Phil Hartman as Santa Claus.

"It was a big hit. People loved it, and we wanted to do an expanded animated version of it for NBC to be like 'The Grinch That Stole Christmas' or something," Franken said. "But when it got to Brandon [Tartikoff], he killed the idea, saying it was 'too Jewish.' Yeah, that's the term— too Jewish."

By now, even Norm MacDonald would have gotten the theme of Franken's anecdotes: Jews censoring Jews—Jewish executives trying to keep Jewish images that had been created by Jewish writers off the screen. But an even deeper resonance was triggered by the term "too Jewish" and the way it seemed to hang in the air between us in that hotel room. It even stopped Franken, who was sitting cross-legged on his bed and had been talking a mile a minute.[4]

The phrase threw me back to one of the very first stories I had heard about Jews on television, just as I was starting my research. It involved *The Goldbergs*, network television's first sitcom with leading characters that were Jews and the first to be called "too Jewish."

Cherney Berg, who wrote and coproduced many of the later episodes of this series created by his mother, Gertrude Berg, remembered one such instance.

"When we began with *The Goldbergs* on television, most of our problem was not from the non-Jews, it was from the Jews, who felt that they really didn't want to be exposed," Berg said. "They wanted to hide. [They] did not want to be part and parcel of a minority group. They wanted to be hidden, hidden away.

"I remember one conference we had with a film company whose president was Jewish, vice-president was Jewish, secretary was Jewish, treasurer was Jewish. We're all sitting around discussing how we're going to make the show. Shouldn't we move the show to Connecticut where Jews would be more American? Should we leave it in New York with Jake still working in what they contemptuously called the rag trade?

"So, we're talking about it. And, if you know the show, you know Uncle David. And Uncle David had a rather thick [Eastern European] accent. And, from the back of the room, comes the voice of one of the vice-presidents of this film company, who says [in an accent even thicker than Uncle David's], 'You doan tink mebbe Uncle David is too Jewish?' "

Berg paused for a second to let the dialect of the Jewish executive and the irony of what he said have some room to resonate.

"And I think that was part and parcel of our problem: How would you present a show about Jews in a non-Jewish way?" Berg said.[5]

"TOO JEWISH" AND SELF-CENSORSHIP

"Too Jewish" is an expression that echoes all too loudly across the history of Jewish characters on network television in its use—most often by Jewish programmers and network executives—as a tool to distort, disguise, or altogether eliminate depictions of Jewish identity from American prime-time television.

First heard in connection with *The Goldbergs* more than fifty years ago, it was used in 1997 by then ABC Entertainment president Jamie Tarses to describe what she didn't like about a sitcom starring Richard Lewis, *Hiller and Diller*, that was on the network's prime-time schedule that fall before quickly being cancelled.[6] Tartikoff had also used it in 1991 in trying to explain why he wanted to cancel *Seinfeld*—a series that would become one of television's biggest hits ever—after just one episode.[7]

"Too Jewish" is the linguistic expression of the phenomenon described by sociologists as "surplus visibility"—the feeling among minority members and others that whatever members of that group say or do, it is too much and, moreover, they are being too conspicuous about it.[8]

"Surplus visibility" is an important concept in this book. In media studies, one hypothesis that has become conventional wisdom without the benefit of rigorous testing or historical examination is that as membership by a given minority group increases in a particular community of production, so will images of that minority group tend to become less stereotyped and more representative of social reality. The popular metaphor for such enhanced membership in the decision-making process is "having a place at the table."

But that is not what happened with Jews and television. The counterintuitive finding of this book is that "surplus visibility" can lead to members of a minority group policing each other's visibility and, in some cases, striving for invisibility.[9] The dynamic was already in play when it came to *The Goldbergs*, with Jewish community groups outside the culture industry and Jewish gatekeepers within it trying to make it "more American" or get it off the air. Cherney Berg is right when he says, "Most of our problem . . . was with the Jews."

Berg's anecdote about the meeting that he and his mother had with Jewish film executives sounds a number of the major themes of this book, starting with self-censorship—the peculiar history of Jewish gatekeepers from William Paley and David Sarnoff, the founders of CBS and NBC, respectively, to Tartikoff and Tarses five decades later keeping Jewish images off the air.

What I set out to do in 1991 was an image study of Jewish characters in prime-time network television. I expected to be working primarily with the shows in which characters like Molly Goldberg, Bernie Steinberg, Rhoda Morgenstern, Michael Steadman, Dr. Joel Fleishman, Paul Buchman, and Fran Fine appeared. I expected to be looking for patterns to the images much as Patricia Erens and Lester D. Friedman had done with their books on Jewish characters in feature films, *The Jew in American Cinema* and *Hollywood's Image of the Jew.*

But one of the first things I found in a preliminary survey of series with Jewish characters is the puzzling fact that from 1954 to 1972 there was not one prime-time show on network television featuring a leading character who was clearly identified as Jewish. An obvious question that could not be overlooked: why? But, to answer that, I had to leave the realm of textual analysis and engage the world in which network television is made. In other words, I had to also study what was *not* on the screen, and that proved to be more difficult in many ways than investigating what was.

I wound up interviewing 114 writers, producers, actors, and network executives for this book, which ultimately came to link a study of production with a study of content to show how persistent images arise and keep getting reproduced in the television industry.[10]

This book tries to map part of the terrain where television and ethnicity meet in our culture. But, whereas most studies of ethnic images in media involve groups whose members have been generally outside the community of suppliers and distributors of such images—for example, African-Americans—this study shows how ethnic identity was invented and depicted when members of the same ethnic group by and large controlled the creation of those images and the delivery system that brought them into America's living rooms.

Up until the mid-1980s, when the founders sold the three major broadcast networks—ABC, NBC, and CBS—they were Jewish-owned. William Paley founded and owned the controlling interest in CBS until 1986, when the Loews Corporation took over. David Sarnoff founded and ran NBC until he retired in 1970; he was succeeded by his son, Robert. In 1985, General Electric bought NBC. Leonard Goldenson was the top officer at ABC from its founding in 1953 until his retirement in 1986, shortly after Capital Cities Communications bought the network.

Throughout the first four decades of network television, the Big Three determined most of the television programming made in Hollywood as a result of their positions as principal buyers of it. Furthermore, many of the leading suppliers—the producers and writers of networks series—were Jewish.[11]

Did the fact that they were Jews affect the way in which Jewish identity was represented on television? The most widely cited answer we have to that question comes from Todd Gitlin's 1983 study *Inside Prime Time*. While the book, which looks at network programming in the 1970s and 1980s, spends only a few pages dealing with Jewish characters, Gitlin concludes: "Given the large number of Jews who hold top positions in the networks and production companies, it seems surprising that Jewish characters are scarce on the screen. But . . . the ethnicity of executives and suppliers doesn't necessarily determine characters. In the end, the networks fall back on their marketplace predilections compounded perhaps by self-protectiveness against any real or conceivable anti-Semitic charge that Jews are too powerful in the media."[12]

Gitlin had other priorities in the book and quickly dropped the issue of Jewish executives and Jewish characters. Furthermore, since the sale of the networks by their Jewish founders in the mid-1980s, truths have appeared that were still hidden in 1983. But this study finds that the ethnicity of the "executives and suppliers" *did*, in fact, "determine characters" in the case of television characters that were Jews.

This book shows that when it came to Jewish images, the generation of Jews who founded the broadcast networks behaved in much the same way as did the immigrant Jews from Eastern Europe who founded the film industry—the moguls chronicled so astutely by Neal Gabler in *An Empire of Their Own: How the Jews Invented Hollywood*.[13] Just as the tension between Jewish identity and assimilation on the part of studio bosses and producers manifested itself when it came to Jewish images on the big screen—especially in the matter of suppressing such images—so it did on the smaller screen of television. And this is not so surprising considering that Sarnoff, for example, was identical to the Hollywood Jews in terms of background; he was an immigrant to the United States from the same small patch of Eastern European turf that spawned such a remarkable number of the men who founded the feature film industry.

On the one hand, like their Hollywood counterparts, Jewish owners and network executives kept some of the more vile anti-Semitic images that had been circulated in print and stage from ever reaching the small screen. Anyone familiar with the Shylocks and sheenies of nineteenth- and early-twentieth-century American theater will appreciate that this is no small matter.[14] But the larger story is one of censorship that resulted in no clearly identified Jewish leading characters in a weekly network television series from 1954 to 1972, and then again from 1978 to 1987. This ethnic whitewashing of television is all the more remarkable when you consider the explosion of films, books, and plays featuring Jewish characters and exploring Jewish identity that so enriched the rest of our popular culture starting in the 1960s.

This book in part examines those periods and explains how such censorship was enforced as it chronicles the lengths to which the founders and some of their network lieutenants went in trying to keep Jewish characters off the air lest their networks appear "too Jewish." One of those lengths involved executives at CBS telling producers that the network had "research" clearly showing that American viewers did not want to see "people from New York, men with mustaches, and Jews" on television (as series co-creator Allan Burns described to me in an interview on November 18, 1997). The first documented mention of such "research" by a CBS executive came in 1969. Thirty years later, Hollywood producers and executives were still citing that CBS "research" in interviews with me. My research into the CBS "research" is one of the stories this book tells.

While the larger story of this book concerns the suppression of Jewish images, it is not the only story told. Once the Big Three networks were sold by the late 1980s and the Jewish gatekeeper-founders had relinquished control, the narrative takes a different turn. The departure of the founders allowed a more "normal" relationship between television images and social reality to start to kick in. Leading Jewish characters start appearing with *thirtysomething* in 1987 on ABC and *Northern Exposure* in 1990 on CBS.

While the Peabody Award–winning *thirtysomething* explored Jewish identity overtly in only a handful of episodes during its four-year run, it did so with a thoughtfulness and intensity unrivaled before and rarely seen since, as creators Marshall Herskovitz and Ed Zwick worked out an answer onscreen to the question of what it means to be a Jew. *Northern Exposure*, a wise and funny drama about a Columbia Medical School graduate forced to go west to the Alaska frontier as a means of paying for his education, continued in the same tradition as it examined problems and complications attendant to assimilation.

By 1991, with such corporations of no particular ethnic bent as General Electric and Capital Cities running network television, there was an explosion of prime-time network sitcoms featuring leading Jewish characters. But being visible does not automatically mean being known. In the context of historical invisibility, what is the vision of Jewish identity and Jewish life that these characters project?

The relationship between television images and social reality is a complicated one, but we do know that there is never a direct reflection. Any notion of social reality is always processed through the perceptions and sensibilities of those members of the Hollywood creative community who make the television shows. And weren't most of the top producers in Hollywood in the late 1980s and 1990s men and women who had learned their craft under the founders' rule? Even though the networks were sold and Jewish characters were at least allowed to exist, vestiges of the culture that the founders helped create remained—indeed, remains today—and contributed to a persistent set of images largely created by Jews of Jews on television.

This book also explains how it could be that Jewish producers create and Jewish network executives buy shows in which Jewish women characters are largely typed into three categories—ugly ducklings, "Jewish-American princesses," and smothering mothers—if they are depicted at all. The most striking aspect of female Jewish identity on network television is the near-total absence of Jewish women characters during the 1990s despite narratives that clearly have space for them. And then comes *The Nanny*, proving that in the end Jewish women really only want the same thing as Jewish men: a non-Jewish partner.

Jewish male characters don't fare all that much better. The dominant patterns: passive husbands married to domineering women, nebbishy boyfriends lusting after non-Jewish women of whom they are often in awe, inferior but loyal sidekicks to non-Jewish men, and, most troubling of all, the effeminate male. And then comes *Seinfeld*, the first Jewish character to become number one in American television. But what kind of Jew are we talking about here anyway?

This book also finds the emergence of new Jewish images in such characters as Max Bickford in *The Education of Max Bickford* on CBS and Joe Rifkind of Sidney Lumet's *100 Centre Street*, a legal drama on the Arts & Entertainment (A&E) cable channel: both debuted in 2001. While neither show was a success in the ratings, Bickford and Rifkind, played by Richard Dreyfuss and Alan Arkin, respectively, transcended most stereotypes of the TV Jew and offered one answer to the question of how you create an authentic Jewish character on television when Jews are so successfully assimilated in American life, with those traits that once identified them as Jews so washed-down. New and different images of Jewish femininity are also identified and examined in this book as they appear in such popular series as NBC's *Friends* and *Will & Grace*.

ETHNICITY AND ASSIMILATION

Two other important themes sounded in the Cherney Berg anecdote about Uncle David and *The Goldbergs* are those of ethnicity and assimilation. That is the subtext to the discussion that the Jewish film executives were having in Berg's anecdote about moving the Goldbergs from the Tremont Avenue apartment where the fictional family had resided since the debut of *The Rise of The Goldbergs* on network radio in 1929 to Haverville, Connecticutt, where Molly and her family would spend their last unhappy years on television in 1955 and 1956.

Ethnicity and assimilation, which form one of the central story lines of the American experience, are also found to intersect in this study to form a stunningly persistent narrative pattern for Jewish characters on network television. From the 1970s through the 1990s, the overwhelming majority of sitcoms and drama series with Jewish characters have shared a pattern of Jewish male characters involved in relationships with or married to non-Jewish women.

Literary critic Leslie Fiedler says the pattern of Jewish men pursuing non-Jewish women in literature is a metaphor for assimilation.[15] Fiedler does not offer an explanation for the lack of a corresponding pattern of Jewish women pursuing non-Jewish men.

This study explores the ways in which ethnicity and gender have driven network television's version of this narrative of intermarriage, while showing how Jewish male characters are literally transformed through their relationships with non-Jewish women. This promise of transformation is especially potent within the flow of commercial network television, filled as it is with advertisements that promise a similar kind of transformation through consumption.

Just as television promises young men that they can be like Michael Jordan through the purchase of Nike athletic shoes, so does it promise Jewish men that they can go from being insecure outsiders to confident, fully vested participants in mainstream American life through a relationship with a non-Jewish woman, preferably one who is blond. This is the overriding message of 1990s sitcoms like *Mad About You*, and now we have the female version of the transformation-through-intermarriage narrative thanks to *The Nanny*.

How does such a narrative told over and over to tens of millions of Americans week after week affect the way in which Jewish women and men see themselves? How does it affect the way in which non-Jews see Jews, or Jewish men see Jewish women? And what role has television's constant telling of this story played in an intermarriage rate that has that jumped from less than 8 percent prior to 1965 to more than 50 percent today—a period during which television became the principal storyteller of American life?[16]

Even though we all understand that Jewish television characters are fictional creations, they still have profound real-life consequences as we use them in the formation of ideas and attitudes about ourselves and others. What meaning, for example, did so many young Jews make of Jewish identity as they played "Jew/Not-a-Jew" with characters on-screen? Was it the one Berg suggested—that Jewish identity was something that had to be "hidden away" if you wanted to be welcomed into America's living rooms, like homosexuality?

This book does not claim to cover the entire range of Jewish identity on American television. I limited myself to fictional Jewish characters, as opposed to Jewish actors and performers, because of the total constructedness of a fictional creation: the more invention that is involved, the more of a chance we might have of understanding the process of inventing the television Jew.[17]

I also limited myself to leading characters appearing in network sitcoms or drama series, as opposed to characters appearing in made-for-television movies, variety shows, or televised plays like those presented on *Studio One* or *Playhouse 90*. I made this choice for two reasons: first, manageability—this is already a huge study in that it covers fifty years; second, as Ella Taylor points out in explaining why she limited herself to half-hour sitcoms and hour-long dramas in her exemplary study of families in network television, *Prime-Time Families*, they formed "the characteristic genre of the first two decades of network television."[18]

Furthermore, in Taylor's words, these weekly series "foster the gradual buildup of viewers' attachment to individual characters and their relationships," thus "generating the fullest possibilities for a meditation" on the realms such characters symbolically purport to represent—in my case, Jewish identity. Leading characters, the group on which I focus my inquiry, maximize all these possibilities.[19]

So, I am dealing only with fictional characters, like Rhoda Morgenstern of *The Mary Tyler Moore Show* and *Rhoda* or Bernie Steinberg of *Bridget Loves Bernie*. I am not dealing with characters played by comedians in skits on variety shows, like Mel Brooks as the 2,000-Year-Old Man on *The Ed Sullivan Show*. Such distinctions might seem obvious to some, but the simple fact of identifying characters as Jewish—the point at which this study starts—proved far more complicated that I imagined when I began.[20]

IN THEIR OWN WORDS

Beyond the history of the characters and their chronology, the goal of this book is to recreate through the words of those involved in making these images some sense of the milieu in which Jewish images were created or censored for prime-time viewing, thus explaining that history. I try to use the words gathered in my 114 interviews to translate a theory into a demonstration of how television production actually worked.

Speaking at the level of theory in trying to explain the production process of prime-time network television, sociologist Richard Butsch described an "imaginary feedback loop" between producers and network executives, saying:

> Because programming decisions are risky and costly and network executives' careers rest on their ability to make the right decisions, they are constrained in their own interest to . . . stick to tried and true formulas and to producers with a track record of success . . . The result is a small, closed community of proven creative personnel (about 500 producers, writers and directors) closely tied to and dependent on the networks. This proven talent then self-censor their work on the basis of a product image their previous experience tells them the networks will tolerate, creating an "imaginary feedback loop" between producers and network executives.[21]

Henry Bromell, a Hollywood writer and producer, spoke from his first-hand experience, but he described the very same kind of "loop" in explaining how Jewish characters had been kept out of prime time for decades and what a landmark it was in 1990 when Joshua Brand, the co-creator of *Northern Exposure*, made it clear that the lead character was going to be named Dr. Joel Fleischman and would be clearly identified as Jewish:

> Josh said he was Jewish, and that was a very ballsy thing at the time, because the networks would never say characters were Jewish. It was Jewish executives making the decisions, and they were very uncomfortable with saying the characters were Jewish. So you have this weird loop from the Jewish executives to the Jewish producers to the characters—this very weird loop. But I remember when Josh said, "Yes, we can say he's Jewish." It gave us a whole new way to think about it as writers: "Oh, yeah, it's Woody Allen in Alaska." It was totally liberating.[22]

Anecdote is the narrative form favored by most of the Hollywood producers and executives I interviewed. As Gitlin pointed out in his study of prime time, "Anecdote is the style of industry speech." I encouraged producers, writers, and network executives in my interviews to speak in the language they regularly used in talking about and doing their work. Gitlin felt that by "recounting a number of stories at some length, and often in the words of the people telling them," he was able to make the claim for *Inside Prime Time* that "Much of this book is what the anthropologist Clifford Geertz calls 'thick description,'" conveying a sense of "not only how and why I think the networks do what they do, but a sense of ambiance and texture of the industry's life-as-it-is-lived."[23]

I am uncomfortable with such grand claims, but there is regularly a thickening of the narrative in this book, with anecdotes told from different points of view intersecting to provide a real sense of the way Jewish identity was actually depicted or censored at specific moments, as with the Tartikoff and Franken anecdotes. There is also a converging of answers that goes beyond the sounding and re-sounding of phrases like "too Jewish" across the years to suggest shared beliefs, sensibilities, and internalized attitudes among many of the people to whom I spoke—a culture, if you will. The explanation Franken gave of Lorne Michaels asking him not to do Jew jokes is representative in this regard: "I mean, there's a feeling among some Jews that, 'Hey, let's not get too out front in our Jewishness, because people might not like it.'"

That mindset is described again and again by persons interviewed for this book, often in the very same words. Marshall Herskovitz, the co-creator of *thirtysomething*, said the central issue in any discussion of the history of Jewish characters is "the level of self-censorship that has gone into the depiction of Jews by Jews over the years." When asked to elaborate, he said:

> It's really historical. It's about what it means to be Jewish in Holly-wood—what it means to see yourself as a minority, yet having this enormous power of communication tools that effect the whole society . . . You know, even back in the 1920s, these guys—Louis B. Mayer and the rest of them [Jewish immigrants who founded the motion picture industry]—had carefully scrubbed out any ethnicism . . . So, self-censorship began back then. They were in some sense trying to create a world that America would accept. There are a lot of people who say that generation of Jews in Hollywood created America's conception of Middle America, Presbyterian America. We [the current generation of baby boomer Jews in the television industry] just in-herited that in some ways. If you sit in the meetings, sit with the networks or go to the [production] studios, you just feel the sense of fear in the room of what it means to be a Jew, the fear of putting yourself too far out there—that you will in some way make a spectacle of yourself, you will embarrass. In these meetings, people still say, "Is it good for the Jews?" You hear that all the time. There is this sense that we are an endangered minority, and, if we stick out necks out too far, we are going to be in deep, deep trouble, because historically that was true.[24]

One aim of this book is to take readers inside some of those meetings, as well as inside the meaning systems of some of the Jewish executives, producers, and writers at those meetings. In this weird loop, if the Jewish writer or producer didn't self-censor, there was often the Jewish execu-tive like Tartikoff ready to step up.

Lynn Roth, executive producer of *The Paper Chase* on Showtime and former head of comedy development at 20th Century Fox, put it this way:

> On television, our culture, which is such a vast culture, is reduced to either these shopping, non-intellectual, gabbing women, or these neu-

rotic, frightened men. So where is the pride? Is there a lack of pride in the creators, or is there a pervasive mentality of don't bring too much attention to us because we've had such a bad history and we don't want it to happen again? You know, is that the mentality at the root of it? . . . The creation of Jewish characters is still an area where they [network executives] are very, very careful . . . I'll tell you the truth, I've been in the television industry for twenty years, and I still don't understand where they're coming from. I know that when I was in comedy development, I always wanted to put Jewish characters in, and there was that phrase I would always hear . . . about being "too Jewish."[25]

refused. The show would be nothing if I watered it down. I write about middle-class Jewish people because I know them, love them, am one of them."[3]

This two-year run without a sponsor came at a boom time when NBC radio's roster of sponsoring companies rose from 39 in 1928 to 343 in 1931, the year Berg finally found a sponsor in Pepsodent toothpaste, one of the companies that had been sponsoring *Amos 'n' Andy* from its beginning.[4] Clearly, Molly was too Jewish for some tastes from the moment she arrived in American broadcasting.

Amos 'n' Andy is also there in the story of how *The Goldbergs* came to network television. In 1948, CBS announced that it was bringing the controversial serial to television as a sitcom. Gosden, Correll, and CBS president William Paley attempted to blunt African-American criticism of the show by promising that it would not be done in blackface. A talent search would be launched, and the show would not go into production until the "finest black actors were signed to play the lead roles." The result was that *Amos 'n' Andy* would not premiere on CBS until 1951.[5]

Meanwhile, CBS wanted to try the same kind of ethnic material that had worked in serial form on radio in its new situation comedy format. Based on its radio history, you might think *The Goldbergs* would have been a natural for CBS, especially since *Me and Molly*, an adaptation for the stage written by and starring Gertrude Berg, was playing to full houses on Broadway in 1948 and 1949 when television was desperate for programming to fill its schedule. But neither CBS nor NBC—then the two main games in town as the only national networks—was interested. In the words of Berg:

> *The Goldbergs* had been on radio for almost 20 years and there were people who just couldn't see it as television material. "It wouldn't translate," was the way they expressed it . . . My agent would call me one day to tell me that NBC didn't think *The Goldbergs* could be a television show. Well, that was their opinion. I knew different. So I told my agent to get to work on CBS. He did and he called back a few days later to say an audition was all arranged. Good! I started to think about a script. Then I got another call from my agent—the audition was off. They also thought the show wasn't for TV. I got annoyed. I was also worried. If you're turned down by NBC and CBS

Learning to Be "More American" –
The Goldbergs

Goldbergs, The—Gertrude Berg had conceived the role of Molly Goldberg
and made her a popular radio character for almost 20 years. In 1949, the
entire clan moved to television . . . They were a middle-class Jewish family
with middle-class problems. Molly's husband Jake was in the clothing business, and their two children, Sammy and Rosalie, were active teenagers
. . . Also living with the family was the educated and philosophical Uncle
David . . . Molly was a good soul and constantly involved in trying to help
everybody in the neighborhood solve their problems . . .

*The Complete Directory to Prime Time Network
and Cable TV Shows 1946–Present*[1]

When *The Goldbergs* premiered as a radio serial titled *The Rise of The Goldbergs* for NBC on November 20, 1929, it had another ethnic program to
thank in part for its existence—*Amos 'n' Andy*, which featured African-
American characters created by Freeman Gosden and Charles Correll,
who were white. The two actors did the voices of the characters in the
accents of nineteenth-century minstrel show performers.[2]

Advertisers had seen their sales soar since sponsoring *Amos 'n' Andy*
and wanted more ethnic radio. NBC, dancing to the tune it thought
advertisers were playing, added *The Rise of the Goldbergs* to its schedule in
response. But, in a pattern we shall see repeating itself in television, more
ethnicity did not necessarily mean more Jewish ethnicity.

As Berg tells the story, "When I first started *The Goldbergs* back in
1929, we were without a sponsor for two years. The network executives
began to think Molly Goldberg might get a sponsor more readily if I
softened her accent and called her Molly Smith or Molly Jones. But I

then you're out of business, and that was something I decided I wasn't.[6]

Berg knew she was getting the runaround, and she also knew the "wouldn't translate" reason was a lie, since NBC and CBS were in a bidding war to lure radio stars and shows to television. Furthermore, she knew CBS was particularly interested in ethnic shows since, beyond *Amos 'n' Andy*, it was negotiating a deal to bring the book *Mama's Bank Account*, which had already been produced as a movie and Broadway musical, to television as a sitcom titled *Mama*, starring Peggy Wood as the matriarch of a working-class Norwegian family in San Francisco. What CBS and NBC were not interested in was Berg's Jewish ethnicity. Paley, who once turned down a chance to back *Fiddler on the Roof* by explaining that it was "too Jewish,"[7] was more comfortable in 1948 putting a series with African-American characters on his network than he was a Jewish sitcom.

To understand how *The Goldbergs* ultimately found a place on CBS's prime-time schedule in 1949 despite Paley's discomfort with an overtly Jewish series, it is necessary to recognize that the production realm of prime-time network programming in 1949 differed from that of today. Primarily, advertising agencies and sponsors played a much greater role in determining prime-time programming from its beginning in 1946 until about 1958, following the quiz show scandals.[8]

In fact, if an advertising agency acting on behalf of a potential sponsor wanted a show on network television in the late 1940s and early 1950s, it would often be on the schedule whether the network wanted it or not. In some cases, advertising agencies, which then had their own television programming departments, essentially programmed certain time periods and nights for the networks by buying blocks of time on behalf of their clients and then putting their shows in. There was almost no shared sponsorship as is the norm today.[9]

In the case of *The Goldbergs*, Paley reluctantly authorized a television audition for the series in response to Berg's personal plea for a chance to show sponsors what she could do.[10] Paley is said to have been more surprised than anyone when General Foods immediately bought the show and told the network through Young & Rubicam, its advertising agency, that it wanted a spot for *The Goldbergs* in the CBS Monday night lineup that included some of the most popular shows of early televison—

Arthur Godfrey's Talent Scouts, Candid Camera, and *Studio One*. What General Foods wanted from network television, in those days, General Foods got.[11] Sadly, as we shall also see when the blacklist struck *The Goldbergs* in 1951, what General Foods did not want on the networks did not get on the air in those days, too.

The most important point, though, is that the Jewish president of CBS resisted putting *The Goldbergs* on the air despite the fact that it fit the very model for the kind of ethnic sitcoms with a history of radio success that his network was looking to add. Meanwhile, a major advertising agency—often described as WASP (White Anglo-Saxon Protestant)[12]—put *The Goldbergs* on the air. It is the first of many examples in this book and in the history of prime-time network television of Jewish gatekeepers in the television industry trying to keep shows with Jewish characters off the air or, at least, modify the characters so as to keep them from being "too Jewish."

THE POWER OF MOLLY

The series that premiered on CBS at 8 P.M. on January 10, 1949, was not much of a departure from the radio version of *The Goldbergs*. At the center of the family living in apartment 3B at 1038 East Tremont Avenue in the Bronx was Berg's Molly. As one reviewer described her: "Like a long-lost relative, a pen pal finally met in the flesh, Molly looked like Molly talked. Gertrude Berg—with her sad, twinkly eyes, her basset hound face, and her potato sack body—was Molly Goldberg."[13]

Usually wearing a dark dress—size 46—with a brooch and some kind of lace at the collar, Molly opened each show by raising the shade, leaning out of one of the windows of the Goldbergs' apartment, and shouting, "Yoo-hoo, Mrs. Bloom," to one of her neighbors across an airshaft.[14] During the CBS years of General Foods' sponsorship, there was always a Sanka coffee can with a flower in it on the kitchen window sill.

As the final notes of the opening theme "Toselli's Serenade" waned, Molly would address the television audience before speaking to any of the neighbor ladies who might appear in their windows on the other sides of the airshaft in response to her voice. The opening of an episode that aired on August 9, 1949, featuring a story line about the family's return from summer vacation at Pincus-in-the-Pines, is representative of

Gertrude Berg as Molly Goldberg in her trademark opening, leaning out the window of her Bronx apartment, to each episode of *The Goldbergs*. It was one of several ways she pushed boundaries and challenged traditional notions of feminine domestic space and behavior. Debuting in 1949, *The Goldbergs* helped establish the template for television's family sitcom genre. Berg created, produced, wrote, and starred in the series. Library of American Broadcasting, University of Maryland the early years and the way Berg merged sitcom and commercial reality in those openings.[15] Pincus-in-the-Pines was a resort in the Catskill Mountains that the Goldbergs visited each summer. It was based on Fleischmann's, a Borsht Belt hotel run by Berg's grandfather. Berg had many happy childhood memories of time spent there, and the hotel reappears continually in her work. Much of the voluminous body of work she created between the mid-1920s and her death in 1966—more than ten thousand radio, TV, and stage scripts for *The Goldbergs* alone— is connected to that hotel in the Catskills that her family ran.[16]

Putting her left hand to her cheek, a frequent gesture, Berg leans out of the window and smiles into the camera at the opening of the Pincus-in-the-Pines episode, saying:

Oy, oy, have I got stories for you from Pincus Pines . . . The old people were irritable because the mattress is not so soft. The kids were restless because they want to do everything in two weeks. And the husbands, *oy, vey.* So, I didn't hesitate to tell the other women and Mr. Pincus himself, too—same as I tell you—about Sanka Coffee. That it's good for restlessness. Good for irritability. Those that didn't know I told them [that] 97 percent of the caffeine is removed—97 percent. Imagine! And, so, you can drink as much as you want as often as you want, and the sleep is left in . . . Mr. Pincus tried it and he says he thinks the Sanka gets into the disposition. "I don't get so many complaints," he says. So, you try it at your house, too, and see if you don't feel better. And maybe you won't get so many complaints. Just try it, please, and see—for me.

Over the years, the sponsors changed, but not the heavy-handed Berg pitch. In 1954, on the DuMont network, she was sponsored by the Vitamin Corporation of America with its Rybutal Vitamin B Complex. In the opening for an episode that aired on May 4, 1954, she appears in the window wearing a bathrobe:

Oy, hello. You'll pardon my kimono, but I'm going out dancing. People ask me, "How can you go out in the middle of the week dancing after doing housework all day?" Here's my answer: Rybutal. You should only know how it helps me not to feel tired or nervous. Everybody needs the important elements in Rybutal—twenty-two important vitamins and minerals. Right on the label here it says "High Potency," and that means extra good and strong. If Columbus didn't discover, what would we have? So, be a Columbus and discover Rybutal.

Berg wrote the copy herself and always tried to link the commercial to the subject matter of the particular show. The Rybutal ad opened a show about Molly being a wallflower at the Shoe Manufacturers' Ball and then finally deciding to take rumba, samba, and tango lessons from an instructor named Ricky in a flamenco shirt with puffy sleeves so she could be "more modern." (Ricky, by the way, speaks with a Hispanic accent just like another Ricky in the CBS sitcom starring a woman named Lucy—a sitcom that was being held up to Berg at the time as the model for what a "modern" sitcom should be.) The episode concludes with Molly back in the window hawking Rybutal:

> So, you see anybody can learn to dance. But what's more important is to feel like dancing. But how can you feel like dancing if you're nervous all the time or tired or just not feeling so good? This can be because you're not getting the twenty-two important elements in Rybutal. Try it. Try Rybutal, and in one little week you should feel like a new person—dancing, bubbling all over. There's a fancy scientific name for this. Should I say it? Body chemistry. This means in plain English in *mein* vocabulary feeling very well. Remember the little cells in your body may wear out faster if you don't get the twenty-two elements in Rybutal. So, get Rybutal and be dancing tomorrow.

The extent to which Berg shilled for the sponsor is important for number of reasons. One, it demonstrates how essential it was that a series first and last serve the sponsor in the early days of television—a point perhaps not so easily understood today. General Foods estimated that Sanka sales rose 57 percent during the time Berg served as their pitch person on CBS.[17]

As for Rybutal, the following letter to Berg from the head of the advertising agency handling the account suggests equal success: "May I just say thanks for the wonderful job you did on behalf of Rybutal. The results speak for themselves. Rybutal is today the leading B Complex Vitamin in America, and you helped put us there."[18] In her collection of papers at Syracuse University, there is far more correspondence between Berg and her sponsors and advertising agencies than between Berg and the networks on which she appeared with *The Goldbergs*. The letters overwhelmingly demonstrate a network role that was far more passive in the three-way process than it would be today.

In the commercial sense, *The Goldbergs* is a prime example of television using a character in Molly who strongly evokes the immigrant past to sell postwar consumer culture to a mass audience. The hard sell is a direct reaction to the knowledge of advertisers that many in the audience held values antithetical to buying on credit, for example, thanks in part to their experiences of living through the Great Depression and rationing during World War II.[19]

While television directories and histories often refer to Molly Goldberg as the "lovable Jewish Mother,"[20] the "eternal mother,"[21] or some other designation suggesting the maternal, motherhood is not one of the primary ways in which Molly is actually defined in the episodes themselves. She is primarily defined, as the commercial messages cited above indicate, by her language, which is also used to suggest the Jewish immigrant experience at the start of the twentieth century. Berg herself touches on some of this in her version of who Molly is and how Molly came to be in *Me and Molly*: "Molly was an amalgam of my mother and my grandmother, Czerny. Into that combination I put a few characteristics of some of the guests at the hotel that I thought Molly should have. Some of the people who stayed at Fleischmann's experimented with the English language and from them Molly developed a manner of speaking that put the horse in the cart and the eye in the soup."[22]

Much of the humor in the series also came from language. Molly had her own version of the malapropism that came to be known as the Mollypropism:

"When we get to the bridge, I'll burn it."
"David, throw an eye in the soup until I get back."
"Rosalee, the guests are here. Bring in the raw-derves [hors d'oeuvres]."
"Rosie, don't talk smart. I don't like your latitude one bit, young lady."
"Rosalee, I'm your mother and I'm giving you an ulimata."
"Jake, slow down. Don't be a hasty pudding."
"It's late, Jake, and time to expire."
"Sit down. Take your feet off."

Language is one of several ways that Molly is linked to a tradition of American humor dating back to the eighteenth century and seen in such forms as the wise fool and the commonsense philosopher. In terms of language, the precedence can be found in southwestern and rural Yankee dialect humor. Later more specific examples would be Finley Peter Dunne's Mr. Dooley, Langston Hughes's Jess B. Simple, and Leo Rosten's Hyman Kaplan.

Overall, *The Goldbergs* was a domestic sitcom in many ways not much different in terms of subject matter and structure than a family sitcom like, say, *The Cosby Show* would be thirty-five years later. The structure of most episodes followed the classic sitcom progression from order or "normality" to disorder or disruption and then back to order or normality restored. Usually, in the case of *The Goldbergs*, the disruption happened within the family or the home. One episode literally begins with Molly saying, "Jake, the whole house is topsy-turvy." But solving the problem often necessitated Molly going outside the home. And almost always it was Molly, not Jake, the father, who solved the problem.[23]

Rosie wants to have plastic surgery on her nose, and the family wants to stop her without saying no. Molly enlists the plastic surgeon in a plot to change Rosie's mind. The son of Mrs. Jerome, one of the neighbor ladies across the airshaft, is so disappointed with his new dental practice that he is going to quit unless he gets some customers. Molly coerces each family member and most of their neighbors into becoming new patients. Cousin Simon, "the rich one," is coming to dinner, and Jake needs to ask him for money to open his own business making dresses. The dinner is a disaster, but Molly has been secretly saving and she can give Jake the money herself. The ladies' club needs money, and Molly decides they can stage *Die Fledermaus* and sell tickets. She ranges throughout the neighborhood finding performers, including a singing butcher for whom she decides to play matchmaker.

Beyond language, the commercial openings of episodes from *The Goldbergs* cited above also suggest the ways in which Berg, the *auteur* of *The Goldbergs*, subverted some of the traditional expectations for women of the time. For example, the kitchen window is the one she leans out of— indicating her domestic place in the home. But the act of leaning out and giving advice to those outside of the home and family shows her pushing into other realms. Moving into the then predominantly masculine realm of business, for instance, she gives advice to Mr. Pincus about what kind of coffee to serve at his hotel, and it immediately results in fewer complaints from his customers. A recurring theme of the series is

Molly using her intelligence, persistence, and aggressiveness, as well as her network of neighborhood women friends, to solve problems that the more self-important men in their business suits like Jake Goldberg cannot solve.

In the commercial messages cited above, Molly is giving advice on keeping customers happy, keeping a marriage workable, and staying healthy and having fun despite the drudgery of housework—not to mention her simple B complex solution to "feeling nervous all the time" in the Age of Anxiety. But there is very little about being a mother.

This is not the Jewish mother of modern-day popular culture anyway. Maurice Berger is the only critic or television historian to have taken any notice of this when he wrote, "While Jewish female characters are rare on American television, they usually appear as overbearing mothers, self-hating *schleps*, or spoiled princesses. Although Molly Goldberg (Gertrude Berg) of *The Goldbergs* (1949–1955) or Sophie Berger (Marion Ross) on *Brooklyn Bridge* (1991–1993) are portrayed as powerful and considerate women, most Jewish television mothers come off as controlling and hypercritical monsters."[24]

The key word is "powerful." Molly Goldberg offers one of the most complicated and challenging depictions of Jewish and feminine identities in the history of the medium. Cutting dead against the conventional wisdom of 1950s' popular culture as a time of laughably repressive images of women on television, Molly Goldberg is one of the most empowered images ever of a Jewish woman in prime-time network television.

She is often overlooked in feminist analyses of Jewish women in popular culture, despite the fact that she was onstage in American life as a star of radio, film, television, and Broadway for more than thirty years—a run unequalled by any other female Jewish character. In fact, the only female character with a longer run is Lucille Ball's Lucy Ricardo. As a TV character, she serves the same function that has been attributed to some movie stars, namely that of embodying "certain paradoxes or contradictions inherent in the larger social formation."[25]

Molly's empowerment is the result of several factors starting with the way Berg's large body physically dominated the television screen especially when she shared the frame with the frail Uncle David. But, ultimately, Molly's power comes from her ability to provide money—the role reserved for men in the prime time of the 1940s and 1950s in such series as *Father Knows Best*. It would have, perhaps, been too much on several levels for Molly to have actually been the breadwinner of the family, the role Berg had assumed in her own marriage in 1929 at the start of the Depression when her husband, Lew, found himself out of work. But there is a narrative that Berg used in many variations at almost every key point in the twenty-seven-year history of *The Goldbergs* on radio, stage, film, and television. She used it so often it becomes the *Ur* story of *The Goldbergs*, and it was at the heart of the plot of the very first radio script written in 1929. This is how Berg described it:

> The first script in what I called *The Rise of The Goldbergs* was taken from a real-life situation. It was the one about Jake working in the dress business and wanting to go into business for himself. He needed some money to rent a loft and some machines. There was some money in his own home that he didn't know about—hidden away in a teapot in the dish closet. Molly had been saving it for a rainy day . . . The saved money idea came from my grandmother, who was always putting away a penny here and a penny there for when something would be needed. Jake's desire to be his own boss was that of my father and grandfather; the details of the situation and the solution came from me.[26]

The same situation can be seen in Berg's hit play, *Me and Molly*, and several of the key television episodes, particularly "Moving Day," which saw the Goldbergs moving from the Bronx to the suburban community of Haverville in 1955, *The Goldbergs'* final season on television.

Me and Molly, the stage play, is set in 1919; again the premise is that Jake wants to start his own business. And, like the first television version of the narrative done in 1949, Molly's rich cousin Simon is expected to loan him the money to rent a loft and sewing machines. But again, Simon says no. Ultimately, Molly again saves the day, this time by "playing with an idea she had for a long time." The idea: "Manufactured dresses didn't fit her and she wondered about why there weren't the odd sizes—'half sizes,' she called them." So, "without Jake's knowing," she starts making half-size dresses "for neighbors with the same problem she had." And, of course, the dresses are a hit, and Jake sees his future business in half-sizes.[27]

"Moving Day" is one of the most important episodes in the history of the television series. For the 1955–56 season, when no network would have *The Goldbergs*, Berg went the relatively rare route in those days of first-run syndication. She struck a deal with a New York filmmaker, Guild Films, to record thirty-nine episodes on film and, in effect, create their own network by selling the show themselves to stations on a city-by-city basis. But Guild Films wanted some changes if it was going into business with Berg: *The Goldbergs* had to move from the Bronx to the suburbs, and the title had to change to *Molly*. In short, it had to get less Jewish.

Because she had no other choice if she wanted to stay on television, Berg went along with most of the changes. But she expressed her concern about them on the eve of the premiere of *Molly*, saying, "I don't think you erase differences among people by ignoring them. My belief is that the only way we will break down barriers is to give people understanding of one another. If I do this on *The Goldbergs*, then I am satisfied. And I do not think we would have lasted for these 26 years . . . if I didn't accomplish this. That is why I include religion on my show."[28]

Berg's reluctant acceptance of the changes is referred to in a 1955 letter to her from R. R. Kaufman, the Jewish-American president of Guild Films and the man responsible for trying to make the show less ethnic:

> This doesn't mean the show as it is now being written and produced represents a conflict with your philosophy . . . The fact that the show has been modernized to keep in step with the growth of America and all its people, without hurting the fundamental appeal, is a tribute to your genius and to the versatility of Molly's way of life . . . Our rapidly growing financial interest in Molly does not transcend my personal admiration for her and the way she is growing in stature and in her relationships with people, no matter where they live or what they are called . . . [29]

Kaufman's effort to change the title and to force Molly into "relationships with people, no matter where they live or what they are called," meaning she had to lose some of the Jewish friends and make new gentile ones, was nothing new. In fact, it was part of a dominant pattern of behavior on behalf of Jewish-American entertainment industry executives, as well as representatives of organized Jewish life, toward the series, as suggested by the following entries in the "Stone Reports" from 1950 and 1951. The Stone Reports was the name given within the American Jewish Committee in New York to the bimonthly reports filed from Hollywood by the Motion Picture Project, which policed Jewish images and met regularly with studio and network executives as part of their monitoring and lobbying efforts. In addition to the American Jewish Committee, other groups participating in the project included B'nai B'rith and the Anti-Defamation League. The project was self-described as a "Jewish Legion of Decency."[30] One 1950 report from John Stone, author of the reports, says:

> Paramount [Hollywood film studio] has bought the rights to film the popular radio-TV show, "THE RISE OF THE GOLDBERGS." Knowing that there is a difference of opinion among some of our major organizations on the subject of the Goldbergs, I spoke quite at length to the people involved [executives at Paramount], and cautioned them about the danger of falling into the error that was so disastrous to "ABIE'S IRISH ROSE." I explained the difference in concept as discussed by members of the American Jewish Congress and the American Jewish Committee, and others ... It seems the "Daily Peoples' World" is also interested in the production. In its Hollywood column, that was brought to my attention, "The Tattler" says, "The Goldbergs characters are warm, sympathetic and could easily be translated to the screen as a portrait of the Jewish people facing the problem of today's America. Unfortunately, Paramount has not the will to portray the real problems of the Jewish people in America on the screen—and the Goldbergs is destined to rely for its drama on trivia, and for its humor on the accents, malapropisms and stereotypes ... The danger is that Jewish people will be held up to ridicule." I talked to Paramount about this, too. The Goldbergs will be represented as an American family that mingles with other families that make up the American pattern of Democracy. There will be no reference to their Jewishness, Catholicism—or any other creed.[31]

Six months later, Stone updated the New York office on the status of the feature-film version of *The Goldbergs* after again meeting with Paramount executives, including Adolph Zukor, the immigrant founder: "The studio is holding back the release date on 'The Goldbergs' for an indefinite date pending a probable change of title to 'Molly.' As Variety expressed it [January 10, 1951]: 'It's felt that the Jewish connotation of the title, "The Goldbergs," might hurt its chances, and the two test shows *apparently have borne out* this theory' [emphasis is Stone's]."[32]

Kaufman was merely reproducing for television the kind of de-ethnicization that the Jews who invented Hollywood—like Zukor—had practiced for decades in the feature-film industry. In a lecture at the Jewish Museum in New York City, critic David Marc characterized the changes wrought by Kaufman:

> In 1955, the title of the only emphatically Jewish series on television, *The Goldbergs*, was changed to *Molly*, in an attempt to give it a more "mainstream feel." Moreover, the Goldberg family moved that season from the Bronx tenement, which had been its home for some 20 years of radio and television broadcast. The moving van took them from Tremont Avenue to a mythical town called Haverville. Yes, Molly and Jake Goldberg, who had struggled all those years in the Bronx, were now admitted to Haverville: the Village of the Haves? The Goldbergs lived in their own house now—just like Ozzie and Harriet.[33]

The actual move took place in the episode titled "Moving Day," and it must be noted for the record that there was no moving van to take the Goldberg family from Tremont Avenue to their new home at 1021 Central Avenue in Haverville. It must be noted because the specifics of the move are carefully laid out by screenwriter Berg so that the deus ex machina of deliverance for the family is again Molly and her ability to provide money.

This time Jake is opening a dressmaking factory in Haverville. He needs to have the factory up and running before the family moves—a process he believes will take about three months—because all their money is tied up in the transition. So, his plan is for him to live and work in Haverville during the week and commute back to the Bronx on weekends until he can get the factory established, get some orders, and have the money to finance the home they want in Haverville.

Molly hates the idea but says nothing to Jake. To David, she says, "This is no way for a family to live. I'm going to walk out to Haverville if I have to with a pan on my back." Naturally, Molly has a plan for how they can get the money to pay down on the house in Haverville without waiting three months. She and David will sell all their furniture in the Bronx apartment. When they get to Haverville, they can buy new furniture from Macy's on the installment plan—an especially convenient idea since the closing credits for the 1955–56 season include the following statement: "Molly Goldberg's home furnishings by Macy's New York."

And so they do sell the old furniture, which Rosie calls "old junk," to friends and neighbors, earning $1,587.25. But on the very next day as Molly is getting dressed to head out to Haverville, Jake arrives unexpectedly with very bad news. He has run out of money and the factory is in danger of closing. "I thought Simon could give me a couple of thousand dollars," Jake says, slumping into a chair and waving his hand in a gesture of utter defeat and loss. That is when Molly takes the $1,587.25 out of her purse and hands it to Jake. Tearfully, he asks her where she got it. "Jake, we've been married twenty years—a little here, a little there, it adds up," Molly says, echoing the words of Berg's grandmother Czerny.[34]

Unlike the schemes of Lucy Ricardo, Molly's schemes always work. She never has to beg her husband's forgiveness; he is the one tearfully thanking her for once again saving the day. This, too, is an important element of Molly's empowerment, as well as an aspect of her femininity that makes her character groundbreaking for television in the 1950s.

Molly's Jewishness was defined in other ways besides language, ethnicity, money, and power—for example, food. In one particularly strange episode from the 1955 season in which two fugitives from a maximum security prison wind up holding Molly hostage in her Haverville home during a stormy night, she offers to make blintzes for them ("Desperate Men").[35] While the episode and the blintzes seem strange on a literal level, on a symbolic level, they are perfectly logical. The story is a comic captivity narrative expressing a fear and sense of isolation that Berg, the author of the script, clearly felt in connection with moving her beloved Goldbergs to suburbia and life among the gentiles. There is a similar darkness to several of the Haverville scripts. The fact that she softens the menacing attitude and actions of the alien invaders (one of whom wears a crew cut and has the very American name of Butch) by making them the very Jewish treat of blintzes is telling.

Even though Berg and the various networks for whom she worked often tried to depict her as the Jewish mother cooking Jewish foods through publicity photos of her standing over the stove or telling *TV*

Guide readers how to make blintzes and borscht,[36] she rarely appeared in such a role in any of the episodes themselves. It was usually Uncle David who did the cooking.[37]

UNCLE DAVID: THE FEMINIZED JEWISH MALE

Molly was also defined in part by her relationship to Uncle David, her father's brother. While it would be convenient to explain "too Jewish" statements like the one quoted by Cherney Berg as being the product of a peculiar and individualized form of ethnic self-hatred on the part of the speaker, the executive from Guild Films was not alone in his assessment of Uncle David. The character was "too Jewish" for some tastes in a number of ways.

In addition to the thick Old World accent, his lines were delivered in such a whiny voice that it seemed as if the character was often going to break into tears. More striking is the fact that he is most often shown wearing a neck-to-knee-length frilly apron and spending most of his time in the kitchen cooking and cleaning under Molly's direction. In general, he is mainly depicted in the feminine terms of the times.

First played by vaudeville comedian and Yiddish theater actor Menasha Skulnik and then by Eli Mintz, who are both slight of build, Uncle David is a variation on a character type found in European anti-Semitic literature stretching back at least as far as the seventeenth century, when folk belief held that Jewish men menstruated.[38] He is the television archetype of the feminized Jewish male that continued in various, less-obvious forms in the world of prime time with such characters as Stuart Markowitz (Michael Tucker) of *L.A. Law* or Miles Silverberg (Grant Shaud) of *Murphy Brown*.

The extent of the feminization of this character is remarkably consistent throughout the history of the series. Numerous episodes open with David in the kitchen in an apron standing at the stove. He takes over most of the domestic duties one might have expected Molly to handle. Here is how Berg, the creator of Uncle David, described the character's history:

> Uncle David . . . was born when I heard Menasha Skulnik in a Yiddish play on Second Avenue. Menasha's voice, soft, gentle, with a squeak in it when he got mad, suggested exactly the kind of man I was

looking for; a small man with a big temper and feelings that could get hurt in the twinkling of an eye ... Sometimes I would examine the lonely old man who had a doctor for a son called Solly, the Doctor, and who was very successful. David would think that Solly had deserted his old father because he had gotten rich and nothing could be further from the truth—it was only that David liked to feel sorry for himself and Solly was a good excuse.[39]

None of that is very flattering, but the textual construction of David is even worse; he is treated by Molly almost as if he were her maid or cook. For example, "The In-Laws" opens with David in the kitchen in an apron at the stove. He is tasting and seasoning a pot of soup.

"David, the girls will be here soon. Stop fussing with the soup," Molly says irritably. "Fussing" is the key word. David fusses a lot, and fussing is a not a masculine trait. The (future) in-laws of the episode's title are Sammy's fiancée, Dora, and her parents, Carrie and Jerome Barnett. David greets Dora and Carrie, saying, "If you ladies care to get fresh and wash up, I'll bring in some refreshments."

The episode titled "Molly's Wedding Plans" opens with the family— Molly, Jake, David, Sammy, and Rosalie—seated around the kitchen table. Again David is wearing the apron. They are discussing the guest list for Sammy's wedding.

"Will somebody tell me why all mothers cry when they hear the word 'weddings'?" Rosalie asks, even though Molly is not crying.

"If I was a mother I'd tell you," Jake says.

"All I know is I'm a father, and I cried plenty when my Solly, the doctor, got married," David says.

Sammy, Dora, and Rosalie depart, leaving the adults to work out the details. While Jake and Jerome move to the living room, David stays with Molly and Carrie in the kitchen. "So, what is it, girls?" Jerome asks when the trio comes into the living room with their final guest list. The men and women break into separate groups a number of times during the episode and each time David goes with the women.

In an episode from August 17, 1954, that involved the Goldberg family helping out in the kitchen and then joining the talent show at Pincus-in-the-Pines, Molly is told that the vegetable woman just quit. Before Molly can answer, David volunteers, saying, "I can be a vegetable woman."

The June 29, 1954, episode opens with Molly again calling out to David, who is at the ironing board, "David, did my dresses come out of the cleaners?" Later, after a dinner that he serves in the Goldberg apartment, David sits down in the living room with the men, the first time this has happened in any episode. But it is only to set up a joke. When cigars are passed around, David joins in only to choke on his first puff and collapse in a violent coughing fit before the other men take the cigar away from him. Sometimes a cigar is only a cigar, but not when it is too much for David to handle.

The feminized Jewish male—an unmanly and powerless Jew—has been called "one of television's most insidious stereotypes . . . a sexist and anti-Semitic construction designed to allay fears of Jewish intelligence, wealth or political power."[40] The feminization of Uncle David is not the same as the burlesque transvestitism of comedian Milton Berle on *The Milton Berle Show*, a variety show that ran from 1948 to 1956 on Tuesday nights on NBC. Judith Butler argues that questioning the complexities of one's sexuality through drag is acknowledging the extent to which sexual identity is a mask.[41] There was a lot of that in Berle—drag that challenged the boundaries of gender.

But there is none of that in Uncle David's feminization. Coupled with the apron, the kitchen, and the fussiness is an utter submissiveness. For example, in "Rosie's Nose," the five family members are again sitting at the kitchen table. Jake and Sammy wear ties, but David wears the apron. They are talking about Rosie's "love of money," which Jake blames on Molly's side of the family. "Your grandfather had the reputation of being the stingiest man in the town," Jake says to Molly. She protests.

"A generous man he wasn't," David says. "I remember once . . ."

"David, please," Molly snaps, and David immediately stops, looks down at the table and then looks up, head still bowed, through his eyebrows at Molly. This hangdog, head-bowed look is a frequent one for David when he is in Molly's company.

Remember this is 1949 to 1955, and questions about how the horror of the Holocaust could have happened are still very much in the air. Did the submissiveness of David—the most Old World of the Goldbergs— provide an easy and false answer for some viewers? David's presence as the archetype of the feminized Jewish male on American television de- mands that the question at least be raised.

It should also be noted that there was one other series during the

1950s that featured a Jewish actor playing a character who was identified as Jewish by name: *Menasha The Magnificent*, a short-lived summer series that debuted on NBC July 3, 1950, and was cancelled September 11, 1950. It starred Skulnik as a character named Menasha, a restaurant manager who started each episode singing "Oh, What a Beautiful Morning," only to slide into deeper trouble and catastrophe as the day wore on.

Earle Brooks and Tim Marsh in their directory of prime time shows offered the most succinct description of the series when they wrote: "Menasha, a little fellow with a hoplike walk and a tragicomic mien, was cast as the meek manager of a restaurant owned by the domineering, Amazonlike Mrs. Davis. His fate was to be pushed around constantly."[42]

Skulnik, who had played Uncle David in the radio version of *The Goldbergs*, joined the television cast of Berg's series after *Menasha The Magnificent* was cancelled. The transition was an easy one: he was playing essentially the same submissive Jewish male.

ROSALIE AND HER NOSE

Rosalie, the teenage daughter, would also become a template for Jewish identity on TV. Often defined by her body, she is created in the image of the ugly duckling—most clearly in one memorable episode, "Rosie's Nose," in which Rosalie wants to have plastic surgery performed on her nose. But she is also television's first "Jewish-American Princess," a particularly destructive and durable stereotype.[43] As the ugly duckling, Rosie lives on in characters like Rhoda Morgenstern (as played by Valerie Harper) and the other feminine sidekick characters that are defined negatively in terms of their body. But, as the "princess," Rosalie can also be seen in Fran Fine, the character played by Fran Drescher in *The Nanny*— a character who largely defines herself in terms of physical adornment and her capacity to consume while avoiding any productive labor.

Here is how Berg described the roots of Rosalie in *Me and Molly*:

The children, Sammy and Rosie, were myself, my cousins, my own children and some parts of all the friends I had grown up with. They also expressed a point of view: that of the first generation Americans who were trying to make sense of growing up in one world, America, but coming from another, the European world of their parents. They were being pulled by the new and held back by the old... Sammy and Rosie were important to *The Goldbergs* because they helped to teach their immigrant parents how to become American.[44]

Rosie did do some of that teaching, though "American" to her mainly meant being "modern" and joining the consumer society. Some of the clearest examples are in "Moving Day," when Rosie calls the family furniture "old junk" and tells Molly the modern thing to do is buy new on credit. She goes with Molly to Macy's and corrects her mother when she calls a tree lamp a "branch lamp." And Molly "learns" from Rosie, buying all new furniture. Rosie's advanced consumerist tendencies, as well as her tendency to cry or get extremely upset at the slightest disturbance to the Goldberg's household, go a long way toward defining her in terms of the "princess" stereotype.

But nowhere is Rosie more strikingly defined than in "Rosie's Nose," which was written by Berg.[45] The episode opens with Sammy solving the mystery for the other family members as to why Rosie is babysitting every night and asking that family members give her only money for her upcoming birthday. "She wants a plastic job on her nose," Sammy says. "She's got an inferiority complex; she thinks she's an ugly duckling."

"I gave her a complex? Such a beautiful girl and I made her inferior?" Molly asks, alarmed. Later, in her bedroom, Rosalie bursts into tears when she is confronted by Molly. "I know every time I look in the mirror that I could be pretty, Ma, if I didn't have this nose," Rosie says. "I've always hated my nose. For years, I hated it. I'm going to have a plastic operation on my nose, Ma, and that's final." She throws herself on the bed, sobbing. "I'm going to see Dr. George Harris. Irene's mother went to him and he made her look beautiful."

Molly calls Dr. Harris and concocts a scheme with him to thwart Rosie's planned operation. But what is important for the purposes of this book is the way the script talks about Rosie and Rosie's nose versus ideals of feminine beauty. Seldom has the American notion of re-inventing the self been so neatly played out in a TV sitcom. Molly tells the family that Rosie doesn't need a nose like those of Leslie Caron or Audrey Hepburn. And then, in the doctor's waiting room with Rosie, Molly starts leafing through a magazine.

"Look, Rosie, that's Zsa Zsa Gabor, no? Maybe the doctor can give you her nose," Molly says.

"She's beautiful," Rosie replies.

"Maybe Ingrid Bergman's nose would be better for your personality, Rosalie," Molly says, holding up another page of the magazine.

When Rosalie agrees, Molly puts down the magazine and says, "Rosalie, I'm your mother and listen to me. Rosalie, you're not an actress in a magazine and for all normal purposes, you're pretty enough."

Just as Molly finishes, in walks a striking woman with a small, slender, Audrey Hepburn sort of nose. The camera gives us a classic profile shot of it as she sits down.

"He did a beautiful job on your nose," Rosie says to the woman.

"Thank you," the woman replies. "He did a beautiful job on yours, too."

"No," Rosie protests, "this is my own."

"It is?" the woman says, surprised. "It's lovely. I wish I had my nose back."

The woman then breaks into tears and confesses to Molly, Rosie, and the rest of the waiting room: "I'm going to have a baby, and my husband doesn't know about my nose. He's so handsome. He has a lovely Grecian profile. Don't you see how embarrassing it will be if the baby is born with my old nose?"

The woman goes on for quite a bit about what a tragic situation she is in, her only option being to get the before and after pictures, show them to her husband, and "Let him do what he likes." Turning to Rosie, she says, "Take my advice, young lady, when you get your new nose, don't keep it a dark secret. Just shout it out to the world." At which point, Rosie announces she doesn't want the operation and runs from the waiting room.

The doctor then walks in and introduces the woman to Molly. "Mrs. Goldberg, I'd like you to meet my wife . . . Mrs. Harris used to be an actress." Molly thanks Mrs. Harris, who also takes her leave. The scene ends with just Molly and the doctor.

"Doctor, can I ask you one question?" Molly says. "Was that your nose or her nose?"

"Well, I can state for a certainty it's not my nose," he says. Then, after a pause, with a chuckle, he adds, "On the other hand, I'm not too sure it's hers either."

Rosie rejects plastic surgery, but not necessarily because she feels her nose is beautiful. In fact, what you have here is Rosie's nose, the Jewish nose, defined in opposition to a number of noses held up as ideal and all belonging to gentile actresses—Audrey Hepburn, Leslie Caron, Zsa Zsa Gabor, Ingrid Bergman, and Mrs. Harris. The doctor's wife validates her fictitious husband's "Grecian profile," while the camera does exactly the same for her nose through its long, loving profile shot of her nose as she enters. The joke at the end about whether it is real or plastic further validates Mrs. Harris's nose as so perfect that Molly has to ask whether it is real.

Meanwhile, the best Molly can say to her daughter is essentially, "No you're not as pretty as them, but, for you, your nose is pretty enough." In the 1970s, we'd see that message about Jewish women reproduced in Rhoda Morgenstern, who was pretty enough but certainly no Mary Richards. And, starting with Bridget of *Bridget Loves Bernie* in 1972 and going straight through to *Mad About You*, we see it reproduced and, in fact, reified in the choices generally made by the Jewish men of prime time when it comes to the objects of their desire.

SAMMY, JAKE, AND THE BLACKLIST

Sammy Goldberg was the most American and least developed character in the Goldberg family. During the television years, he was always shown in shirt and tie or slacks and sweater. His story arc is college, the Army, and then engaged to be married during the last year of the show. He graduated college as an engineer. He had a bar mitzvah during the radio years but was already too old by the time the series came to television.

The episode in which he is most prominent is "The In-Laws" from 1955. The episode is about Molly wanting Sammy and his fiancée, Dora, to live in "one of the nice ranch houses" in Haverville—near her—after they are married. She thinks it is a done deal when Sammy gets a job offer in Haverville. But Sammy turns down the job offer, telling Molly, "We just think Haverville is a little too close to home." What is noteworthy is how cool, calm, and confident Sammy is while standing up to Molly on this very important matter. Uncle David is downright submissive, and husband Jake at this point in the series is somewhere between passive and henpecked, while Sammy presents a new, more assertive image of Jewish masculinity in relation to Molly. If nothing else, one can safely say Sammy is not a mama's boy.

Molly, of course, is beside herself after the showdown with Sammy.

Interestingly, Berg, the screenwriter, ends the series of scenes involving Sammy's rejection of Haverville in the bedroom of Jake and Molly just as they are about to turn out the lights for the night. After listening to Molly, the passive Jake says he can't make Sammy change his mind, "So resign yourself. *Oy*, good night."[46]

In the next scene, we see Dora's mother, Carrie, exulting over the good news that Sammy now has a job offer in New York City where she and her husband, Jerome, live. Furthermore, an apartment just two blocks away has a vacancy. But Carrie's joy is short-lived when Sammy and Dora decide that New York is too close to home, too. More passive-father humor here when Carrie demands Jerome make Dora change her mind, saying, "Jerome, are you her father or not?" Jerome's response: "I'm going to shave." Shaving is a masculine act, but it is positioned here as a move of escape or avoidance by a man who can't control his daughter.

Molly, with David in tow, comes to visit Carrie to try and hatch a plan to keep Sammy and Dora somewhere nearby after they get word that Sammy is about to accept a job in the Belgian Congo. As Uncle David puts it, "The Belgian Congo with cannibals and gorillas, *oy*." At which point Sammy and Dora walk in on the conspirators, and Sammy loses his temper. The episode ends with Sammy and Dora telling both sets of parents how much they love them, but that Sammy is accepting a job in Oklahoma. It is not Haverville and it is not New York City, Molly says, but it is a lot closer than the Belgian Congo. It is one of the least tidy endings in the history of the series, but it does seem to be a practical ending for an episode that was really about a negotiation of power between Molly and her grown son, and, if nothing else, it offered a more assertive image of Jewish masculinity than had been seen on series television up to that point.

Jake, the father, as played by Philip Loeb in 1949 and 1950, started out as a fairly strong, traditional male figure for the times—a hard-working, honest dresscutter who wants to start his own dressmaking business. But, after Loeb was replaced as a result of being blacklisted, Jake progressively became a passive, subordinated, weak father in the hands of actors Harold J. Stone and Robert H. Harris. He lives on in characters like Martin Morgenstern (Harold J. Gould) on *Rhoda* and Jules Berger (Louis Zorich) of *Brooklyn Bridge*, respectively.[47]

Jake was never Molly's equal and, as discussed in the analysis of Molly, the bottom line was money. There is a suggestion of that in Berg's own less-than-laudatory description of the character: "Molly's husband Jake, too, was a combination of people . . . He had touches of my father Jake's stubbornness and ability to go from one mood to another without reason or explanation. He also had a bit of Lew [Berg's husband] in him. He was a stickler for being correct in his dealings with everyone and he was too kind to be a good businessman."[48]

Not exactly a glowing recommendation for someone whose dream was to own his own business and, with Molly's help, did during most of the television years. While the economic power was always with Molly, the Jake that started the series as Papa Goldberg in 1949 was a much stronger one than the Jake who ended the series in Haverville in 1956. With the early Jake on CBS in 1949 and the early 1950s, his bite was much less than his gruff demeanor might suggest, but Molly's relationship with him was much more a matter of power negotiated than it was of her dominance.

By 1955, however, it is a different story. Typical of Jake's role and stature in the Haverville household is a scene that unfolds in "Rosie's Nose" after Molly hangs up the phone, having confirmed that Rosie has an appointment for a consultation with a plastic surgeon.

"Well, my teenage miss is going to have a consultation with me right this minute. I'll put an end to this," Jake announces angrily.

"Oh, Jake, please," Molly says, waving him away with a dismissive gesture of her hand and heading off on her own to deal with the matter. In times of crisis, he is mainly ignored by Molly.

The decline is best illustrated by comparing that treatment to the Jake we see in an untitled episode from 1949 that centers on young Rosalie writing a composition for school about her family. In this time of sitcom "crisis," rather than ignoring Jake, Molly repeatedly turns to him for guidance and direction. He is as much at the center of the household decisionmaking process in 1949 as he is at the periphery in 1956.

The very first words of the episode, which aired on CBS October 10, 1949, come from Molly, who says, "Jake, Jake, the whole house is topsy-turvy." It is topsy-turvy because of the school assignment and Molly's fear as to what Rosalie might say about her family in an essay that could well be read on parent-teacher night. As Molly puts it, "Jake, Jake, I'm trembling already. Should we be worried at this moment? Shouldn't we have confidence that our child will write what we would like to hear?"

Everything is addressed to Loeb's Jake, and everything flows to him in the Goldberg household. In the early years of the series with Loeb, one of the key sources of drama and tension was how Jake would react— specifically, whether or not he would raise his voice or lose his temper. In this episode, instead of trying to calm Molly in her "trembling," Jake gives voice to his own worries in a booming voice as he storms around the living room: "Ah, if I was the father I should be? Did I ever sit and read to the child? Did I ever take her to the park or the zoo or the botanical garden or planetarium? Shouldn't a man of my age be able to control his temper? Yet, what right have I got to bring my business worries over my threshold? Shouldn't the child be protected from the storms of the world? The trouble is you only get one chance to be a good parent."

Molly says, "They should have parent-teacher meetings before the child is born, not after." But when she fails to join Jake in the breast beating, he says, "So, Molly? From you I hear only silence. Are you so contented?"

"Did I say?" Molly asks.

"So say," Jake commands.

"What should I say?" Molly counters.

"If you don't say it, I will," Jake threatens. "I know my faults, Molly. Do you know yours?" Jake then enumerates Molly's faults: she is "always mixing" too much in the neighborhood and "gossiping" with the neighbors, not staying home and paying enough attention to her own family. The conversation escalates as the tone of Jake's voice rises and he does more stomping around the apartment.

"My mixing is not just mixing," Molly insists. "My interest is in people, not just gossip. My interest is in interest."

Jake appears not even to hear, as he demands, "So, I'm not a father? Tell me. So, when I holler, I holler because I like to holler, I want to holler? Tell me. No, when I holler, I holler because I love my family and I want to do for them beyond my power and strength. That's why I holler."

At which point Rosalie enters the room, and everyone tries to act as if everything isn't topsy-turvy in the Goldberg household. After several complications in the form of essay rewrites by Rosalie, the episode ends happily with Rosie reading an essay that talks about how much her parents love each other, how happy the family is, how well Molly "knows the neighborhood," and how much Molly "loves" their neighbors and vice versa. The essay also mentions Jake's "temper," but says it is only because he "loves" the family so much and is such a good father. The final camera shot shows Jake and Molly beaming at Rosalie as she reads, with Molly then looking at Jake and Jake looking down at her face approvingly. In the visual language of television, that would make Jake and Molly at least equals, with the final shot suggesting a position of slightly more authority for Jake. Again, a far cry from the Jake we see routinely dismissed by Molly in later years.

But it is impossible to understand the decline in the authority of Jake onscreen without also having some sense of the history of the actors who played Jake over the years and the blacklisting of Philip Loeb.

In May 1950, at the end of that television season, *The Goldbergs* appeared to be riding high as the seventh highest-rated series on television.[49] Furthermore, Berg won the Emmy that year for Best Actress,[50] while Loeb was voted "Television's Father of the Year" by the Boys Clubs of America.[51] But all was far from well backstage. The paperback book *Red Channels* had been published the previous month, listing names and dossiers of actors who were allegedly Communists or "friendly to Communist causes." Loeb was listed in *Red Channels* and pressure began building immediately from the sponsor, advertising agency, and network for Berg to fire Loeb.

Berg used all her clout and wiles to keep Loeb on the show through the next season. Typical of Berg's response was her announcement in April 1951 that at the end of the television season she was going to "tour GI camps and bases at her own expense."[52] She was naive enough to think that showing her own patriotism could somehow save Loeb as long as she stood behind him. She hired a publicist to make sure her announcement was reported as widely as possible, but it was not nearly enough. Less than a month later, the entertainment industry trade paper *Variety* reported that General Foods—the same advertiser that had previously showered Berg with notes and letters of gratitude and praise—was dropping *The Goldbergs*.[53] Before Berg even left for Europe and her tour of GI bases, CBS announced that it too was dropping the show.[54] The official CBS statement saying that the cancellation "was strictly business" was widely quoted,[55] though no one bothered to ask how canceling the seventh highest-rated series on television could possibly be good business.

Billboard magazine, the most aggressive publication at the time in re- porting on the blacklist, did offer a bit of analysis, saying that there were "political undertones" to such cancellations.[56] That is as specific as any- one would get in print until January 1952, when the *New York Times* reported that NBC was picking up the series that CBS had cancelled. The headline on the *Times* story: "Loeb Dropped."[57] In February 1952, John Crosby, the television critic for the *New York Herald Tribune*, gave the fullest account of the story of how Loeb had to be dropped so that *The Goldbergs* could get back on the air:

> *The Goldbergs*, once one of the most highly rated shows on television
> . . . limped back on the air again last week, mighty subdued, its earning
> power diminished, its chief male actor missing, its format extensively
> rearranged. At that, I suppose it's lucky to have got back on at all.
> *The Goldbergs* had become the most dreaded word in broadcasting—
> controversial . . . At the center of the controversy was Philip Loeb, a
> very fine actor, who played Jake Goldberg, husband of Molly or Ger-
> trude Berg who writes, stars in and owns *The Goldbergs*. Back when it
> was on CBS, General Foods, the sponsor, and the network both tried
> hard to get rid of Mr. Loeb whose name appears in *Red Channels* . . .
> Mr. Loeb was offered $85,000 [two years' salary] to quit. He refused.
> Mrs. Berg refused to discharge him. Finally, General Foods dropped
> the show . . . It [the series] switched to NBC-TV. Normally, this would
> have been quite a coup for NBC, *The Goldbergs* being worth roughly
> $3,500,000 a year in billings at the time. But as time passed and con-
> troversy waxed, it became worth a lot less than that. NBC held open
> prime evening time for the show, but no sponsor would touch it with
> Mr. Loeb, who protested futilely that he was not and had never been
> a Communist.[58]

Loeb did take $85,000 from Berg in January to leave the series. In February, he issued a statement, saying, "Although I believe a grave injustice is being done to myself and others in the entertainment industry by the blacklist, I appreciate Mrs. Gertrude Berg's position throughout."[59]

But, even without Loeb, the series was now controversial, and NBC could still not find a prime-time sponsor. RCA (Radio Corporation of America), which owned NBC, was the first sponsor, with Berg standing in her window hawking RCA television sets to her viewers just as she had coffee and vitamins: "RCA, huh? Not just initials but a name to remember when you want the best. *Oy*, what RCA did for the world! Mavelous! Mavelous!"

The series ran Monday, Wednesday, and Friday on NBC from 7 to 7:15 P.M.—a very strange format. Structurally, Berg was trying to write a sitcom in what was essentially a serial or soap opera radio format. It was a strange time period, too, since it was not prime time and many local affiliates around the country ran their own programs from 7 to 8 P.M. The result was that *The Goldbergs* was not seen in many cities even though NBC had affiliates in those cities—thus, it had a smaller potential audience to sell to advertisers.

Despite all of that, the series did eventually attract Necchi sewing machines, Ecko packaged goods, and Rybutal vitamins by the start of the summer of 1952. But, by July, Necchi and Ecko pulled out—Necchi said it did not have enough business to afford the show,[60] while Ecko cited the lack of 100 percent clearance for the show among NBC affiliates.[61] The Necchi letter of cancellation is especially telling, with treasurer Milton Heimlich calling his letter "an unashamed confession of love" for Berg praising her for "presenting Jews who act as Jews" in her program. The bottom line, though: Necchi was pulling out. What the letter reads like more than anything else is an apology by Heimlich for caving into pressure to cancel Necchi's sponsorship of the series.

After taking *The Goldbergs* off the air in July 1952 because of the advertiser pullout, NBC brought it back as a summer replacement in July 1953. But, again unable to find a sponsor, the series was permanently cancelled by NBC two months later, at the start of 1953–54 television season. Bouncing down the ladder from top-rated CBS to second-place NBC, the next stop for *The Goldbergs* was the almost-bankrupt DuMont network, where it ran from April to October 1954 as a summer replacement for *Life Is Worth Living*, the religious talk show featuring Fulton J. Sheen, a bishop in the Catholic Church.

The final gasp was in syndication, with Berg and Guild Films selling it city by city with different sponsors in each one—a hopelessly complicated way to do business. In that final 1955–56 television season, it was often smaller, regional Jewish advertising agencies and local sponsors that kept *The Goldbergs* on the air.[62]

On September 1, 1955, Philip Loeb killed himself by taking an overdose of sleeping pills. He died at age 61 alone in a room in the Taft Hotel in New York City. He had been struggling to find work since leaving *The Goldbergs* and had been living in the months before his death with the family of actor Zero Mostel, who was also blacklisted.[63] A tribute in the *New York Times* said, "Philip Loeb died of a sickness commonly called 'The Black List.' "[64]

What the story did not say is that it was two Jewish network founders, Paley and Sarnoff, who accepted and enforced that blacklist in the broadcasting industry. The lessons of the blacklist and self-censorship were not lost on Berg, who said in a 1956 interview, "You see, darling, don't bring up anything that will bother people. That's very important. Unions, politics, fund-raising, Zionism, socialism, intergroup relations. I don't stress them. And after all, aren't all such things secondary to daily family living?"[65]

A RARE RELIGIOUS MOMENT

In *The Goldbergs*, then, Jewish identity was depicted in several ways: first and foremost through language, but also through the body (Rosie's nose), objects (the menorah on the mantel in the family living room), geography (the Bronx), surname (Goldberg), food (blintzes and gefilte fish), and occupation (Jake as dresscutter in the garment industry).

There is one other highly important way Jewish identity was constructed in the series: religion, or Jewishness as Judaism. On October 5, 1954, in what would be her last month on network television, Berg gave American viewers the most Jewish episode of any series in the history of network television. The entire episode is about Yom Kippur, the holiest of Jewish holy days.

The episode opens with Molly, Sammy, and Rosie hurrying about the apartment trying to get things done before sundown. Molly tells Sammy, "You just have time to run down before the stores close for the holiday ... Go, before the tailor closes." As he leaves, Molly turns to Rosie, "I want to be dressed before sundown ... Did you decide what you're going to wear to temple?" As Rosie goes off to get dressed, a neighbor lady, Mrs. Ellenbogen, walks in. The zipper on her dress is stuck, and she wants Molly to help her zip it. "*Oy*, it's tight," Molly says. "*Oy, oy, oy.* Take away your hand a little."

Mrs. Ellenbogen says, "I like to be in temple before the first star is in the sky." As Molly fights the zipper, she says, "Mrs. Ellenbogen, if through the year, I said something or did something, I want to say excuse me." Mrs. Ellenbogen hugs Molly. "Likewise, Mrs. Goldberg, if I said anything." Molly responds, "You didn't. Always a good neighbor."

This is the Yom Kippur practice of atonement—asking forgiveness of those whom you have hurt during the year. To underline that message, Molly yoo-hoo's to Mrs. Silvertone and then asks her if she has offended her in any way, explaining, "This is the kind of holiday when people have to ponder. It's a time when people ask for forgiveness, darling."

Meanwhile, the main plot starts to take shape. Uncle David always goes to temple for Yom Kippur with his son, Solly, the doctor. But Solly has called to say he can't go with his father tonight. The reason he can't go is that his baby has a temperature of 104 degrees. But Solly doesn't tell David that, because he doesn't want to upset his easily excitable father. Instead he tells David that he is going with his father-in-law. This, however, also upsets David and leaves him thinking his son has rejected him, as well as a sacred ritual that the two had shared.

A subplot surfaces when it is discovered that the tailor gave Sammy the wrong suit for Jake—one too small and so old it shines. Moments after the discovery, in walk Mr. and Mrs. Ellenbogen, who are leaving for temple. Mrs. Ellenbogen had confided to Molly that they were having financial problems.

"My Joe's a salaried man, not self-employed like your Jake," she says, adding that she is embarrassed by her husband's one old suit.

But Mr. Ellenbogen is not wearing an old suit. He is wearing a fine-looking one and looking fine in it. When he and his wife leave, Jake says, "A suit without a shine, it does something for a man's psychology." But a confused Sammy says, "Wasn't that your suit he had on, pop?" When Jake says it was, Sammy asks, "So, why didn't you tell him?" Jake's reply: "Because I liked the way he looked in it." A holiday message about charity and kindness.

Back to David, Solly, and Molly. Just before David is about to leave for temple alone, Molly picks up the phone and insists Solly explain to David why they won't be going together. The next shot takes us inside a packed and brightly lit synagogue. The camera focuses on Jake and David in prayer shawls and yarmulkes with the men. Then it goes up to the balcony to show Rosie and Molly with the women. The cantor is singing "Kol Nidre," and the camera moves slowly up and down the rows of men on the main floor, showing the faces of old men and young boys standing side by side, suggesting generational continuity. Then the same visual treatment is given the women. Rosie is looking solemnly at Molly, who has a look of sadness on her face. The neighbor ladies, Mrs. Ellenbogen and Mrs. Silvertone, are standing nearby and both are crying. Some of the men and women are davening. The cantor's concert ensemble is singing now.

This sequence, in which we see the Yom Kippur service while hearing the cantor and the choir sing, goes on for six minutes and nine seconds. At the end of it, Solly, wearing yarmulke and prayer shawl, comes rushing in to take his place next to David. "She's all right. The baby's going to be all right," he whispers happily to David, who bursts into tears of joy at the news. The episode ends with a long shot from the ceiling down that takes in the entire temple and suggests the majesty of the Yom Kippur service as the choir and congregation join in song.

The show ends with Molly back in the window talking to her TV audience: "Dear friends, that we all wish on you God's blessings on this day and greetings from our family to your family. Good night."

It is the same kind of treatment for a Jewish holiday that we have seen hundreds of times on television for Christmas with fictional families like *The Waltons* wishing us a happy holiday from their house to ours and God's blessings.

We have not seen the Jewish version in a weekly network series since that night on DuMont in 1954. Nor would America see another leading Jewish character in any prime-time network program for eighteen years following the cancellation of *The Goldbergs* by DuMont the following month.

"Write Yiddish, Cast British" –
From Dick Van Dyke to Mrs. G

Imagine CBS with a man with all that money and all that power being in a non-competitive business for all those years! Not only was television itself a monopoly with only the three networks then—no cable, nothing else—but he didn't even have any real competition . . . The monopoly of television was far more influenced by the fact that there was really only one player, and that was Paley.

Michael Dann, former NBC and CBS programming executive, on
the power of William Paley and CBS in the 1950s and 1960s.[1]

Following the cancellation of *The Goldbergs* by DuMont at the end of the 1954 television season, it would be almost two decades before American viewers would have another chance to become acquainted with a leading character in a weekly network series who was overtly Jewish. That character was Bernie Steinberg (David Birney) of *Bridget Loves Bernie*, which premiered on CBS in 1972 and was cancelled at the end of the same season despite being a Top 10 series in the Nielsen ratings.[2]

This void is one of the most striking aspects in the history of Jewish characters on network television, yet it has never fully been explained. There is some consensus among television historians and analysts that the 1950s and 1960s were a time in which all forms of ethnicity were essentially excluded from a prime-time landscape that became overwhelmingly suburban, white, middle-class, and Protestant, reflecting larger social trends. *Leave It to Beaver* and *Father Knows Best* are the series most often cited to make the case.

David Marc, author of *Comic Visions: Television Comedy and American Culture*, articulates the position as well as anyone:

As the Age of Television dawned, the vision of the promised land of social mobility shifted from the vertical Olympus of the Manhattan apartment tower to the horizontal utopia of the tract development ranch house . . . One by one, the old inner city ethnic sitcoms were cancelled in the mid-fifties . . . By the early sixties, sitcom America, dominated by shows such as *Father Knows Best* and its many clones, had become so white, so Anglo-Saxon, and so Protestant that even the Andersons' seemingly Hispanic gardener—played by an actor named Natividad Vacio—goes by the name of Frank Smith.[3]

There are two things wrong with such an analysis of 1950s television: by generalizing, it oversimplifies the situation and ignores large exceptions. It also seems to accept a "reflection" theory of television, which says that TV series reflect social reality in a direct way. As much as the television industry itself would like us to see the medium as a "window to the world" or some sort of "mirror" of it, the relationship between television and social reality is far more complicated.

In terms of ethnicity, while there was less of it than during the periods immediately preceding and following the years 1955 to 1972, there was still a considerable amount of it on network television during those years. There just wasn't *Jewish* ethnicity. What I am saying here is that the absence of Jewish characters from 1955 to 1972 can only be fully explained by looking at the milieu of network production during those years. What such an investigation shows is tremendous network resistance toward, if not an institutional policy against, series featuring Jewish characters by the dominant television institution of the era, CBS.

The three-network universe of the time, which also included NBC and the fledgling ABC, was run by Jewish chairmen who had both the inclination and the power to keep Jewish characters off their airwaves. This is particularly true in the case of Paley, the founder and autocratic chairman of CBS, whose deep ambivalence about his Jewish identity has been well documented.

I am not ignoring those arguments that try to explain the absence of leading Jewish characters from 1955 to 1972 on network TV by linking it to larger social trends such as movement to the suburbs, a rapidly expanding middle class, and assimilation. But what I cannot stress enough when it comes to network television is that between social reality and the on-air programs themselves there are always gatekeepers in the persons of the writers and producers who create the shows and the network executives who determine what sorts of programs will be bought and broadcast into America's living rooms.

Even if they are not actively functioning as gatekeepers, they still serve as a filter between the two realms. Understanding the psychology and actions of key gatekeepers is essential to understanding how the relationship between television programming and social reality is actually shaped. In this book and particularly in this chapter, "warped" is a far more appropriate way of describing the role played by Jewish gatekeepers like Paley and Sarnoff, who kept virtually all Jewish leading characters off the network landscape that they controlled from 1955 to 1972.

First, some context and often-ignored facts about ethnic images from 1955 to 1972. While it is true that ethnicity in network prime-time series was in decline for a period of about ten years from the late 1950s to the late 1960s, the exceptions to Marc's "so white, so Anglo-Saxon and so Protestant" thesis are major. In terms of leading characters, you can start with Ricky Ricardo (Desi Arnaz), the Cuban-American bandleader and husband of Lucy Ricardo (Lucille Ball) on *I Love Lucy*, the most popular series on network TV from 1951 through 1957 during its run of weekly original episodes. The series stayed on CBS in prime time through 1961 in one form or another, with Ricky's ethnicity constantly before the viewer in his accent, Spanish-language epithets, occupation, and comments from Lucy. In fact, to a lesser extent, Lucy's ethnicity was also made plain through references to her maiden name of Lucy Mac-Gillicuddy and her Scottish background.

Another major exception often ignored altogether in the "so Anglo-Saxon and so Protestant" analysis is *The Danny Thomas Show*, also known as *Make Room for Daddy*, which ran from 1953 to 1957 on ABC, and from 1957 to 1965 on CBS, before returning to ABC for the 1970 and 1971 seasons.[4] *The Danny Thomas Show*, which dealt with the on-stage (at the nightclub)/off-stage (the family apartment in Manhattan) lives of entertainer Danny Williams (Thomas) was drenched in ethnicity, and Semitic ethnicity to boot, with constant references to Williams's Lebanese ancestry. In fact, from 1956 to 1971 one of the most popular recurring characters on the series was Williams's Uncle Tonoose (Hans Conried), the patriarch of the Williams clan, who held to old country ways, spoke with a thick accent, and is referred to in one reference book as "Danny's wacky Lebanese relation."[5] Another recurring ethnic character was the elevator operator in Williams's building, Jose Jiminez (Bill Dana). Even the ethnicity of Williams's wife from 1957 to 1971, Kathy (Marjorie Lord), was constantly referenced in the series via Williams's pet names for her, "Clancey" and "Irish." She is referred to in one reference book as the "Irish lass" and "the former Kathy O'Hara."[6]

And, like *I Love Lucy*, this was not a minor series. From 1957 to 1964, *Make Room for Daddy* consistently finished among the ten most popular series on all of television, with much larger audiences than *Father Knows Best*, *Leave It to Beaver*, or *The Donna Reed Show*, the series often cited as examples of "so white" hits in the bygone days of Consensus America and a three-network universe.[7] So, there clearly was an audience for Semitic ethnicity.

There was other ethnicity, too, in the 1960s. The very Irish police officer, Francis Muldoon (Fred Gwynne), was featured in *Car 54, Where Are You?*, a sitcom by Nat Hiken that ran on NBC from 1961 through 1963. In 1965, prime time got its first African-American leading character in Alexander Scott (Bill Cosby) of *I Spy*, an adventure drama. In 1968, there was another African-American leading character in Julia Baker (Diahann Carroll) of the sitcom *Julia*. In 1969, add Pete Dixon (Lloyd Haynes), an African-American teacher, to the list in *Room 222*, a drama about an integrated big-city high school. As contested as race was in the 1960s, you might wonder how a medium known for playing it safe could accommodate three leading African-American characters but no Jewish ones—especially given the example in 1956 of many NBC affiliates in the south refusing to even air *The Nat "King" Cole Show* because the star was African American.

One of the first indications that there might be a sign saying "No Jewish Characters" hanging somewhere at the networks during this era involves a 1960 CBS sitcom pilot titled *Head of the Family*, which would become *The Dick Van Dyke Show* in 1961 and go on to enjoy a six-year run that would make it a television classic.

Carl Reiner, a writer and second banana to Sid Caesar on *Your Show of Shows* and *Caesar's Hour*, wrote *Head of the Family* as a sitcom in which he would star. He wrote the pilot and twelve episodes—all at his own expense, with no advance payment from any network or production company—during the summer of 1959, when he saw the popularity of the variety show genre in which he had worked for over a decade starting to wane. The autobiographical nature of the sitcom is impossible to miss.

As Ginny Weissman and Coyne Steven Sanders explained in their book *The Dick Van Dyke Show*, Reiner was a sitcom writer, and the character he would play, Rob Petrie, was a sitcom writer. Reiner lived in New Rochelle and worked in Manhattan, and Rob lived in New Rochelle and worked in Manhattan. Rob's wife, Laura, was a dancer who had given up her career to be a wife and mother. Carl's wife, Estelle, was an artist who had given up her career to become a wife and mother. Rob and Laura had a son named Ritchie. Carl and Estelle had a son named Rob, who would go on to play Mike Stivac on *All in the Family* and then enjoy a successful career as film actor, director, and producer. The Petries lived at 448 Bonnie Meadow Road in New Rochelle, and the Reiners lived at 48 Bonnie Meadow Road. Reiner said he added the four to his address "so nobody would come visit me."[8]

Reiner, of course, recognized the parallels: "I was examining my life and putting it down on paper. [I was trying to create] the first situation comedy where you saw where the man worked before he walked in and said, "Hi, honey, I'm home!'"[9]

Reiner's agent, Harry Kalcheim of the William Morris Agency, was shocked when he found out that his client had written a total of thirteen episodes of *Head of the Family*, when the accepted formula was to write only the pilot "on spec," as it is called in the industry, and then try to get a network or independent producer to pay for the production of the pilot. Kalcheim quickly found a backer for the pilot in Joseph Kennedy, whose son John F., a U.S. senator, was running for president. Initially, Kalcheim had sent the script to actor Peter Lawford, brother-in-law of John F. Kennedy, who had let it be known he was interested in producing a television series. Lawford took the script for the pilot to the family patriarch—who once served as chairman of the Keith-Albee-Orpheum theater chain and personally financed a never-released film version of *Queen Kelly* starring his intimate friend, Gloria Swanson—for approval. Joseph Kennedy had to approve any such family expenditure, according to Reiner. The elder Kennedy liked *Head of the Family* so much that he decided to finance the pilot himself.[10]

The pilot was filmed in New York with Reiner as Rob Petrie, Barbara Britton as Laura, and Gary Morgan as Ritchie. Sylvia Myles and Morty Gunty played Rob's coworkers, Sally Rogers and Buddy Sorrell. The fictional series, the show-within-the-show, that they worked for was called *The Alan Sturdy Show*. It was later changed to *The Alan Brady Show*, when it was decided that some viewers might hear Alan Sturdy as "Alan's dirty."[11] Despite the backing of the Kennedy clan and the thirteen extra scripts, CBS barely gave *Head of the Family* a look—a highly unusual reaction, given the full package, that was never explained. The pilot aired July 19, 1960, on an anthology showcase called *Comedy Spot*. Such summer series were dumping grounds for failed pilots. By the time it aired, Reiner knew *Head of the Family* was dead in the water.

Reiner was ready to put the failed series on the shelf and move on, but Kalcheim was not. When Reiner resisted resubmitting the scripts to other producers and networks, Kalcheim took it upon himself to send the package of thirteen scripts to another of his clients, a highly successful Hollywood producer, Sheldon Leonard, who was then producing *Make Room for Daddy*. After reviewing the material, Leonard called Reiner out to California to give him the good news and the bad news: Leonard felt that he could get the series on CBS's schedule in the fall, but first he had to "rewrap the package."[12] Rewrapping meant recasting all the parts, including the lead. Once Reiner agreed, a talent search began. The final two candidates to play Rob Petrie were Dick Van Dyke and Johnny Carson. Nothing Jewish about either of them, for sure— volumes have been written about the Midwestern, heartland look of each man.

Oscar Katz, former head of programming for CBS in New York, described the "rewrap" by saying, "They de-Jewishized it, midwesternized it and put Dick Van Dyke and Mary Tyler Moore in the leads."[13] When Reiner himself was asked about the change and whether saying he was "too ethnic" was code for too Jewish, he said, "Look, it wasn't a big secret. In those days, there were just a lot of important network and agency people who thought that way . . . The funny part is, that version [*Head of the Family*] wouldn't have succeeded. Dick was better as me. If they'd said in the first place not 'he's too Jewish' [but rather] 'he's not talented enough,' it would've been fine. *That* I could buy."[14]

And the lesson was not lost on succeeding generations of Jewish network executives. Thirty-five years later, in a discussion on the larger issue of Jewish identity in popular culture, Tartikoff, the former head of NBC programming, would say, "The maxim of show business is, you know: write Yiddish, cast British. Which, you know, was the thing that was always said to Jewish writers. You know, Carl Reiner wrote *The Dick Van Dyke Show* for himself, and then he filmed the pilot and everybody said, 'Carl, we want somebody less ethnic.' So, they got Dick Van Dyke."[15]

THE JEW AS SIDEKICK AND FOIL

While the leading character in *The Dick Van Dyke Show* would be decidedly not Jewish, there was a supporting role for a Jew, that of Buddy Sorrell. He could be called a sidekick, but in truth he was more of a foil. Rob is tall, Buddy short. Rob is fair, Buddy dark. Rob is an optimist, Buddy a pessimist. Rob is married to the lovely and sexy Laura, while Buddy is married to a woman named Pickles who was never seen but was the constant butt of Buddy's jokes about her weight and lack of sexual appeal.

The name Pickles works on another level in that food was often used in the series as an indicator of Jewish identity. For example, in an episode titled "The Ugliest Dog in the World," Rob rescues a stray dog and brings him into the office. Buddy gives the dog part of his corned beef sandwich, while Rob offers some milk. But Buddy pushes the milk away, saying, "That ain't kosher. For him, it's cream soda or nothin'." To which Sally says, "Rob, he's trying to kill the dog." Rob delivers the punch line, saying, "No, he's trying to convert him."

Buddy is not a leading character, but one episode, "Buddy Sorrell—Man and Boy," must be explored in this book, because it has become one of those popular touchstones revered in shared memory by many Jewish viewers. The episode centers on Buddy going back to have the bar mitzvah he never had as a boy, because, according to the rabbi with whom he studies in the episode, "Mr. Sorrell was too poor as a boy to be confirmed." The episode is often celebrated, because it is said to be the first time a Jewish religious ceremony was seen in a prime-time network series. It is also often praised for the elevated tone with which the bar mitzvah itself is treated.[16]

It is not the first series to show a religious ceremony; *The Goldbergs* did Yom Kippur a decade earlier. Prior to the ceremony, most of the jokes in "Man and Boy" are drawn from the interface of religion and show business. For example, when Buddy comes to the rabbi's home to study, both men put on yarmulkes, and the rabbi's wife brings them each a glass of dark wine. "Gee, I hope I'll be able to learn all this stuff by Saturday," Buddy says.

Morey Amsterdam played Maurice "Buddy" Sorrell as the Jewish sidekick and comic foil to Dick Van Dyke's Rob Petrie, the leading man in *The Dick Van Dyke Show* on CBS. One of Buddy's few elevated moments came at his bar mitzvah in an episode titled "Buddy Sorrell, Man and Boy." Photo: Dallas Times Herald

"You better, Buddy," replies the rabbi. "There are no cue cards in the synagogue."

After the rabbi corrects Buddy on the pronunciation of a Hebrew word and then praises Buddy for his improved effort, Buddy says, "By George, I think I've got it."

"Give bar mitzvah lessons to a comedy writer," the rabbi says, shaking his head.

"Sorry, rabbi, I just couldn't resist," Buddy says, completely out of character from his usual wise-cracking, spritzing persona.

"Don't apologize, Buddy. There's nothing wrong with a little humor even in confirmation lessons," the rabbi says portentously.

"How's the lesson going today?" the rabbi's wife says, entering the room to remove the glasses.

"Buddy's doing just fine, dear. The only problem is he started thirty years too late."

"It's not my fault," Buddy says. "It took me that long to save up for a blue suit."

The main source of tension in the episode is that Rob and Sally think Buddy is having an affair because of the messages the rabbi's wife has been leaving at the office and Buddy's lame excuses for his absences (he doesn't tell his coworkers about his bar mitzvah lessons).

Finally, Rob confronts him by handing him one the message slips and saying, "Forget about her. She's no good for you. Besides, you're married and she's, she's another man's wife, Buddy."

"Yeah, my rabbi's," Buddy says.

Rob gasps, "You're running around with your rabbi's wife?"

"No, I'm running around with my rabbi. Where did you get such a crazy idea [that] I gotta set you straight? I'm not running around with anybody."

"Well, what are you doing?"

"I'm taking bar mitzvah lessons."

"Aw, Buddy, it's bad enough. Don't be blasphemous," Rob says.

"I couldn't be that. I don't even know what it means. Look, when I was kid, I missed out on my confirmation, and my mother never forgave herself. That's all. And she wanted, well, I'm just going through the whole thing for her, the whole schmeer."

"Buddy, you mean the phone calls, the messages, the meetings?"

"Strictly kosher."

As for the ceremony itself, it totals only one minute and forty-five seconds versus the more than six minutes for the Yom Kippur service in *The Goldbergs*. Half of the ceremony is devoted to the cantor's singing, which is jarring to an ear attuned to the previous twenty minutes of colloquial English and quick-paced banter of the sitcom. At almost a minute, the singing does seem to go on for a very long time by sitcom standards. In fact, the singing seems alien enough that it could certainly contribute to a construction of "otherness." The cantor is positioned so that we see the Star of David and a menorah behind him in case anyone doesn't get the message: "This is a Jewish ceremony."

The ceremony has its elevated moments, including the rabbi addressing Buddy as Moshe Selig Sorrell, and Buddy addressing the congregation and asking for God's help in being worthy of the support he's received. As the camera shows us an elderly woman smiling through tears, and a lone violin starts to play, Buddy says, "Well, momma, you've waited a long time to hear this: Today I am a man." The camera then cuts to Sally, Laura, and the yarmulke-clad Rob sitting in the front row. As Buddy says "man," Rob leans forward and is about to applaud—only to be stopped by Laura, who looks at his hands and rolls her eyes. As Rob freezes in mid-gesture on that last show business moment, we hear the rabbi say, "Now, let us pray," and the episode ends.

Looking back thirty years later, the "man" statement and the "man and boy" of the title seem to have a special resonance in that Buddy was the adolescent always mouthing off and getting in trouble with the boss, while Rob played the adult, reining Buddy in and time and again saving Buddy's job. This is the sort of depiction often used for minority or working-class male characters, insofar as it shows them incapable of management or leadership positions in the workplace or society.[17]

Outside of the constant cuts to Rob and Laura, the concluding one minute and forty-five seconds of "Buddy Sorrell—Man and Boy" is unusual, elevated, and touching, though not nearly as profound or as elevated as *The Goldbergs'* rendering of Yom Kippur. It is worth noting that Reiner waited until the final month of the series' six-year run to paint Jewishness in such bold, religious strokes, revisiting the autobiographical material he had to leave behind to get *Head of the Family* off the shelf and on the air at CBS as *The Dick Van Dyke Show* in an era when Jews were not considered acceptable as leading men in prime time.

There is another story from the 1960s involving a landmark series that more than any other single factor helps explain the absence of Jewish characters during this period. It involves Allan Burns and Jim Brooks in 1969 trying to sell their idea for a new series about a single woman working at a television station in Minneapolis to CBS. Burns and Brooks flew to New York from Los Angeles to meet with CBS executives about getting the series on the air. Burns set the scene this way: "There's a very womblike room at CBS in New York that had black felt or something like that on the walls. You go in and you feel like you're in the abyss. You sit in this room and there are special ceiling lights shining down. It was like being in a Kafka-esque kind of play."[18]

In that room, the writers laid out their concept for what would become *The Mary Tyler Moore Show*. Central to the concept, according to Burns, was the fact that Mary Richards (Moore) was divorced. She would be the first divorced female character in a network television series. According to Burns:

> The people from CBS wrung their hands, and said, "You cannot do this, you cannot do divorce." And we said, "Yes, we can. Divorce is something that Americans understand, because almost everybody is touched by it one way or another." But it wasn't working. We weren't convincing them at all. Finally, they just turned to this guy from research and he just reeled off this litany, saying CBS had research that showed there were four things American viewers simply would not tolerate. One was divorced people. The others were people from New York, men with mustaches, and Jews . . . I looked around the room and what you had mostly were divorced Jewish guys from New York. Not too many mustaches, though. But we just sat there stunned.[19]

While the story has been told by others over the years in one form or another,[20] no one has tried to ascertain whether there really was any industry research that said American viewers did not want to see Jewish characters on TV. If there was, in fact, such research, it would certainly offer one possible explanation for the void. If valid, it would also possibly tell us something about anti-Semitism in America at the time. Burns, for one, says he never doubted the network had such research. In fact, he says he still believes it to this day:

On the face of it, it seems so stunning in its stupidity that what can you say? We sat there stunned. But there he was [the CBS head of research], flipping through his, well, I don't know if he had papers with him or not. I don't remember exactly. But I had the feeling that they thought they were giving us facts. I don't think they were making it up. I don't know why they would. I don't think they were that Machiavellian about it. I think they were just saying to us, "We hate the fact that you have a divorced character, and we want to convince you against it. So, here's a guy who we trust that does research for us, and you should listen to him."[21]

As the story has been retold over the years both in Hollywood circles and scholarly accounts, it has taken on the aura of fact. Twenty-seven years later, in an interview with me, Tartikoff would cite it as a reason that he and other executives were reluctant to develop series featuring Jewish characters. But, in fact, after interviewing as many of the people who were in that meeting as were willing to talk, as well as the CBS executives who would be the persons most likely to know about the existence of any such research, I believe the evidence shows that the CBS executives in that meeting were lying to Burns and Brooks about having data that said American viewers did not want to see Jews on television.

Bob Wood, who was then president of CBS, is dead. Letters to Mike Dann, who was head of programming for CBS when the meeting took place, requesting an interview for this study were returned unopened with the "refused" box checked by the post office. Dann was the person in charge of the meeting Burns described. Jay Eliasburg, the former head of CBS research who until now has never been identified as the man reportedly making the statement about Jews and people from New York in accounts of the meeting, said that no such research ever existed but that lying about the existence of such research was often done by CBS programmers.

"I'm not aware of any research of any kind that I knew about—and, presumably, I should have known about it if it existed—that said any of those things," Eliasburg told me in a 1999 interview. "You know, a lot of times, the guys in programming would offer as an excuse, you know, to back up their opinion about a show or whatever, they would say, "Well, our research shows . . ."[22]

Fred Silverman, who took over as head of programming for CBS a few months after the meeting in question in 1970 when Dann was fired and, in fact, saved *The Mary Tyler Moore Show* from a time period that all but guaranteed it would be cancelled before most viewers ever had a chance to sample it, was adamant in saying he never heard of any such data regarding Jews, New Yorkers, or men with mustaches either.[23]

David Poltrack, who joined CBS research in 1969 and was senior vice-president in charge of it twenty-eight years later when interviewed for this study, would seem in the best position to know about such data. He, too, denies its existence:

> I haven't seen anything along those lines. At one point, we had some research that said people don't like people with foreign accents. But that's the only thing even remotely like that. I've never seen anything in that regard [the statement about Jews, men with mustaches, and people from New York]. In fact, *The Nanny* is a classic case, because, when *The Nanny* was in development, there were people who were speculating that the show might be "too New York" and "too Jewish." And, in fact, the research showed the opposite. It showed that the show was more popular outside New York in the middle of the country than it was even in the major markets. In that case, the research was actually correcting a misperception by some of the people involved.[24]

Poltrack succeeded Eliasburg in 1982 as head of CBS research, so between them they cover the full history of the CBS research division at least back to 1955, when Eliasburg returned to the network after being laid off in 1949. Eliasburg first joined CBS in research in 1947. The only element not common to all story variants about the meeting is who made the statement—Eliasburg, Dann, or some other CBS executive.

While some of the persons interviewed for this study believe it was Dann, Burns is very specific in his memory of the speaker being "a researcher." However, the consensus among those who were in the room and a number of former network executives familiar with the men in that room is that, if it was Eliasburg, he was lying at the behest of his bosses, who believed they were carrying out the wishes of their boss, William Paley, the founder of CBS. Two former CBS executives say without equivocation that it was common knowledge in the executive suites that Paley did not want shows featuring Jewish characters on CBS.

The "research" claim was the way executives like Dann could enforce the edict without leaving their boss open to criticism on a subject about which he was highly sensitive.[25] Dann was interviewed in 1996 for the Oral History of Television Project at Syracuse University. While not asked specifically about this meeting, he did say in connection with "taboos" for network television in the 1960s, "There was a rule that you couldn't have shows from New York, because everybody hated New Yorkers, and, so, you could never have that as a background. It had to be from the Midwest. It always had to be *Father Knows Best* or an *Ozzie and Harriet* background."[26]

There are two aspects of that statement that require context. First, by the 1920s, New York had become shorthand for—if not synonymous with, in show business circles, at least—Jewish. The case is best made by Stephen Whitfield in his book, *In Search of American Jewish Culture*. He starts with the fact that while Jews were less than 3 percent of the national population, they were almost ten times that percentage of the New York City population during most of the century.[27]

The other important aspect of Dann's statement involves his use of the word "rule" in connection with shows set in New York. By virtually every account of those years at CBS, only one person laid down such rules: Paley. Dann, who worked with and saw Paley on an almost daily basis during his years as a senior programmer at CBS from 1963 to 1970, says:

> When I was there, everything on the air at CBS was influenced totally by the man who called the shots: Bill Paley...Bill Paley loved programming and was actively involved with every single show on the air. He would call at eleven at night about a show, and you had to take the call. He would call me on Saturday mornings. If I wasn't going to be in the office on Saturday, I knew to check in while shopping. And the operator would say, "Mr. Paley is looking for you." It would be 9:30 on a Saturday morning and I'd be in a phone booth at Sears talking to him about a show that was on CBS the night before. That hands-on attitude by Paley permeated the whole company... but programming was his passion.[28]

Or, as Paley biographer Lewis J. Paper put it, "But no one ever forgot who made the ultimate decisions. As one CBS program executive used to say, 'Well, we have people who are experts in statistics, and we have people who have creative ideas and are experts in programming, and then they all call Mr. Paley and he tells them what to put on the network.' "[29]

THE POWER OF PALEY

Most of the roads back through the history of this era of network television eventually lead to Paley, and almost no one wants to talk on the record about Paley and Jews, even though Paley has been dead since 1990. His power in the world of television and his sensitivity to any mention of his ambivalence about being Jewish were so great that they are still feared by the men and women who worked for him at CBS. But there is little doubt that Paley is one of the primary reasons there were no Jewish characters on network television from 1955 to 1972. A large part of the answer to the riddle of Jewish screen invisibility for almost two decades—despite all the Jewish writers, producers, and network executives working during that era—is found in looking at both the incredible power Paley wielded in television during those years and his psychology as a Jew. No one in the history of television policed against surplus Jewish visibility like Paley.

The *New York Times* said of Paley, "He is to American broadcasting as Carnegie was to steel, Ford to automobiles, Luce to publishing and Ruth to baseball."[30] But a more apt comparison is that he was to television as Adolph Zukor, Carl Laemmle, William Fox, Louis B. Mayer, and the Warner brothers were to the motion picture industry. In fact, even though they were immigrants from Russia and Paley was a first-generation American Jew, he admired them as businessmen, loved the glamour of Hollywood, and, in some ways, modeled his network on their studios. As Dann puts it, "Paley was just crazy about Hollywood... He adored Hollywood people."[31] Biographer Sally Bedell Smith says that when Paley spent $30 million in 1964 to acquire rights for one hundred Hollywood films for CBS, "He was indulging a fantasy that had its roots in 1929 when Adolph Zukor offered him a job as his assistant at Paramount. Paley had been friends with Hollywood moguls and producers since the '30s."[32]

Gabler says that to understand the films that came out of the studios of Zukor and the other Jewish founders—and especially the absence of

Jews in those films—you have to understand something about the "psychology" of the men who ran the studios:

> There is, of course, a school of thought that says it doesn't make any difference who makes the movies. Whether they were made by gentiles, Jews, whether they were made by Italians or Russians, it's all the same. I don't subscribe to that school. I believe the fact that every major American studio was founded by and controlled by an Eastern European Jewish immigrant is significant. I believe that the fact that each of these individuals operated within a certain kind of psychological environment is reflected in the kinds of movies they made. So, I mean, the short answer is there's a connection between the creator and the product . . . Unless you believe that people are completely divorced from their own psychology, their background, where they came from and what they do, you can take it on faith . . . there's a relationship [between creator and product].[33]

And so it is with television in the 1960s. In the fragmented TV universe of the late 1990s, it is difficult to conceive of life in a three-network monopoly. But for the time period in question—1955 to 1972—when there were no images of Jews on network television, it was almost a one-network monopoly. CBS was number one in prime-time ratings from 1955 until 1976—a period during which it was known as "The Tiffany of Networks," an image Paley loved and cultivated. In the words of Dann, who had worked in senior management positions at NBC from 1951 to 1963 before joining CBS: "His dominance was so total that CBS was often responsible for 85 percent of total profits for all three networks for many years."

The psychology of William S. Paley when it came to his Jewishness is no simple matter. In *The Powers That Be*, David Halberstam writes:

> Paley never ceased to be a little ambivalent about his origins, both about being Jewish and being a Russian Jew. He was proud of his background, but as he grew older and more successful he did not necessarily want to be reminded of it. As he tried to put it aside, hang around not just with Wasps but super-Wasps, it somehow always lurked in the background. It worked on him so powerfully that it could even warp his normally keen sense of popular entertainment.

His aides secured an early option on *Fiddler on the Roof,* which they were sure would be a smash hit. They were surprised when Paley, after reading the script and listening to the music, turned it down. To Mike Burke [a CBS executive], one of those who suggested he buy it, Paley said, "It's good, but don't you think it's too Jewish?" Burke, startled by the comment, answered that no, as a non-Jew, he did not. The Jewishness was always there, he was always aware of it and sensitive to it.[34]

Paley biographer Smith writes:

Paley was ambivalent about his Jewishness, courting socially prominent WASPs and blending eagerly into their milieu. Many people thought he was an Episcopalian. But he did not turn his back entirely on his heritage. He was known to drag attenuated socialites into the kitchen of a Jewish delicatessen after the theater. He gave modestly to Jewish causes and prided himself on having the mayor of Jerusalem, Teddy Kolleck, as a friend . . . Bill Paley subtly adopted WASP ways. He never actually tried to hide his Jewishness. But he never flaunted it and in large measure withdrew from it.[35]

Paley's father, Sam, and mother, Goldie, were both born in the Ukraine, the same area as the founders of the motion picture studios, and immigrated to the United States with their parents in the late nineteenth century. They were married in Chicago in 1898. As Halberstam asserts, Paley's Russian roots were a source of sensitivity. In a book about CBS titled *CBS: Reflections in a Bloodshot Eye,* author Robert Metz described Paley as a "Russian Jew." Paley had his chief of public relations, Kidder Meade, include in a long list of "factual corrections" sent to Metz and his publisher the statement that Paley was not a Russian Jew, he was a "native American." The list of so-called corrections was subsequently sent out with all copies of the book as part of an agreement aimed at precluding a lawsuit threatened by Paley.

Describing Meade as "Paley's PR man whose great value as a public relations man stemmed in part from the fact that he was *not* Jewish," Halberstam said:

Well, yes, he [Paley] was [an American Jew] . . . but in the world of American Jewry, Bill Paley was a Russian Jew, which in those early days was not as good as being a German Jew. German Jews were a good deal more acceptable, and they were viewed both by the Wasp establishment and by themselves as being more upstanding and respectable than Russian Jews, who were generally regarded as long of hair, disheveled of dress, and radical of thought. Those who knew Bill Paley when he first came to New York thought that he would have liked to be taken up by Our Crowd, the bastion of German-Jewish respectability. But Our Crowd was having none of it. The smell of cigars was still on his money and radio was new and flashy and perhaps vulgar.[36]

The distinction between German Jews and Russian Jews, especially during the first part of the century when Eastern European Jews were flooding into America, is important for trying to understand Paley. Paley's father, Sam, who spoke with a thick accent, was a millionaire by 1910 by all accounts, but it didn't automatically bring respectability even within Jewish circles. In 1919, just after the family moved their cigar manufacturing operation from Chicago to Philadelphia, Goldie gave a party and invited members of the city's Jewish elite, most of them German Jews. None accepted.

As Smith tells it, "Bill, only nineteen, tried to soothe her feelings. 'They don't really count,' he said. 'I'm going to New York and I'll not only make lots of money, I'll marry a Vanderbilt.' Later in life, Sam Paley told the story of Goldie's party and Bill's reaction ... Sam's account revealed not only the depth of Bill's resentment but his early equation of WASP acceptance with success."[37]

Smith writes of another snub involving Paley's application to join the Philmount Country Club, which was founded by the Gimbels and Loebs in response to them being rejected by gentile clubs. After Paley's application lingered for an unusually long time, a friend made discreet inquiries and discovered that, "while the membership committee had no objection to Bill, they were afraid his father would come and play golf. 'They didn't want any part of him because of his thick accent,' recalled Lester Degenstein, who made the inquiry. Bill was eventually admitted, but after paying his initiation fee and first year's dues, he resigned."[38]

Paley did not marry a Vanderbilt, but for his second marriage in 1947 he wed Barbara (Babe) Cushing, who was from a prominent WASP family, and it was close enough.

As he grew richer, Paley's world grew smaller. In the postwar years he seemed to concentrate on climbing the social ladder in America and Britain. His world was the realm of Jock Whitney [his new brother-in-law] and Alfred Gwynne Vanderbilt, of dukes and viscounts, of beautiful, decorous women and dashing gentlemen, where bloodlines and social standing were all. "They will get rid of every Jew," an old friend of the Paleys from a prominent Jewish family predicted after Bill and Babe's marriage. That was not quite true; the Paleys remained friends with the Selznicks and the Goldwyns [Hollywood Jews], but they seemed to be the exceptions.[39]

Paley was in no way a religious Jew. He was confirmed in a Reform temple, which required reciting the Ten Commandments in Hebrew, but the words and rituals held little interest for him. As he put it, "When I was fourteen years old, I started asking questions and couldn't get decent answers. I said, 'My God, that's a lot of bull.' " He had memorized his confirmation statement and had virtually no idea what he was saying. His only goal was to be free of these obligations as an adult. Not surprisingly, Bill Paley made few visits to temple after those early days in Chicago.[40] There was little identification with Jewish religion or culture in the household of Bill and Babe Paley; she was an Episcopalian, and neither she nor Bill went to temple or followed Jewish traditions.[41]

In the end, Paley's sensitivity to his Jewishness is perhaps best illustrated by his reaction to Halberstam's account of the *Fiddler* story that first appeared in a series of articles in the *Atlantic* monthly magazine in 1975. Meade, the public relations whiz and vice-president of corporate affairs for CBS from 1957 to 1981, who worked with Paley in attacking the accuracy of Halberstam's work, described Paley's reaction by saying, "He really hated those *Atlantic* articles. One thing about Halberstam, he was Jewish, and Paley was Jewish. But Paley didn't like Jewish people. I don't understand it, but if a Jew criticized him, Paley took it more personally."[42]

Paley was obsessed with the articles, which he saw as the first major crack in a carefully constructed public image that he had fully expected would hold up beyond the grave. Halberstam called it Paley's "neurosis about the Jewish question." As Lewis Paper describes it, "Paley was so troubled by Halberstam's description of the *Fiddler* incident that he had his lawyers contact the writer and threaten a lawsuit. Halberstam was not one to be intimidated so easily. He telephoned Mike Burke in London to receive confirmation of the story's accuracy, and the threat of a lawsuit vanished. Still Paley could not put the Halberstam articles out of his mind. They gnawed at his insides, diverting his attention from almost every other matter."[43]

Paley "hired a small army of public relations aides" to work with Meade in attacking the Halberstam articles, which would later be published as *The Powers That Be*. He also carried the articles around with him for months, explored the possibility of buying the *Atlantic* to make sure no more Halberstam pieces were published in the magazine, and threatened Alfred Knopf with legal and economic actions if the offending passages were not removed from *The Powers That Be* before publication.[44]

Paley's feelings about Jews did carry over into his sense of image for CBS, not only on air but in the executive suite. CBS had only one Jewish president in its history, Louis G. Cowan. When Cowan became president in 1958, Paley told him he would not have gotten the job had his name been Cohen, which it was before it was changed.[45] The person who actually gave Cowan the news of his appointment as president was Frank Stanton, Paley's right-hand man over the years. Cowan's reply when given the news: "But, Frank, I thought you knew: I'm a Jew."[46]

As for Sarnoff, Paley's counterpart at NBC, who counted among his earliest memories Cossacks riding into a group of Jewish protesters and trampling women and children under the horses' hooves, the drive to assimilate was also intense, though he was more openly Jewish than Paley. "Paley was put off by Sarnoff's more obvious identification as Jew, and Sarnoff was irritated by Paley's WASP pretensions," according to Smith. Or, as David Adams a former NBC executive and intimate of Sarnoff put it, standing on the other side of the fence, "To Sarnoff, Paley wanted to operate in a gentile, fast-paced high society world. He basically gave up being Jewish. Sarnoff wasn't much of a Jew either, but he was a member of Temple Emanu-El."[47]

Sarnoff was in every respect—from his birth in 1891 on a shtetl in the Russian Pale to his childhood of hard work on New York's Lower East Side—cut from exactly the same biographical cloth as the Hollywood moguls described by Gabler in his study of the motion picture industry: "Above all things, they wanted to be regarded as Americans, not Jews; they wanted to invent themselves here as new men. The movie Jews were acting out what Isaiah Berlin, in a similar context, had described as 'an overintense admiration or indeed worship' for the majority . . ."[48]

The continuity from Cohn and Goldwyn to Sarnoff and Paley is best described by Stephen Birmingham in *The Rest of Us: The Rise of America's Eastern European Jews*:

> In Hollywood, the great movie producers had deep ambivalence about their Jewishness ... Harry Cohn, the despotic head of Columbia Pictures, entered life a Russian Jew and left it a Roman Catholic. Sam Goldwyn's Catholic wife once said that her husband had expressed the wish that they both become Episcopalians. "After all," he said, "Goldwyn doesn't sound like a Jewish name"—which of course is why he had chosen it. In the world of radio and television, this conscious non-Semitic facade had become if anything even more pronounced, as though the new media had decided to follow the de-Semiticized guidelines laid down by the Hollywood of old. Though the boardrooms of the three major networks had become largely populated by descendants of Russian Jews, the out-front faces that the public saw would be the Christian ones of Walter Cronkite, John Chancellor, David Brinkley, Chet Huntley, Dan Rather, Roger Mudd, Harry Reasoner and Howard K. Smith. As a result, the public would not think of television as a Jewish enterprise.[49]

Writing in 1971, critic Les Brown reproduced the standard network response to Jewish ownership of all three networks in a three-network universe:

> As to the idea that the three networks are Eastern, liberal and Jewish, it is largely a myth. While it true that the heads of the three parent corporations are Jews, the fact is that William S. Paley's identification with his ethnic origins is slight and Robert Sarnoff's even slighter. Both move in the high social circles thought of as Anglo-Saxon Protestant. Leonard Goldenson and Si Siegel are not quite so assimilated, but neither do they own the controlling stock in ABC, Inc. . . . With the exception of Lou Cowan, who had a fairly brief tenure at CBS, there has never been a Jewish president at any of the three television networks, nor is there likely to be until there no longer is Jewish top management in the corporations. Hyperconscious of the suspicions surrounding the coincidence of three Jewish generalissimos in the three great broadcasting corporations in America, Paley, Sarnoff and Goldenson appear to have taken such extreme caution against fueling the idea of "Jewish networks" that they have in fact discriminated

against Jewish executives who might have qualified for leadership posts ... If top management had ever handed down a Jewish point of view (whatever that might be) to the next tier of executives—some command or commandment subversive of Christianity or basic Puritan American values—or put the interests of one ethnic group above that of the others, the scandal would certainly have broken out by now, considering how many executives have left the companies. So much for the "Jewish control" ...[50]

In arguing against the notion of "Jewish control" of network television, Brown ironically winds up offering more support for the case that the ethnicity of the network founders resulted in them taking unusual actions to avoid having their networks thought of as Jewish. If they were willing to "discriminate" by keeping qualified Jewish executives out of the more highly visible jobs in the boardroom, why wouldn't they also keep Jewish characters off the screen? After all, which would be a greater threat to the "non-Semitic facade" that Birmingham says they were trying to create with all those Christian anchormen from places like Texas, Missouri, and Nebraska in the American Heartland? Again, contrary to Gitlin's suggestion (see p. 8), the ethnicity of the executives *did* determine characters—in this case, the exclusion of Jewish characters.

Or, as it was given voice in the "pitch" meeting at CBS on the concept that would become *The Mary Tyler Moore Show*, the ethnicity of the executives resulted in the exclusion of people from New York, men with mustaches, and Jews. It resulted in the "rule," as Mike Dann put it, that turned Carl Reiner into Dick Van Dyke before the comedy writer from New Rochelle would be judged ready for prime time by the powers that be at CBS in 1961.

If I am overstating Paley's power in the 1950s and 1960s, it is only in not giving Sarnoff his due. Together the two ruled with such power that they were able to make or break the industry-wide blacklist of those accused of ties to the Communist Party in the 1950s that destroyed Philip Loeb and others. Carl Dreher described their role in *Sarnoff: An American Success Story*:

Blacklisting, in its mature phase, peaked synchronously with the cold war, [and] spread from the movies eastward. The theatre offered the most resolute resistance, radio-TV least. There was also less excuse for the TV tycoons, since they had early warning from Hollywood and could have prepared an effective defense . . . Sarnoff and NBC were more culpable in the institutionalizing of radio-TV blacklisting than William S. Paley, Frank Stanton and CBS. Forming a united front, with or without ABC, the two networks could have probably stopped the invasion at the outset. Instead, both collaborated with the invaders . . .[51]

Brown is right about Goldenson's power at ABC being far less than that of Paley and Sarnoff at their networks. Furthermore, ABC was a woefully weak network until the 1970s. But, for the record, despite Brown's claim that Goldenson was less "assimilated" than Paley and Sarnoff, the truth is that the head of ABC was just as ambivalent about being Jewish and just as inclined to keep explicit Jewish subject matter off his network's airwaves, though his involvement in programming was not as great as Paley's.

Tom Moore, a former ABC executive, says *The Jerry Lewis Show*, a 1964 version of Johnny Carson's *Tonight* show, was cancelled by ABC because of "Jewish jokes" and on-air references to "Leonard's lineage" made by Lewis.[52] Moore was the executive sent by Goldenson to warn Lewis, who refused to self-censor and was cancelled in midseason.

There is also the case of *All in the Family* being rejected by ABC in 1969, three years before CBS premiered the landmark series. ABC turned down *All in the Family* twice in part because "the pilot had some very unflattering words about Jews and blacks," according to Michael Eisner, then a young ABC executive.[53] Goldenson acknowledged that he voted against buying the series, which Lear had created for ABC, because he felt "it would antagonize certain ethnic groups."

I focused on Paley because he was the most powerful and by far the most involved in on-air programming of the three Jewish founders. Furthermore, his ambivalence about being Jewish was the most high-profile, widely documented, and acute of the three. But I do not want to suggest that his attitude toward Jewish identity was some sort of strange, eccentric, personal, and isolated pathology. Though I would place Paley near one end of the spectrum, his attitude could be placed within the range of thinking called "assimilationist"—a view that deemphasized ethnic uniqueness, avoided attracting attention to one's ethnic group identity, and stressed blending into some notion of an American mainstream. This is the very attitude described by Cherney Berg in the introduction.

And while American Jewish responses to the postwar situation were widely varied, this was one of the predominant views, as historian Jeffrey Shandler pointed out in discussing the difficulty of trying to bring Holocaust stories to television in this era. He described it as "a period when American Jews are particularly circumspect about being distinguished as Jews..."[54]

I am in no way trying to justify or soften anything Paley, Sarnoff, or Goldenson did, especially in the case of instituting a blacklist for the television industry. I find that morally reprehensible. Furthermore, I am appalled by the horrible symmetry of the Hollywood moguls starting the motion picture blacklist in 1947 and the Jewish network bosses Paley and Sarnoff bringing it to radio in 1949 and television in 1951. Then, closing another weird loop, Jews like Phillip Loeb were the ones most horribly victimized by it. But the climate of anti-Semitism in which these men acted also needs to be acknowledged as the very real force it was.

Historian Holly Cowan Shulman—the daughter of Louis Cowan, the only Jewish president in the history of CBS during Paley's ownership— said she had no direct knowledge of Jewish images being kept off the air during the years her father was an executive at CBS (1955 to 1959). But she added, "I don't find that in any way surprising—that those images were kept off the air. I would think that television paralleled movies in that respect." In trying to explain the mindset of such men of her father's generation, she explained: "These are men who knew that the world was an anti-Semitic place. You don't tempt fate. These are men who are concerned that the best foot always be put forward. So, you simply don't assign a television character a Jewish name like Seinfeld in that kind of climate. That's going out of your way, asking for trouble, if you will."[55]

DOING BUSINESS IN A CLIMATE OF ANTI-SEMITISM

When the House Un-American Activities Committee (HUAC) first started formally looking for Jews in the motion picture industry in 1946, its acting chairman was John Rankin of Mississippi. Even though John Parnell Thomas was the chair when hearings were actually convened in 1947, Rankin was still the driving force. Film historian Neal Gabler, among others, describes Rankin as a "vicious anti-Semite."[56]

Forty-three subpoenas were issued as the HUAC hearings opened. Of those, twenty-four went to persons considered "friendly" witnesses. Of the remaining nineteen, who had been prejudged as "uncooperative," ten were Jewish.[57] Ring Lardner Jr., one of the nineteen, said, "There was considerable feeling that this was a force in which anti-Semitism played a considerable part."[58] Lardner, who was blacklisted, would after many years without work win an Academy Award for the screenplay of *M*A*S*H*.

Lester Roth, a vice-president at Columbia when the hearings began, described what the film moguls were feeling as it became clear that Jews were being targeted by the committee: "Every executive in the business knew it was just a question of time before a drive would be made to take it [the motion picture industry] away from them. There's always the complexion that, 'Hell, we're the Jews and we built this thing up. They wouldn't let us get into the banks. They wouldn't let us into the insurance companies. They wouldn't let us into any of the nationally wealthy hard industries. Now we've built this one up, and they want to take it away.' "[59]

The fledgling networks were even more vulnerable than the film studios in the early 1950s, because television was so dependent on Madison Avenue. As we have seen, in terms of programming, the advertising industry controlled prime-time television up until about the quiz show scandals of 1958, and Madison Avenue was decidedly WASP.

If anyone did not realize that Jews were going to be targeted in the television industry just as they had been in film, they did by the spring of 1950, when one of the first shots fired at Network Row in New York was the naming of Loeb in *Red Channels*. What is amazing in retrospect is that Gertrude Berg was able to keep him in the show—and the show on the air—for another year until the spring of 1951.

Though not reported until May, the decisions by General Foods and Paley to cancel the series had actually been made in early April, shortly after the conviction on March 29, 1951, of Ethel and Julius Rosenberg as spies for the Soviet Union. Their three-week trial in New York and subsequent death sentences made daily headlines across the country. To the best of my knowledge, the connection between the conviction of the Rosenbergs and the cancellation of *The Goldbergs* has never been made, but the timing is such that one cannot help but wonder if the official branding of the Rosenbergs as spies at the height of the Cold War didn't have a direct impact on what happened to *The Goldbergs*. Both were, after all, young Jewish families with two children. Would gentile viewers think of the Rosenbergs when they saw *The Goldbergs* on their television screens?

Jonathan Rosenbaum, author of the book *Movies as Politics*, describes some of the links being made in viewers' minds at the time: "There became an identification in peoples' minds of things that went together: intellectuals, Jews, Russians, communists," he says. "If you look back at any of the depictions of what communists were, all of these things kind of get merged together in the public imagination."[60]

This context can also help explain the fervor with which an immigrant like Sarnoff and a first-generation Russian Jew like Paley embraced assimilation in their own lives and went out of their way to insure a "non-Semitic facade" for their networks. "Of all the things the anti-Semitic tracts said about Jews around the world, the one thing that's always been true is that the Jews always dominated the movie business and the television business from the beginning," Marshall Herskovitz said. "It's an overwhelmingly Jewish medium. And, so, you have all these Jewish people who for sixty years had to reign themselves in out of some fear from really revealing who they were."[61]

Gabler explained the overdrive toward assimilation on the part of the moguls by saying, "When you're trying to make yourself American and you're trying to prove to the powers that be—which frequently threatened them, frankly—and the general audience that you have no hidden agenda. When you're trying to prove that there's only one agenda and the agenda is we love this country, we subscribe wholeheartedly to its values—even though, of course, parenthetically, we're creating these values—the last thing in the world that you want to do is to raise your profile and say, 'Look, we're also Jews.'"[62]

Whatever their reasons and the psychology underlying it, what really matters here is seeing the ethnic self-consciousness of the Jewish founders and understanding their ability as gatekeepers to keep virtually all explicitly Jewish leading characters off American television screens throughout the 1960s despite an explosion of ethnicity—including Jewish ethnicity—elsewhere in the culture during that decade.

I say "virtually" because there were two short-lived series during the seventeen-year stretch from 1955 through 1971 that deserve mention as possible exceptions to the statement that there were no network series with leading characters who were Jewish during this time. Furthermore, there was some Jewish identity on network television during these years not only in terms of supporting players like Buddy Sorrell but also in made-for-TV movies and guest appearances. Shandler, for example, offers a wonderful history of how television treated the Holocaust, but it is crucial to understand that he is dealing with a relative handful of one-shot productions across the entire fifty years of network television.

For example, a Paddy Chayefsky TV drama like *Holiday Song*, the story of a cantor who questions his faith, played two hours on the *Philco Television Playhouse* one night in 1952 and then was gone. On the other hand, a weekly series like *thirtysomething* would play an hour a week for twenty-two weeks a year and then be repeated for another twenty-two hours in the summer. And that happened for three years. Or take *The Holocaust: The Story of the Family Weiss*. This landmark 1978 miniseries ran just four nights on NBC, whereas *Seinfeld* ran nine years with twenty-two episodes played twice each year on NBC. That's 396 nights on the network in first-run. The days and nights that *Seinfeld* plays on hundreds of stations across the country in rerun are beyond calculation.

I cannot stress enough the difference in audience sociology between a leading character in a weekly series and a character who appears once or twice in a guest role in such a series or even as a leading character in a movie or miniseries that airs only once or twice. There are critics who point to an episode here or there that deals with Jewish identity, especially on long-running series, as if that is an argument against the case I make at the heart of this book. But it is, in point of fact, only more support for my argument as to how the Jewish founders suppressed Jewish identity.

The most eloquent testimony in this regard comes from Shimon Wincelberg, a writer and producer active in Hollywood on such series as *Bonanza* and *Have Gun Will Travel* from the 1950s through the 1970s. "They [the network bosses] rationed you: one Jewish character a year, one black a year," Wincelberg said. "Back in the '60s, there was a sort of informal quota on westerns, police shows, detective shows; they let you do one Jew a year, usually as an innocent victim of the bad guys."[63]

As for the possible exceptions to the claim of there being no leading characters who were Jewish during this era, CBS introduced a series in the fall of 1961 titled *Mrs. G Goes to College*, starring Gertrude Berg. In it she played a senior citizen who goes back to get her college degree. But first she must get past her freshman adviser and professor of English, the formidable Englishman W. W. Crayton (Cedrick Hardwicke).

Berg described the series and her character by saying, "I was finished with *The Goldbergs* and couldn't sell them again. So what would you do? I had to sell something else. It's the same old Molly, just older."[64]

But it wasn't the same old Molly, and therein lies its importance to this book. The actress who had been known as Molly Goldberg for more than thirty years to radio, television, film, and theater audiences suddenly is transformed into a character named Sarah Green. The surname is one of Hollywood's favorite Jew-not-a-Jew names. It was the name of Gregory Peck's character in the feature film, *Gentleman's Agreement*, only a few years earlier. Today it is the name of the character played by Jennifer Aniston on the NBC sitcom *Friends*.

To further confuse viewers familiar with Molly and *The Goldbergs*, in the pilot titled "First Day" Sarah describes her late husband as someone who "used to manufacture ladies' dresses." The "used to" draws an expression of sympathy from the listener, but Molly responds by saying, "That's all right. If I know my Sam, he's up there designing half-size robes."

So, it's the old "half-size" business from the earliest days of *The Goldbergs*, and the husband is a dress manufacturer too. But here he is named Sam instead of Jake, and this Sarah suddenly believes in a Christian cosmology with a heaven populated by beings in robes! And remember how Molly's ethnicity was occasionally defined by food in *The Goldbergs*? Here, during her darkest hour in her first day in the rooming house where she lives, she starts to cook soup for the "house mother" and one of her fellow students. But no *matzoh* in the new world of Sarah Green; here it's alphabet soup. Sarah does manage to slip a Mollyism in as she's warming the soup when she says, "Look at me, I'm dangling a participle in my alphabet soup."

As the series struggled and failed to find an audience, CBS renamed it *The Gertrude Berg Show*, only adding to the confusion about this character named Green who believed in angels. Mercifully, *Mrs. G Goes to College/ The Gertrude Berg Show* was cancelled after just six months. But it suggests the strange and convoluted lengths to which CBS would go during this period to mask Jewish ethnicity.[65]

Before there was Bernie of *Bridget Loves Bernie* in 1972, there was one other young, hip, clearly Jewish character in prime time, though he was not technically the lead in the series. The character was Aaron Silverman of *The Young Lawyers*, which had a short run on ABC during the 1970–

71 television season. Silverman was played by Zalman King, who is today most widely known as the director of Showtime's stylish and steamy *Red Shoe Diaries* series.

In premise, *The Young Lawyers* was a courtroom version of *The Mod Squad*, which had established itself as one ABC's more successful series during the previous season. The young lawyers were law students operating a "neighborhood law office" in Boston that provided free legal assistance to indigent clients. They worked under the direction of crusty supervisor David Barrett (Lee J. Cobb).

During the first half of the season, there were two young lawyers, Silverman and Pat Walters (Judy Pace), an African-American woman. Whereas Silverman was radical in his politics, Walters was more middle of the road, but both were on the side of those they saw as oppressed. Most of their legal work involved taking on those identified as oppressors—slumlords, corrupt police officials, and socially irresponsible corporations. As this series went on, a third young lawyer was brought in, Chris Blake (Philip Clark), an earnest, upper-middle-class WASP who was often in direct conflict with Silverman. The series was cancelled in May 1971.

"Actually, what happened is that they began to feel it was too controversial at ABC and they brought in another lawyer, a gentile lawyer," King said.[66] When asked if he thought ABC felt the series was too controversial because his character was Jewish, King said, "Oh, completely. Yes." King said he always thought it strange that of all the characters only Silverman was not given a family or a personal life. The character existed only at work, and mainly what he did with his knowledge of the law is make trouble for the powers that be.

That facet of the characterization also was not lost on King: how the concepts of Jew and radical were wed in Aaron Silverman. Halberstam's description of the way German-Jewish members of Our Crowd saw Russian Jews—"long of hair, disheveled of dress and radical of thought"—is not a bad description of Silverman, who never wore a tie and almost always appeared in the same rumpled corduroy jacket. This is an especially important connection, because, as King himself came to understand, *The Young Lawyers* was, in large part, ABC's way of responding to the social upheaval of the 1960s. One possible reading of *The Young Lawyers* in this regard was that Jews and blacks were the radical ones. And, of the two, it was the Jew who was really driving the radical politics of the 1960s.

King said he was told at the time that ABC was cancelling the series despite fairly strong ratings because of its controversial nature and the resistance both from viewers in the Midwest and managers of ABC-affiliated stations in that region of the country, particularly as it concerned his character; again, the old bromide of being "too Jewish." With the series being set in Boston, at least, no one could say it was "too New York."

But, again, there is no evidence of resistance or controversy in terms of research data or any executive from the era claiming to have knowledge of such data. When it came to cancelling series with prominent Jewish characters, it seemed as if all you had to do was point to the Heartland bogeyman. In 1983, Gitlin appeared to be referencing that when he wrote, "But in network and advertiser parlance, 'the market' is still personified as a hypothetical anti-Semitic Midwesterner ready to switch channels at the first sign of a Stein."[67]

That is a large generalization, and, if CBS's Poltrack can be believed, by 1992, when *The Nanny* was being developed, at least one network was not personifying the market that way based on its research. But such conventional wisdom does die hard in Hollywood and on Network Row. Just as CBS's make-believe research about audience resistance to Jewish characters was still being cited by Tartikoff and others during the 1990s as if it was true, so too was that anti-Semitic Midwesterner still invoked by those trying to play the "too Jewish" card.

In the end, that is the greater truth about "people from New York, men with mustaches, and Jews." Even though it is not very difficult to show it was a lie told by network executives carrying out what they thought was the will of their all-powerful boss, the lie became an operational truth for the industry, passed from one generation to another of network programmers and used to keep Jewish characters in the shadows or altogether absent from America's main stage of prime-time network television for almost two decades.

Prime-Time Intermarriage 1 –
Bridget Loves Bernie

True, it's 1972, but *Bridget Loves Bernie* is still obnoxious and offensive.
Leonard Davis, letter to the *New York Times*[1]

It is in the liberal Jewish tradition to oppose all forms of censorship . . .
But, in the end, faced with CBS' shocking insensitivity to the religious
beliefs of six million Americans, we've had to draw the line here.
Rabbi Balfour Brickner (Commission on Interfaith Activities)[2]

Bernie Steinberg did not have a mustache. But he was from New York, he was a Jew, and he was a leading character in the sitcom *Bridget Loves Bernie* on William Paley's CBS schedule in the fall of 1972.

Although there was an explosion of sitcoms with other ethnic characters and episodes exploring such formerly taboo topics as birth control and abortion that year, *Bridget Loves Bernie* became so controversial that CBS cancelled the series despite it being the fifth most popular show on network television, with a bigger audience than *The Mary Tyler Moore Show*. In fact, *Bridget Loves Bernie* is the highest-rated series in the history of network television to have ever been cancelled.

Bridget Loves Bernie was only on the air for eight months, but it is an extremely important series in the peculiar history of Jewish characters on network television. Its embattled run highlights another form of censorship keeping Jewish images off America's center stage of prime-time network television for many years: the actions of Jewish pressure groups that did not like the Jews they did see onscreen. The series was also prime-time television's first clear sounding of the themes of intermarriage and assimilation through the depiction of a relationship between a Jewish man and a non-Jewish woman. The backlash to the marriage of Bridget

Fitzgerald and Bernie Steinberg was so great that it would be fifteen years before any network would allow such a relationship between leading characters onscreen again, as ABC did with the debut of *thirtysomething* in the fall of 1987.

Prime-time network television was changing dramatically in the early 1970s when *Bridget Loves Bernie* arrived on the scene. *Time* magazine described the network landscape in the fall of 1972:

> TV has embarked on a new era of candor, with all the lines emphatically drawn in. During the season that began last week, programmers will actually be competing with each other to trace the largest number of touchy—and heretofore forbidden—ethnic, sexual and psychological themes. Religious quirks, wife swapping, child abuse, lesbianism, venereal disease—all the old taboos will be toppling... No new adventure hero, it seems, will be admitted to the schedule without an ethnic identity badge. ABC's *Kung Fu* is sort of *Fugitive* foo yung—a Chinese priest permanently on the lam in the West of the 1870s... The title character of NBC's *Banacek* is not only a rugged insurance sleuth but also a walking lightning rod for Polish jokes... Indeed, the 20 new series making their bow this fall add up to a veritable pride of prejudices.[3]

Yet, for all that ethnicity, there was only one new series with a leading Jewish character, and even that proved to be too much for prime time.

The explanation often given for the great change that was taking place in prime-time network television in 1972 is the cultural upheaval of the 1960s especially in matters of artistic expression and ethnicity.[4] In many ways, that is absolutely on the money. Social reality was knocking so loudly on the door of network television that some of it had to be let in.

Again, though, a warning against reading that statement as an endorsement of the view that says television directly reflects or mirrors social reality. Social reality was already changing dramatically in America by the mid-1960s. Television did not start to reflect it in a significant way until 1972. I am convinced that such a lag can only be understood by also studying the network and Hollywood gatekeepers during those years and the ways in which they tried to keep that social upheaval out of prime-time dramas and sitcoms as long as they could without losing their audiences.

One of the central arguments of this book is that during the years that the Jewish founders ran the networks the usual relationship between what is shown on television and the larger society was greatly distorted when it came to matters of Jewish identity. Images, tensions, themes, and ideas from the larger society that traditionally find their way onto television screens as they are reworked into drama and comedy by writers and producers living in that society were virtually absent. And no period makes the case more forcefully than the late 1960s and early 1970s, as other realms of American popular culture suddenly started to bloom with Jewish images and leading characters.

Nowhere was that more apparent than in feature films: *The Graduate* (1967), *Bye, Bye Braverman* (1968), *Goodbye, Columbus* (1970), *Where's Poppa* (1970), *Getting Straight* (1970), and *The Heartbreak Kid* (1972). And they showcased a new crop of leading men, Jews regularly playing Jewish characters: Dustin Hoffman, Richard Dreyfuss, Elliott Gould, George Segal, and Richard Benjamin.

Why film and not television? Because by the mid-1960s the studio system founded and controlled by the Jewish moguls had given way to smaller independent film companies often controlled in their distribution needs, if in no other way, by vast corporations with no particular ethnic makeup. Jewish writers and directors reacting to the ethnic awakening and concerns in the larger society of 1960s America could find their voices in a post-mogul Hollywood now willing to allow Jewish identity to be openly explored on the big screen. But in network television the founders still ruled with an iron hand. Jewish images and leading characters by and large would have to wait until the late 1980s, after the founders surrendered control as their film counterparts had done by the 1960s.

I believe the kind of changes seen in the prime-time television lineup of 1972 are as much a result of the business and production practices of network television as they are a reflection of social reality. The single most important industrial factor driving the change in prime-time television circa 1972 was *All in the Family*, a Norman Lear sitcom starring Carroll O'Connor as Archie Bunker, buffoon or hero, bigot or right-thinking American, depending upon your reading of the hit series. *All in the Family* debuted in the fall of 1971 and finished its first season as the highest-rated series on television, a spot it would hold for five straight years as it inspired a slew of spin-offs from Lear and imitators from other producers. Its achievements were unprecedented, as was its average Nielsen rating of 30, which translated into about 50 million viewers each week.[5]

By the fall of 1972, everyone in Hollywood and on Network Row wanted the next *All in the Family*. But only three years before, no one had wanted the original. As described in the last chapter, Lear had first produced the show in 1969 for ABC, which turned it down twice in part because "the pilot had some unflattering words about Jews and blacks," according to Michael Eisner, the chairman of Disney who was then a young ABC executive.[6] Leonard Goldenson, then chairman of ABC, acknowledged that he vetoed *All in the Family* because he felt "it would antagonize certain ethnic groups."[7]

To understand how a character who called Jews "hebes" and "kikes," as Bunker did, then wound up on the network of Paley, you have to look at the agendas of several key players within the production and distribution community of the time, particularly Lear, Paley, and Robert Wood, who took over as president of CBS in 1969.[8] In the case of Lear, he made it clear that he would only produce *All in the Family* for CBS if he could do it his way, which included introducing a new realism to the sitcom. In addition to "hebes" and "kikes," that meant Archie would use such terms as "spades" and "coons" for African-Americans, "spics" and "greasers" for Hispanics, and "polacks" for Polish-Americans like his son-in-law, Michael Stivac, who was played by Rob Reiner. Lear would not compromise.[9]

As for Paley, in the end it turned out that almost nothing mattered more to him than being number one in the ratings,[10] and, as the 1960s ended, Paley suddenly found himself in the unfamiliar position of not having the top-rated show on television. Worse, by 1970, he had only four of the top ten series on television, and each of those had older demographics, which resulted in lower advertising rates. The cash cow of CBS was in danger of going dry if a new generation of viewers was not found.

In 1969, Paley brought in Wood, and, within a few months, the new president of CBS had a plan "to get the wrinkles out of the network without eroding our popularity." The plan was to cancel a slew of rural comedies and variety shows despite their relatively large audiences and find more sophisticated, urban, and contemporary shows that would draw younger viewers. Wood presented his plan to Paley and the other top CBS executives, including Dann, who was the architect of the old schedule of shows, in early 1970. As Sally Bedell Smith reports the meeting: "Shocked that CBS would cancel popular shows, Mike Dann heatedly objected to the plan . . . 'Lower your voice, Mike,' said Paley. 'The room turned to ice,' recalled programming executive Perry Lafferty. Several months later, Dann quit CBS. 'Gentlemen,' Paley told the executives, 'you finally have a president with a vision of what is absolutely correct.' "[11]

Dann was replaced by wunderkind Fred Silverman as head of programming under Wood. Among the shows that Wood and Silverman cancelled were *The Ed Sullivan Show*, *The Jackie Gleason Show*, *The Red Skelton Show*, *Green Acres*, *The Beverly Hillbillies*, *Petticoat Junction*, and *Mayberry, R.F.D.* They would be replaced by *All in the Family*, *Maude*, *The Bob Newhart Show*, *The Mary Tyler Moore Show*, and *Bridget Loves Bernie*. This is about as complete an overhaul as can be imagined. The first and most important of what Wood called the "new look" CBS shows was *All in the Family*.[12]

Paley went along with the drastic changes wrought by Silverman and Wood because he was convinced it was the only way to achieve both the ratings dominance and the prestige he so desired.[13] But, not surprisingly, he at first hated Archie Bunker. Paley found the show vulgar and Bunker's ethnic insults particularly offensive. Wood won Paley over by arguing that *All in the Family* would usher in a new genre of comedy in the coming decade.

Wood was right. By 1974, CBS had nine of the top ten shows again and they included programs like *The Mary Tyler Moore Show* and *M*A*S*H*, which the critics consistently referred to as "smart," "sophisticated," and "quality" productions. As the rising tide of ratings for *All in the Family* lifted other boats in the CBS prime-time lineup, Paley not only stopped hating the controversial show, he fell in love with it. Typical of Paley's desire to have both ratings and prestige, he commissioned a study to find evidence that watching *All in the Family* diminished bigotry. Unfortunately for CBS, its paid researchers found that the series actually reinforced prejudice. Jack Schneider, a senior CBS executive, says he brought the study to Paley, saying, "What shall we do with it? If we release it, we'll have to cancel the show." According to Schneider, Paley's response was, "Destroy the study. Throw it out."[14]

That is how a show with a leading Jewish character finally found its way onto William Paley's schedule in 1972: *Bridget Loves Bernie* was seen to be smart, sophisticated, and, as more than one newspaper critic put it using the jargon of the time, "mod"—so smart, sophisticated, and "mod" that it could be teamed with *All in the Family* and *The Mary Tyler Moore Show* in CBS's powerhouse Saturday night lineup. If Paley could learn to love Archie's ethnic insults, maybe he could accept one leading Jewish character named Bernie, especially if the series he was in so perfectly fit the new programming game plan and, most important of all, preached the very kind of assimilation that Paley himself practiced. And it looked like *Bridget Loves Bernie* was going to be more than okay when television critic John O'Connor of the *New York Times* previewed it and *The Bob Newhart Show*, another new addition for 1972 to CBS's Saturday night lineup:

> For some time, the Columbia Broadcasting System has been on the verge of putting together a blockbuster lineup of situation comedies for its Saturday evening schedule. The network may just have succeeded. Retaining two of the best produced series on TV—*All in the Family*, which goes on at 8 o'clock, and *The Mary Tyler Moore Show* at 9—C.B.S. is inserting two new candidates, *Bridget Loves Bernie* at 8:30 and *The Bob Newhart Show* at 9:30. Based on the first episodes, which will be shown tomorrow night, both are strong contenders for survival in the TV marshland.[15]

THE LOWER-CLASS JEW

The pilot of *Bridget Loves Bernie* opens on Park Avenue with a cab arriving in front of a luxury building and a young, attractive woman getting into it. That woman is Bridget. The man driving the cab is Bernie. A chorus sings "Love is crazy/It's unwise" as she reaches out to pay the fare and their hands touch, and "It may be crazy/But, oh, so sweet" as the next shot shows the cab parked and empty with Bridget and Bernie sitting on a park bench kissing passionately. The overall feel of the music, the New York street shots, and the look of the couple is that of a film version of a Neil Simon comedy like *Barefoot in the Park*. As the theme song and the kiss end, she says, "I don't even know your name." He says, "Bernie Steinberg. What's yours?" She says, "Bridget Teresa Mary Colleen Fitzgerald." He says, "I think we have a problem. How Catholic are you?" She replies, "I think you should meet my brother."

Bridget's brother, Mike, is a Roman Catholic priest. "Well, I guess if you two are determined to go through with this, there's only one thing to do," he says to open the next scene.

"Excommunication?" Bridget asks.

"Breakfast," Mike replies.

"You mean no argument about different ethnic and religious backgrounds, how are you going to raise the children, and the birth control issue?" Bernie asks incredulously. "What kind of priest is this?"

"An understanding one, I hope," Mike says.

"Give me the Pat O'Brien priest any time. At least you know where you stand with them," Bernie says, shaking his head as the scene ends.

This change in location from a nicely furnished rectory is signaled by loud, minor-key music as Bridget and Bernie arrive on the Lower East Side for dinner at the Steinbergs in their flat above the deli. The music, featuring clarinet and fiddle, suggests *Fiddler on the Roof.*

"What kind of name is Fitzgerald?" Bernie's mother, Sophie, asks. "Irish? Oh, not Jewish? What, you don't like gefilte fish? Have some horseradish. Bernie likes it hot."

This is not the Yiddishe-Mama-in-transition of Molly Goldberg. This is the TV version of Sophie Portnoy, known to a mass audience from *Portnoy's Complaint,* which had been published three years earlier, in 1969. This is the castrating Jewish Mother.

"So you're Catholic? Full-blooded?" Bernie's uncle Moe Plotnick asks. Like Uncle David in *The Goldbergs,* Moe lives with the Steinbergs, though he is not feminized in the way David was.

"We're Jewish, you know," Sophie says again to Bridget, apropos of nothing.

Sophie, Moe, and Bernie's father, Sam, start to talk and laugh among themselves, their voices rising, much of the conversation taking place in Yiddish. Sam talks with his mouth full of food, and bits of food fly out. Bridget is not only excluded, she seems somewhat alarmed or intimidated by the volume and foreignness of their words.

Finally Bernie explodes, "I don't believe this. I've lived with you people all my life. Now why is everyone all of a sudden being so Jewish?"

Meredith Baxter and David Birney as Bridget Theresa Mary Colleen Fitzgerald and Bernie Steinberg in *Bridget Loves Bernie*. Despite being a Top 10 show in the A. C. Nielsen ratings in 1972, it was cancelled during its first season in reaction to widespread Jewish protests over the marriage of Bridget and Bernie. Library of American Broadcasting, University of Maryland

At this point, "Jewish" is mainly defined as being as loud, foreign, crude, and rude.

Sophie stands up. She is on the verge of hysteria. "You see, already it starts. Here, Bridget, have a midget Danish—raisins and prunes. I had to go clear across town to get them. But I didn't mind three hours on a bus. I figure for my son nothing's too good."

Bridget takes a bite, tries to swallow, and then excuses herself, rushing off toward the bathroom, covering her mouth with her napkin.

"A gentile and a Catholic with a frail stomach: that combination could ruin any marriage," Sam says.

"The kid better check that out," Moe says. "It could cost a fortune in Blue Cross." Add cheap and insensitive to the definition of Jewish.

"Look at that, you made her sick," Bernie says angrily.

Sophie is now in fullblown hysteria, sobbing uncontrollably.

"Sophie, will you stop with the tears already?" Sam commands.

"It's not only that, I had one of my visions," Sophie sobs. "It was Seder and Bernie and his friend came here with their five children, and three of them were nuns."

Cut to the Upper West Side and through the window of a luxury building to a brightly lit, richly appointed, modern living room with a man and a woman—both dressed in stylish, expensive-looking clothes. They are Walt and Amy Fitzgerald, Bridget's parents. The contrast between the dark, old-fashioned, almost black-and-white look of the Steinbergs' apartment and this one is striking.

"She said he's different on the phone. Oh dear, he's not a Democrat, is he?" Amy says.

Out front we see Bernie and Bridget staring up at the building. "You own the whole building?" Bernie asks, looking stunned. "You're rich. You're stinking rich!"

"You make it sound like a disease," she replies.

Walt hears the doorbell ring and looks down on the street. Instead of Bernie, though, he sees Bernie's African-American friend, Otis, who drove the couple over in the cab that he and Bernie share as drivers.

"Ohhhhh," Walt moans, "he's colored."

"How colored?" Amy asks.

"Very," Walt says angrily as he heads toward the front door.

But when he opens the door, it's Bridget and Bernie, and Walt's first words are, "You're Caucasian." It takes Bernie a second, and then he says, "Oh, that's my friend Otis, he's a rock musician."

Walt excuses himself and leaves the room. Leaning against a closed door in the hallway, he whispers urgently, "You can come out of the bathroom. It's not as bad as you think. He's not black."

"Well, what color is he?" Amy asks from the other side of the door. "I think he's Jewish."

As she comes out of the bathroom she makes the sign of the cross and says, "Thank you, God."

"Listen," Walt says, "I don't think the situation exactly calls for celebration and the lighting of candles."

"Why, is he short?" Amy asks.

"The important thing for us is not to overreact," Walt says as they walk toward the living room. "So just put the fact that he's Jewish out of your mind unless it comes up."

As they enter the dining room and a butler brings coffee and tea, Amy asks, "Now, Bernie, do you take one lump or two in your Jew?"

Dinner starts just as badly as it did at the Steinbergs. "So you're a cab driver?" Walt says to Bernie.

"That's only temporary, Daddy," Bridget answers. "Bernie has ambitions in the theater."

"Oh, as what?" Walt asks.

"A female impersonator," Bernie says.

"He's only joking, Daddy," Bridget offers.

"Oh, we know that, Bridget," her mom says. "I've never heard of a Jewish homosexual."

"You should meet my cousin, Herbie," Bernie says.

As the main course arrives, it is ham for everyone except Bernie, who gets salami. A few moments later, Bernie gets up from the table and rushes out of the apartment, leaving a note for Bridget that says, "Face it, it's not going to work." When Bridget finally catches up with him, he says, "Look, I saw the way you live, the way you were raised. It just wouldn't be fair."

To which Bridget replies, "I'm not going to argue with you."

"You're not?" a surprised Bernie says.

"No, I'm going to get married," she says confidently.

The scene cuts to a civil wedding ceremony for Bridget and Bernie that lasts all of nine seconds, four of which are taken up with their kiss.

It is important to go through the pilot in this scene-by-scene manner, because it is a very well-crafted pilot. In fact, Fred Silverman—who has probably seen more pilots than anyone in Hollywood during a career that included jobs as head of programming at ABC, NBC, and CBS—called it one of the best pilots he ever saw.[16] And a well-crafted pilot will contain most of the major themes and establish the various ways that identity and relationships will be depicted in the series for the rest of the year or even its entire run. Haiku-like in its economy, a well-crafted pilot will make almost every second of its twenty-one minutes and thirty seconds of running time count.

One of the most striking ways that Jewish identity is depicted in the pilot of *Bridget Loves Bernie* is in terms of social class. In the universe of this series, to be Jewish is to be of a lower class. That process starts immediately with Bernie as cab driver being hailed by the elegant-looking young woman on Park Avenue. It is the first image viewers see, and it is the one that *Time* magazine focused on in describing the series in its 1972 season preview as the story of a "well-heeled Catholic girl who falls for a poor Jewish cab driver." The same difference in social class is mentioned in several letters to the *New York Times* during the eight-month run of the series, such as this one on January 21, 1973: "To add insult to injury, most of the 'humor' in the series is based on the sup-posedly ethnic shortcomings of the low-class Jewish and the high-class Catholic families."[17]

And it is class differences that Bernie alludes to ("Look, I saw the way you live . . .") in explaining why he thinks "it wouldn't be fair" for Bridget if he were to ask her to marry him. Critics, too, have commented on differences in social status, as in this analysis of the series in con-nection with what one writer calls the "validated Jewish male" on tele-vision: "On what may be television's most anti-Semitic program, the situation comedy, *Bridget Loves Bernie* . . . Bernie Steinberg, an aspiring writer and part-time cabbie, is married to the wealthy Bridget Theresa Mary Colleen Fitzgerald . . . As their in-laws spew bigoted venom . . . the couple argues incessantly. Bernie invariably yields to his wife's wishes, always the lowly Jew groveling for the approval and attention of his angelic wife."[18]

Even the volume level of the series helps to define the class difference. Whenever the action moves to the Steinbergs' Lower East Side deli, the music gets louder. And the Jews who live at, work in, and frequent the deli speak in loud and emotional voices, often literally yelling at each other despite the fact that they are not angry. The only Steinberg who does not speak this way is Bernie.

But this is not such a subtle sitcom that you have to analyze speech patterns to decode class difference. The scene immediately following the civil ceremony in which Bridget and Bernie are married opens with Moe, Sam, and Sophie standing (literally hat in hand for the men) in the foyer of the Fitzgerald mansion. Bridget's brother, Mike, greets them, and they ask if he has seen the couple as they cannot find Bridget and Bernie anywhere. At which point Amy arrives, looks them over disapprovingly, and says, "Look, I know this is 1972, but you people are just going to have to learn to use the back door." When Mike explains who they are, she says, "Oh, I'm terribly sorry, but I thought you were the caterers." The joke is that they are caterers, and that is the high end of the Steinbergs' business.

Steinberg's Catering is regularly referenced in the series, and often it is tied to social class. For example, in an episode titled "A Funny Thing Happened on the Way to the Vatican," Amy sells Sophie a ticket to a Daughters of Isabella (a female Catholic organization like the male Knights of Columbus) raffle and Sophie wins a trip for two to Rome, including an audience with the pope. Walt is appalled at the thought of Sam and Sophie meeting the pope, and in a fantasy sequence we see Sam and Sophie dressed as nineteenth-century Eastern European peasants standing in front of the pope (again Sam is hat in hand).

"Next time you're thinking of throwing a feed, maybe you'll give us a call, Steinberg's Catering," Sam says to the pope. "Maybe for a crowd that size we'll give you a very special price." As they are taking their leave, Sophie says, "If you don't mind me saying it, Your Holiness, you're too thin." The possibilities for offense are numerous. In addition to Sam and Sophie depicted as peasants groveling before the majesty of the pope, the name Isabella might carry baggage from the Spanish Inquisition for some viewers. Furthermore, anti-Semitic stereotypes of Jews as cheap, pushy, and lacking in social graces could be suggested by the words and actions of Sophie and Sam.

Back in the Fitzgerald foyer near the end of the pilot episode, Sophie announces that she has had another vision: "There's been a terrible accident and Bernie is maimed from the waist down." Yes, Sophie, as the smothering Jewish mother, is once again near hysteria (this time with decidedly Freudian overtones) until Mike, the confidante of Bridget and Bernie, tells everyone that the two have gone off to get married. Moe, sizing up the Fitzgerald foyer, sticks out his hand to Walt and says, "It's kinda exciting, us being relatives through marriage, no?"

"Oh, yes, the mind boggles," Walt says in an icy tone as he walks away. Beyond the putdown from Walt and the suggestion of Moe's crassness, there are more social class semiotics. Walt wears a blazer, rep tie, gray slacks, and white shirt. Moe and Sam are in open-collared shirts covered by mackinaw and parka. Sam still wears his apron from the deli. And whereas Walt speaks the kind of clipped, "proper" English that might be thought of as WASP, Moe speaks with a Brooklyn accent in which "work" is "woik" and "girl" is "goil." There is contrast between Sophie and Amy, too. Sophie is dark-haired, heavyset, and dressed in a dark potato sack of a house dress. Amy is blond, slim, and dressed stylishly in silk blouse, skirt, and heels. As we have seen in prime-time television series ranging from "The Honeymooners" in the 1950s to "Roseanne" in the 1990s, heavyset is often code for lower class.

The big scene in the pilot comes next, back at the deli, as Amy, Walt, Sam, Sophie, Moe, and Mike all enter Bernie's apartment, which is also above the deli, unannounced and head straight for the bedroom. There they find the very happy newlyweds under the sheets.

"All right, Michael, marry them," Walt yells to his son, the priest.

"Wait a minute. Why a priest? Why not a rabbi?" Sam counters.

"Hurry, get Rabbi Golden. Tell him it's an emergency," Moe says, pronouncing it "emoygency."

But Bernie tells them it's "too late," they've already been married in a civil ceremony.

"A civil ceremony?" Sophie screams. "It's like a bad vision."

And, yet, in accordance with the dictates of sitcom resolution, the next scene finds them all downstairs in the deli eating cheesecake, seemingly in good spirits and enjoying a newfound sense of brotherhood until Walt looks out and notices that the hubcaps are gone off his Mercedes. As Walt fumes, we cut to Moe, who takes Amy into a back room and says, "I put them (the hubcaps) here for safekeeping. It's a nice neighborhood, but it's a German car."

In addition to the ways already described, Jewish identity is also defined in the pilot in terms of food (gefilte fish, midget Danish, salami, and cheesecake), an assumed anti-German sentiment (invoking the memory of the Holocaust to get the joke about the Mercedes), and music (nineteenth-century Yiddish folk music).[19]

One of the more convoluted ways that Jewish identity is further depicted is found in the continuum suggested when Walt mistakenly thinks Otis is Bernie. The presumed joke: Jewish is bad, but it could be worse. He could be black. Jewish characters also make jokes about Otis, reinforcing a depiction of African-American identity as the least desirable of all. But, part and parcel of that humor is a depiction of Jewish as not being quite white.

The second episode of the series, "Wake Up, We're . . . ," deals with the two families trying to get Bridget and Bernie married in a religious service. After a lot of fighting, Sophie finally says, "Okay, I'm not happy about it, believe me, but maybe we can take half a loaf," meaning the family will agree to an interdenominational service. But, just as she finishes saying it, Bernie walks in with Otis and says, "Parents of the groom, say hello to my best man."

"*Oy*, we've just been whittled to a third of a loaf," Sophie moans, looking at Otis as the laugh track offers its approval.

That wedding episode opens with Walt and Amy trying to convince themselves that the Steinbergs will be "reasonable" and let them have a religious (read Catholic) ceremony.

"Just because they're Jewish doesn't mean they're not human," Walt says.

"That's right," Amy agrees. "With our son a priest and our daughter practically raised in a convent, what could they possibly say?"

"I think the expression is *oy, vey*," Walt responds.

Amy then takes Sophie to lunch at an elegant restaurant that completely overwhelms the woman, while Walt takes Bernie to his country club.

"Is this your first time in here?" Walt says.

"It may be the first time any Steinberg's been in here," Bernie says.

"Well, it won't be the last. You can bet your mezuzah on that," Walt replies, using Yiddish consistently to reinforce the notion of Jew-as-other suggested by his remark, "Just because they're Jewish doesn't mean they're not human."

At the Amy-Sophie lunch, we get the first concrete depiction of Jewish in any kind of religious terms when Amy says she is surprised to hear Sophie say that Bernie wants a Jewish wedding. "Listen, for a boy who's been bar mitzvahed, who got straight A's in Hebrew class, not important? Listen, every night, you're kneeling at the foot of your bed, he's dreaming of a Jewish ceremony," Sophie explains. The truth, as viewers already know by this point, is that Bernie could not care less about a Jewish wedding.

Through a series of misunderstandings, Walt, Sophie, and Amy all leave their lunches thinking they have won the day. When Walt drops Bernie back at the deli, he is so happy with the outcome of lunch that he says, "Sam, you've got a fine boy there. He's proving you Jews aren't as clannish as people say."

"We've been waiting two thousand years to hear that," Sam says sarcastically.

Jewishness is also defined in terms of extended kinship: like Molly Goldberg in an episode of *Molly* that dealt with her son, Sammy, planning to be married, Sophie cannot settle on "immediate family." She insists on: "Uncle Max, Aunt Rhoda, Cousin Sadie, Cousin Meyer, and Minnie and Ben Goldberg for starters."

There is more social class: Amy wants the Peter Duchin Orchestra for the wedding, to which Walt replies, "For this wedding, I don't see the harm of Borrah Minevitch and his Harmonica Rascals." At the wedding, Walt compliments Sam on his appearance, and Sam replies, "Jacobi's Rental had a field day with us."

The wedding is almost cancelled at the last moment when Walt tries to get Bernie to sign a document saying any children will be raised as Catholic, but this very important matter is quickly dropped, with Bridget saying, "Oh, Daddy, how could you?" And then the wedding is underway, with both a rabbi and a priest presiding. Both are young men. The ceremony takes place in a church, and no glasses are broken as in a Jewish ceremony, but Sam, Moe, and Bernie do wear yamulkes.

"I'm a rabbi and my colleague is a priest, and yet the truth of God never changes," the rabbi begins. "And what is the truth of God, but to teach man to live in harmony with his fellow man?"

The priest takes over, saying, "I, too, am happy to see that two people of different faiths can meet in the common ground of love. Perhaps, this ceremony will not only prove two people can live together in peace and harmony, but point the way to when nations can live together in harmony with nations, people can live in harmony with people, and religions can live in harmony with religions."

Both rabbi and priest give their blessings as the episode ends with the entire wedding party standing in a circle with their hands together "like the New York Knicks just before game time," to quote an analysis that would appear later on the Sunday Religion page of the *New York Times*.[20]

THE JEWISH PROTEST

Reaction to the series was without precedent. One historian suggests that the Jewish protests over *Bridget Loves Bernie* changed the very way Hollywood's feature film industry depicted intermarriage.[21] There is some consensus that the reason the series was so offensive to some Jewish groups was that it made intermarriage look too easy. And, indeed, there is support for that in documents from the times. The following letters are representative of reaction to the pilot episode:

> There above Steinberg's Delicatessen on the Lower East Side of CBS, Catholic Bridget loves Jewish Bernie; and another Jew is lost. While Bernie gets sick over his in-laws' ham and Bridget gets sick over Momma's gefilte fish and miniature Danish, Jewish kids and teenagers see that—after all—it is pretty romantic and chic to make it with a nice gentile. And if the parents are against it, it makes it an even cuter relationship.[22]

> Mixed marriages are considered by a large segment of the Jewish community and leadership as the major threat to the continued existence of the Jewish people in the Diaspora. To base a comedy series on this problem is as tactful as would be, for example, a series about the merry adventures of a Jewish family on their way to the gas chambers ... Even television executives should be sensitive enough to distinguish between criticizing racial and social prejudice, as in the fashionable ethnic comedies [like *All in the Family*], and attacking attitudes aimed at ethnic survival.[23]

By December, an organized Jewish campaign against the show was well underway. Orthodox rabbis met several times with CBS officials, demanding that the show be taken off the air. When that did not work, they picketed CBS headquarters in New York. A Conservative rabbi led a boycott of advertisers of the show. Reform rabbis, too, met secretly with CBS officials in an attempt to get them to change the show. Rabbi

Abraham Gross, president of the Rabbinical Alliance of Orthodox Rabbis and Educators, called the series a "flagrant insult" to Jews, saying, "Intermarriage is strictly forbidden by Jewish law. Yet this series not merely condones intermarriage, but repeatedly suggests it is desirable."[24]

In January, a more direct approach was taken, according to Meredith Baxter, who played Bridget: "We had bomb threats on the show. Some guys from the Jewish Defense League came by *my* house [in Sherman Oaks] to say they wanted to talk to me about changing the show. This is when I found out they had just bombed some place . . ."[25]

That same month, a man was arrested in Santa Monica in connection with threatening phone calls made to the home of Ralph Riskin, one of the producers of *Bridget Loves Bernie*. According to the *New York Times*, "The calls were said to protest the depiction of an interfaith marriage" in the series.[26]

By February, Edward B. Fiske reported in the *New York Times* that "Leaders of virtually the entire spectrum of American Religious Judaism have asked the Columbia Broadcasting System to withdraw the program on the ground that it makes intermarriage look 'mod' and mocks a basic tenet of Judaism." In the words of Rabbi Balfour Brickner, spokesman for the Synagogue Council of America and the Commission on Interfaith Activities, "The program treats intermarriage in a cavalier, cute, condoning fashion and deals with its inevitable problems as if they were instantly solvable."[27] Of his group's meetings with CBS officials, Brickner, a Reform rabbi, said, "They've held us off, and the most eloquent response to our protests has been the re-run of the series' most offensive episode, in which a rabbi and a priest co-officiate at the supposedly religious wedding of the couple."[28]

The production company that made *Bridget Loves Bernie*, Screen Gems, and CBS offered their first official response in February. Calling it an "entertaining comedy show," John H. Mitchell, president of Screen Gems, said, "While we recognize that interfaith marriage is a reality in today's society, I don't for a single moment believe that *Bridget Loves Bernie* is advocating it or that any couple would be influenced by it."[29]

Responding to complaints about the marriage and "alleged offensive Jewish stereotypes," CBS's Wood said, "From the beginning, we've had Jewish and Catholic clergymen as advisers on the series in an effort to make sure we would not be offensive. We realize that those who protest are not cranks, but sincere, concerned people. But if we respond to pressure to cancel the show, we do a disservice to the millions who obviously like it. We simply don't know what to do."[30]

Disservice or not, CBS had decided what to do by late March, when it announced that it was cancelling *Bridget Loves Bernie*. The cancellation was "absolutely removed, independent and disassociated from criticism of the show by some Jewish groups," Wood said. He claimed the protest "had been limited to a very small, though articulate group." On the day of the cancellation, Screen Gems's Mitchell said, "It is entirely possible, and we are doing everything to make it happen, that the program will be picked up by one of the other networks."[31]

But, indicative once again of the peculiar history of series with leading Jewish characters, neither of the other networks wanted the fifth most popular series on all of television. And again, while Wood was the one catching the flak in the press, it was Paley who had made the call behind the scenes. As Wood was to later say in connection with another controversial programming call made by Paley in March 1973, "Someone had to finally bite the bullet ... The decision properly went out over my name, and I stand by it."[32] A big part of being president of CBS was fronting for the boss and making sure you took all flak rather than him.

As for Wood's claim that the protests had nothing to do with the cancellation, few believed it. In the face of instant credibility problems, Wood and other CBS executives refined their explanation of the cancellation by saying yes, the ratings were high for *Bridget Loves Bernie*, but it was creating a "hammock effect" between *All in the Family* and *The Mary Tyler Moore Show*, with too many people tuning out CBS after *All in the Family* and then returning for *Mary*.[33]

This is pure spin doctoring. *Bridget Loves Bernie* performed better in that time period than did the 1970–71 series it replaced, *Funny Face* with Sandy Duncan. *Funny Face* finished as the seventh highest rated series that season, while *Bridget Loves Bernie* finished fifth the next year. Meanwhile, the series that replaced *Bridget* for the 1973–74 season, *M*A*S*H*, finished fourth, losing just as much of the audience from *All in the Family* as *Bridget* did. Furthermore, CBS did not cancel *Funny Face* when it moved the series from Saturday nights to make room for *Bridget*. Instead it was renamed *The Sandy Duncan Show* and moved to another time period on Sunday nights. *Bridget* got no such chance to relocate.

One other matter of memory: while some histories say that Catholics and other religious groups also pressured CBS on the issue of *Bridget*

Loves Bernie, there is no historical evidence to support that. There was one letter to the *New York Times* that said Catholics should also be offended by the series, but Catholics were focusing their protests that year on *Maude*.[34] The *Bridget Loves Bernie* protest movement was strictly Jewish. Looking back some twenty-five years later, Meredith Baxter said:

> At the time, I thought, "Well, gee, *All in the Family* offends everybody, so why should we have a problem? But, as I understood the complaints, as they were explained to me, they [Jewish protesters] did not like that we showed easy assimilation—that it was depicted without difficulty. And they felt that it was inaccurate and that the characters were caricatures . . . I know that the Black Rock Building in New York [CBS headquarters] had been picketed by the Orthodox Jews. Catholics didn't seem to care an awful lot. But [in the end] I think the problem for Jews was that the series just made it look too easy, too unproblematic. They [Jewish protesters] felt it was a serious issue and we were only going after the comedic effect, which is probably true. It wasn't really an *All in the Family* kind of show trying to examine issues. I thought that was what the show could [potentially] do: show the impossibilities of assimilation. But we didn't really deal with the tough stuff, except food issues.[35]

JEWISH RE-EDUCATION

As discussed, "food issues" were only one of the ways Jewish identity was depicted in the series. And, while the various religious groups were quite specific in their objections to how the series treated Judaism, I think one more pattern of imagery in the series needs to be noted, especially when trying to understand why Jews took offense while Catholics did not.

The fundamental dialectic, if you view the entire year's worth of episodes, is not Jewish versus Catholic as much as it is young versus old/ modern versus old-fashioned. The people who have the answers in this series are the young people, most often Bridget's brother, Father Mike, the go-between among all parties. His fundamental role is in constantly siding with the couple and then "teaching" the parents to see the wisdom of the modern or young persons' point of view. The viewer is urged to identify almost as much with Mike as he is with Bridget and Bernie.

The process is clearly seen in the Christmas-Hanukkah episode, titled "'Tis the Season," when Mike comes up with the answer to a conflict between the families as to how the holidays should be celebrated by bringing a young rabbi friend to the deli to "teach" Sam the correctness of celebrating the Christmas holiday with the Fitzgeralds rather than being "pig-headed." As Sam puts it following his re-education, "Even for a man of principle, there comes a time for change." This is especially telling coming from Sam, whose older brother and uncle were rabbis, according to information we are given earlier in the episode. But they were of the "older" generation, so they were wrong, while the younger generation has the answer. The themes of young versus old and Jewish re-education are given comic reinforcement immediately after Sam's pronouncement, with Uncle Moe in full Santa gear being taught by Father Mike how to be a proper Santa Claus.

We have seen this process of children teaching parents before in *The Goldbergs* when Rosalie re-educated her mother away from the lessons of thrift that Molly had learned during the Depression and World War II. Rosalie "teaches" Molly the wisdom of buying on credit. At the very core of *Bridget Loves Bernie* we see television doing the same kind of ideological work on collective memory. But the collective memory being discredited and revised here is not refusal to buy on credit but rather certain tenets of Judaism itself.

Furthermore, in terms of the old versus new dialectic (with new and modern as good, and old as bad), the Steinbergs (Jewishness) are far more closely associated with old-fashioned than the Fitzgeralds (Catholicism). In fact, Father Mike is a constant reminder of how modern and "understanding" Catholicism can be. As shown in the pilot, the construction starts with the darkness versus light of the two households. But it then extends through the decor of the two homes, as well as the modern dress of Amy Fitzgerald versus the positively nineteenth-century peasant look of Sophie Steinberg. The music, too: klesmer at the Steinbergs versus a light, modern sound that matches the theme music when visiting the Fitzgeralds' Park Avenue manse. It is the same with Sophie's visions and superstitions, while Amy is remarkably free of any of them, despite the social reality of Catholicism celebrating visions as much or more than any religion—using them, in fact, as a pathway to official sainthood.

As for Walt—just like Archie Bunker, who immediately preceded *Bridget Loves Bernie* in the CBS lineup—viewers could either revile him for his anti-Jewish remarks or they could revel in the anti-Semitism. The bottom line of the series is that old-fashioned is bad, and nothing is more old-fashioned in this universe than Sam, Sophie, and Moe Steinberg. Walt and Amy Fitzgerald are essentially modern. The modern versus old dialectic is part of a larger ideology in prime-time television that grows out of Madison Avenue using the medium from its earliest days to teach consumerism and finding younger viewers more receptive to the sales pitch.

There is another key distinction that I think matters in this series. Whereas Jewish is depicted as both a religion and an ethnic identity for the Steinbergs, Catholicism is only a religious identity for the Fitzgeralds. Their Irishness—their ethnic identity—is never attacked in terms of negative stereotypes about drinking, for example. Religious identity is something you can change through conversion, if you so desire, while ethnic heritage is something you cannot. So, in that sense, I think the attack on Jewishness in *Bridget Loves Bernie* is more fundamental.

Interestingly, this very distinction came into play in a *New York Times* interview titled "Birney and His 'Irish' Rose," with the actors who played Bridget and Bernie, Baxter and David Birney, when they were asked about their religions: "Why does everyone want to know if I'm Jewish?" Birney says irately. "I really find it offensive, because I don't know whether they're asking about my religion or my background. Actually, I'm an Irish Protestant but I have no organized religious affiliation . . ." "I was raised a Presbyterian, but I have no religion now," Miss Baxter says, somewhat more calmly.[36]

One last distinction involves Baxter using the word "assimilation" to describe what the series was about, whereas every one of the Jews interviewed for this study used the word "intermarriage." As she put it, "We made assimilation look too easy." Specifically, the series was, of course, about intermarriage. But, in a larger sense, she is right about it really being about assimilation.

Bridget Loves Bernie is the first instance in network series television of what would become by the early 1990s an ironclad pattern of Jewish men married to or involved in relationships with gentile women, to the near exclusion of Jewish women onscreen altogether. There is a long history of Hollywood feature films preaching assimilation through intermarriage—usually Jewish men with non-Jewish women. It goes back even farther on the American stage, with one critic calling the "ramifi-

cations of Jewish-gentile romance [a] near obsessive concern in perform-
ances with Jewish characters" by the start of the twentieth century, as
immigrants from eastern Europe poured into New York.[37]

In trying to show change in the way feature films have come to depict
such intermarriages, historian Joseph Greenblum writing in the journal
American Jewish History offered criteria for judging whether a film preaches
an "old-fashioned" melting pot notion of assimilation wherein the Jewish
partner's ethnic identity is often lost, versus a more "pluralistic" sense
of intermarriage. According to Greenblum: "Three issues underlying a
film's depiction of the interfaith relationship should be considered in
determining orientation:

- Whether the film idealizes or accepts interfaith love and
  marriage.
- Whether the film suggests that Jewish identity and group ties are
  undesirable or unimportant.
- Whether the film presents a favorable image of a gentile partner
  who is the key to, or the reward for, the Jewish partner's career
  success, social advancement, and alienation from the Jewish
  group."

Bridget Loves Bernie is a clear example of a show "reverting to the
melting pot model," Greenblum says. It also reverts to one of the most
offensive versions of that model to some Jewish sensibilities, *Abie's Irish
Rose*.[38] Even though Greenblum is discussing feature films and not television series, he included *Bridget Loves Bernie* because he considers the
"demand of Jewish leaders to withdraw the new television hit" as a
watershed in "creating a greater cognizance of Jewish sensitivities in Hollywood" and changing the way such relationships would be depicted.[39]

Or not depicted, as would be the case for fifteen years for prime-time
television series despite a steadily increasing rate of intermarriage in
American life that would climb to one out of every two marriages involving Jews by the time the next Jewish-gentile religious nuptials were
shown in a prime-time series when *thirtysomething* debuted in 1987.[40]

Again, the curious absence of image is best explained in terms of the
"realpolitick" of network television and the actions of Jewish TV executives in the wake of the protests waged against *Bridget Loves Bernie*. Fred
Silverman, head of programming at CBS during the controversy, explained it this way:

I think a lot of people at the broadcasting networks were concerned [about the protests]; they don't need to deal with that. They don't need pressure groups every day. And that's why when *Amos 'n' Andy* went off the air [as the result of protests by the NAACP], you didn't see very many black shows for a long, long time. I mean, people were scared. Who needs that grief? Who needs advertiser boycotts and the NAACP and JDL? It's just needless aggravation. The best thing to do is to just shy away from it—just don't do those kinds of ethnic shows that are going to cause trouble.[41]

One cannot help but appreciate the irony. Ethnicity is exploding throughout the rest of the culture, but not on television. Wood and Silverman convince Paley to go against his best judgment and dip his toe in the water with one Jewish character named Bernie, and what happens? Jews picketing outside CBS headquarters and wall-to-wall-coverage in the *New York Times* of the outrage over the series.

But you also cannot help but appreciate the prescience of those who were so troubled by the depiction of intermarriage; like television, they also were trying to resist social reality—in their case, an intermarriage rate in American Jewish life that was only 8 percent before 1965 but would soar to 25 percent by 1975. Twenty-five years after that, it would hit 50 percent.[42] The Jews marching outside CBS headquarters were feeling the exponential change in their real lives in 1972, as well as, perhaps, sensing the power that television's glamorous and sexy depiction of intermarriage could have on succeeding generations.

CBS and the other networks had done a very good job for two decades of shying away altogether from series featuring Jewish characters. And now the lessons of *Bridget Loves Bernie* would not be lost on them. If there was going to be a Jewish character on network television, you could bet he or she was not going to be in anything that could be called an "ethnic show," even if the leading character was Jewish.

In terms of chronology, this is where CBS's *Rhoda* enters the picture in 1974. Rhoda fits the chronology perfectly, illustrating the gatekeeping climate of this period in the way that the producers consciously avoided dealing with Rhoda's Jewishness.[43] But, to highlight certain themes, I will hold off discussing *Rhoda* until chapter 6, where it can be examined alongside other series featuring Jewish women as leading characters.

Before leaving the 1970s, though, there are two other series that must be briefly discussed: *Barney Miller* (1975–82) and *Welcome Back, Kotter* (1975–79), both of which aired on ABC. *Barney Miller* starred Hal Linden as the captain of a police precinct in Greenwich Village. Because Linden is Jewish, some viewers and reviewers assumed Miller was a Jewish character. But Danny Arnold, the co-creator and executive producer of the series, explained it this way: "We never said Barney was Jewish and we never said he wasn't. We deliberately gave him an ethnic/nonethnic name."[44] Such intentional ambiguity does not seem so strange from Arnold's point of view in light of the trouble he had casting Linden, a man from New York with a mustache, in the role. Arnold says one ABC executive, whom he declined to name, "particularly hated" Linden. "Personally, I think it was because he [Linden] was Jewish," Arnold said.[45]

In explaining the process as it played out in network television circa 1975, Arnold said none of the ABC executives ever came out and said Linden looked "too Jewish." As Arnold put it, "They don't say that. What they do is suggest other people. And the people they suggest are nice, clean-cut, Aryan-looking, you know, obviously WASP . . ."[46] Miller was surrounded by a multi-ethnic cast of cops, and their ethnic identity was the point—except for the two who might be Jewish: Miller and Detective Phil Fish (Abe Vigoda). With those two, viewers had to guess. Miller does not fit the scope of this study, which set out only to examine clearly identified leading characters who are Jewish, because he is not identified as Jewish. It is the same for Fish, who had a spinoff series for half a season in which he starred. A non-Jewish producer who worked on both series explained it this way to me in an off-the-record conversation:

> It [Arnold's reluctance to let the characters be identified as Jewish] became a kind of running joke for us. We would slip stuff in that might identify these guys as Jews, and Danny would go crazy trying to catch it all and take it out before taping. He just believed they couldn't be known as Jews, like there was a law or something with the Jewish network executives. Hell, maybe there was. Whatever, we never said they were Jews. We never said what the hell they were.

Welcome Back, Kotter falls into the same kind of Jew-not-a-Jew/crypto-Jew never-never land for its leading man, Gabe Kotter, a high school teacher in Brooklyn. Again, some viewers might assume Kotter is Jewish, because the person who played him, comedian Gabriel Kaplan, is Jewish.

But you will find no evidence in the series to support that, which is rather astonishing in and of itself. There is, however, one clearly identified Jewish character in the series: Juan Epstein (Robert Heyges), a supporting player.

In the pilot, Vinnie Barbarino (John Travolta) is introducing each of the remedial students known as the "sweat hogs" to their new teacher, Kotter, when he says, "That is Epstein, the toughest kid in the school. He was voted Most Likely to Take a Life."

"Your mother's Puerto Rican?" Kotter asks in response to the introduction.

"No, my father," Epstein says. "My mother's a Bibberman."

"I didn't know there were Epsteins in Puerto Rico," Kotter says.

"Oh, there weren't until the winter of '38," Epstein says, rising to his feet, "when a boat carrying a shivering Lou Epstein from Odessa to the Bronx stopped in San Juan. 'Oy,' my grandfather says, 'look at the palm trees. Feel the heat. Look at this beach. Who need Miami?' From that day on, there were Epsteins in San Juan."

"That's very interesting, Epstein," Kotter says. "What's your favorite subject?"

"Assault," Epstein replies.

Though a comic version of it, this is prime-time network television's first recurring version of what would come to be known as the Tough Jew. A few years later in 1981, we would see another version of it in another supporting player, Detective Mick Belker (Bruce Weitz) in the gritty police drama *Hill Street Blues*. The Tough Jew—as minor a movement as it might be in the symphony of Jewish prime-time identity—is important to note because it plays against the dominant pattern of neurotic, weak, timid, or even effeminate depictions of Jewish men on television. In fact, part of the underpinning for the humor in the construction of Epstein is the very notion of a Jew who is tough, though the idea here is that it comes from his Puerto Rican ancestry. And the humor in that regard relies on another ethnic stereotype, that of Puerto Ricans as violent, part of an uncontrollable, volatile, dangerous, Latino element in American urban life.

In the end, we are left with another curious, albeit minor, moment in the history of Jewish characters—the fact that such specificity is given to a supporting player's ethnic identity, while the leading character who appears to be Jewish is left purposefully undefined. But then again, Kotter was a New Yorker and a man with a mustache just like Barney Miller. And American viewers were supposed to know exactly what that meant without being told, according to the phantom CBS study that some network executives are still citing today.

The Dramas –
thirtysomething and *Northern Exposure*

I'm sure you don't know about this story. But, in the pilot episode, there was an enormous fight with the network because I wore a yarmulke for the first time . . . And, by the way, the network was being run by Jews— not only at the top, but from the top down through many echelons.

Actor Ken Olin, who played Michael Steadman
in ABC's *thirtysomething*[1]

If there is one date for the turning point in the depiction of Jewish identity on prime-time network television, it would have to be September 29, 1987, the night *thirtysomething* premiered on ABC. After another astonishing run by the three networks of nine years without a series featuring a leading character identified as Jewish, suddenly there is *thirtysomething*, with a leading man wearing a yarmulke in the very first sequence in which he appears. While the Peabody Award–winning series would explore Jewish identity overtly in only a handful of episodes during its four-year run, it would do so in those with a seriousness and intensity unrivaled before and rarely seen since, as the Jewish producers worked out an answer onscreen to the question "What does it mean to be a Jew in 1980s America?"

Furthermore, its success in establishing a Jewish leading man whom millions of viewers came to care about helped open the door for what would quickly become a relative flood of male Jewish characters onto the small screen, including Dr. Joel Fleischman (Rob Morrow) in *Northern Exposure*, a CBS drama about a recent Columbia University Medical School graduate forced to go west to the Alaskan frontier as means of paying for his education. *Northern Exposure* and *thirtysomething* were the first prime-time dramas to feature Jews as leading characters. With twice as much time each week as a sitcom and working in a formula that generally dealt with more serious subject matter, the two dramas offered a quantum leap in the exploration of Jewish identity on prime-time television. But they would not have found their way into America's living rooms without a monumental change taking place behind the scenes in the world of network television.

Written by baby boomers Ed Zwick and Marshall Herskovitz, *thirtysomething* looked at the relationships among seven adults, all in their thirties and living in the Philadelphia area. At the center of the seven was the married couple of Michael Steadman (Olin) and Hope Murdoch (Mel Harris). He is a young Jewish advertising executive who had graduated from the University of Pennsylvania. She is a young non-Jewish writer who graduated from Princeton. Their different ethnic and religious backgrounds provided an undercurrent of conflict that was explored in a handful of episodes, as we shall see.

Like Steadman, both Herskovitz and Zwick are Jews who were married to non-Jews at the time. Both of their wives, Liberty Godshall and Susan Shilliday, wrote for the series. Godshall explained the relationship between writers and characters by saying, "Marshall and Susan and Ed and I have used these stories to talk over our marriages, what we fight about, and what we secretly cry over. Sometimes I even suspect we've found ways to articulate in public what we have never been able to put so well when looking into each other's eyes."[2]

The pilot opens on a series of quick-cut, black-and-white scenes of the courtship between Michael and Hope: first meeting, first time in bed together, and separate get-togethers in which they talk about each other to friends. The first time the camera actually slows down enough to let us get a full look at Michael is on his wedding day, the culmination of the opening montage. In that shot, we see Michael in what looks like the vestibule of a church talking to one of his friends, Gary Shepherd (Peter Horton), questioning what he is about to do. And, then, with resolve, Michael pulls a yarmulke out of his coat pocket, puts it on his head, and passes through a door that clearly leads to the altar. The series then formally opens in present time with Hope and Michael as the parents of a seven-month-old daughter, Janey.

The story about the yarmulke is important, because it highlights in terms of its timing the massive changes that were taking place off-camera

Michael Steadman (Ken Olin) and Hope Murdoch Steadman (Mel Harris) with their daughter, Jane, in the landmark ABC drama *thirtysomething*. No network series explored Jewish identity or intermarriage with as much wisdom and courage. Photo courtesy The Kobal Collection

in the world of network television during 1985 and 1986, when Herskovitz and Zwick were developing the concept for *thirtysomething* for ABC. In 1986, ABC officially changed hands, going from the control of Leonard Goldenson, one of the founders, to Capital Cities Communications, which paid $3.5 billion for the network. A year earlier, NBC had passed from the Sarnoffs to General Electric, while Paley's control over CBS had effectively ended in 1985 when Lawrence A. Tisch's Loews Corporation took over.

Those moves in ownership away from the founders constitute the backstage explanation for *thirtysomething*'s arrival in 1987 and the steadily increasing number of Jewish leading characters in subsequent years. The culture that the founders had put in place—what Olin referred to as the "many echelons of Jewish executives" in the quote at the start of the chapter—did not disappear overnight, of course. In fact, in many ways the culture they put in place lives on even as this is being written in 2002. But when Zwick and Herskovitz challenged what Mike Dann in his day called a "rule" about no leading Jewish characters, they found there were no longer any rulers around at the very top who cared enough about the matter to categorically say no the way Paley, Sarnoff, and Goldenson had. The self-censoring founders, who had inherited and passed on the values of the Hollywood film moguls, had sold out, packed up, and moved on. And the decidedly non-Jewish corporations like General Electric and Capital Cities that now controlled the boardroom did not have any such taboos about series with leading Jewish characters.

One of the major goals of this book is to offer this explanation of the departed founders for the networks' about-face with regard to leading Jewish characters that started onscreen with the debut of *thirtysomething*. The explanation—which might be called the "ding-dong, the founders are gone" hypothesis—has not been offered elsewhere. Typical of the kinds of explanations offered for the arrival of more than a dozen leading Jewish characters in the late 1980s and early 1990s is scholar Terry Barr's from the journal *Studies in Popular Culture*:

> But the 1990's is a far different era. Film and TV executives and writers who want to translate the "other" into characters that mainstream American audiences will accept or might even identify with have simply found more nerve, more chutzpah . . . But another reason for the dramatic increase in Jewish characters in film and tele-

vision is surely the desire of Jewish writers, producers and directors to show mainstream America that Jews do have specific cultural and religious traditions that are legitimate subjects for popular media to explore.[3]

Barr offers this explanation without talking to any of the Jewish writers, producers, or directors whose intentions he claims to know from looking at the images they create. I am not arguing against his right to do that. I am arguing that the kind of production study and close history offered here provides a more grounded explanation for this dramatic change in onscreen imagery. It started with the yarmulke on Michael's head, which came just as the transition from Goldenson's regime to Capital Cities was being realized—a transition that took ten months from the time it was announced to become official. It took several years beyond that for Capital Cities to field a management lineup it considered its own rather than the one inherited from Goldenson, which is why *thirtysomething* started out dealing with the old regime and wound up with a new one while it was on the air. Some ten years after the series' premiere, Olin remembered the fight with the network over his character wearing a yarmulke this way:

> The network was run by Jews, because this is ABC before it was bought by Cap Cities. And they were terrified that they would put a leading man in one of their dramas who was Jewish. And people were very surprised about that, because they'd say, "Now wait, wait, wait. I'm sure that someone [some character] has admitted before [Michael Steadman] that they were Jewish." And I said, "But the problem is that it's even worse than saying it, because on film you're showing it." I mean, I was coming out, and it was a visual statement declaring my Judaism [donning the yamulke]. And it was incredibly difficult. I mean, it was a long fight. And I think [ultimately] there was probably some compromise in terms of, if I was going to wear yarmulke, then I wasn't going to speak Yiddish or something. Or there wouldn't be any Hebrew, I don't know. But it was a very long fight. It was a very big deal to those Jewish executives that the Jewish character not announce his Judaism . . . And that's a very interesting thing, particularly since none of them [Jewish characters] admitted to it [being Jewish] for years and years.[4]

In a 1999 interview, Herskovitz remembered the incident in a slightly different way, saying, "My best recollection is . . . that it was more along the lines of, 'Do you have to show him in a yarmulke in the opening?' It wasn't 'you can't' or 'you shouldn't show him in a yarmulke.' It was more, 'Do you have to?' . . . And we said, 'Yeah, we have to.' And, ultimately, they said, 'Okay, if you have to, you have to.'"[5]

But, as Olin said, there was compromise. The vestibule scene prior to Steadman donning the yarmulke and entering the church gives ABC a Steadman without yarmulke as his first full image. Furthermore, by not having the camera follow him through the door after he puts the yarmulke on, Herskovitz avoids having to deal with the legacy of the *Bridget Loves Bernie* furor over how the intermarriage ritual is depicted onscreen. But there are two important points here. First, given the history of Jewish characters, showing a leading man in the first sequence in a yarmulke was a landmark. Second, once Herskovitz and Zwick stood their ground on the essential point—that Steadman was going to announce his Jewish identity to viewers in the very first moments of the pilot—they found that the resistance ultimately melted away, because there was no longer anyone at the top to deliver the ultimate "no."

CHRISTMAS WITH THE STEADMANS

If there were viewers who did not know that Steadman was Jewish after the yarmulke in the pilot, they certainly did after the Christmas episode a few weeks later, titled "I'll Be Home for Christmas." It is virtually all about Steadman being Jewish and his relationship to his non-Jewish wife, their daughter, and the Christian holiday. The hour opens on Christmas carols, which are heard throughout the hour. Early in the episode, Hope is singing "Deck the halls with Michael Steadman" as Michael walks in looking depressed.

"You're cheery," she says sarcastically.

"Just that time of year," he replies.

He notices gifts from her parents on a table, and says, "Hope, darling," with some exasperation.

"Daddy and I just want to make sure Janey has a great Christmas," she replies, handing one of the gifts to him.

"Oh, this is great. This is got to be the reversible yarmulke I wanted so badly," he says sarcastically.

She tries one more time to cheer him up, kissing him as she says, "I could make you like Christmas with tinsel on our naked bodies." But she then pulls away at his coldness and says, "It's supposed to be a good time, Michael. *A Christmas Carol* wasn't written by Kafka, so could we please just have a good time and forget the face." The "face" is a reference to his dour look. But the face only darkens as she mentions them getting a Christmas tree.

"Tree? Tree? I thought we worked that out," he says.

"Michael, you can't hang candy canes on a ficus."

"I'm sorry," he says, "I don't mean to be. I mean, I'm trying, Hope. It's just."

"Just what?" she interrupts, now as angry as he was a few moments before.

"You haven't set foot in a church since I've known you," he says.

"You haven't set foot in a temple," she responds.

"So what's it matter?" he snaps back.

"It's important to me," Hope insists. "Can we talk about it later? I gotta go bake cookies."

The argument ends, but the subtext is explained two scenes later when Elliot Weston, Michael's best friend and partner in the advertising agency they run, says he is not going to stay late that night because he has to get a Christmas tree. On behalf of the agency, Michael has taken on a job doing an ad campaign for a firm that offers aerobics classes for pregnant women, and he has everyone at the agency working right up to Christmas.

"Every year, this is when I get my tree, Mike," Elliot says. "You guys don't get trees, huh?"

"We gotta talk about it, me and Hope. [Pause.] This is so weird. I used to like Christmas. I used to like it with Hope. But now."

"A tree is not just a tree?" Elliot says.

"I see this tree. I see it in my living room," Michael says, "and I see my grandfather rising up from the grave and having another heart attack. I do. And now there's Janey."

"Yeah?" Eliot says.

"What do I want to tell her about who I am? I mean, what if she totally loves this? I don't know where that leaves me."

Janey and what her sense of identity will be become the focus of the argument between Michael and Hope that continues throughout the episode. In the next scene, Hope hears caroling outside and says, "Michael, listen, isn't it beautiful?"

"Very nice, yeah," he says darkly.

"You don't even hear them," she says angrily, and then she starts taking down the decorations she had put up in their living room.

"Honey, what are you doing?" he says once he notices.

"Cleaning up. I am wrong, Michael. I shouldn't have put this stuff up . . . It's just that I want Janey to have what I had: lights, reindeer, and a window to watch for Santa. I mean, for all I care Santa could be a nice Jewish boy. I just don't want us to be scared of giving her all that just because we don't know what we want."

The big, angry fight comes a few scenes later, when Hope says, "Michael, what do you believe in? We never talk about it."

"Okay, okay, you," he says.

"That's all?" she replies.

"That's not enough?"

"No, no, that's great. I mean, you believe in me; that's great. But, Janey, Michael, what's she going to believe in?"

"She's a baby," he replies angrily.

"You know what I mean," Hope snaps back.

"Okay, Hope, fine, what about you? What do you believe in?"

"I used to know what I believed in. It was easy. It was . . ."

"It was what, Hope? What do you believe in?"

"I don't know, heaven."

"Harps and angels?"

"Okay, harps and angels, yeah."

"Okay, but you don't know now?"

"Well, it's changed," she says. "It's you and . . ."

"Wait, I changed it?" Michael asks. "How? I want to know, because it's weird to me, Hope, that we should have a Christmas tree, which is what you want, which is fine. But what about me? Because I don't see you polishing any menorahs, Hope."

For all the talk, the most eloquent moment in the episode is a visual one. Standing outside in the cold and dark, Michael sees Hope and Janey framed in the warm glow of one of the front windows of the Steadman home, looking up and out at the falling snow or, perhaps, for Santa. We see it from Michael's point of view, and then the camera pulls back further to show us Michael looking very lonely. For Michael, being Jewish is something that alienates him from the holiday season, and now he fears it is alienating him from his wife and child. In this episode, there is little joy in being Jewish.

This being network television, the conflict between Michael and Hope does find some resolution before the hour ends. But, like the Christmas episode of *Bridget Loves Bernie*, it mostly involves the Jewish character coming to embrace Christmas to an extent that he previously had been unwilling to do. On the day of Christmas Eve, Michael calls his employees at the advertising agency into his office and announces they are all on paid holiday break as of that moment. For the first time, Michael says "Merry Christmas" rather than "Happy Hanukkah," as he tells them that the client will have to wait for the aerobics campaign or can fire the agency if he does not like it.

The next scene opens at night with Michael in an SUV with a Christmas tree on top pulling into his driveway. A light snow is falling, while "Silent Night" plays softly on the soundtrack. As he enters his home, he comes upon Hope lighting Hanukkah candles in a menorah. She is holding Janey, and standing at her side is Michael's cousin, Melissa (Melanie Mayron). Hope explains that Melisssa brought the menorah. As tears fill Hope's eyes, Michael, Melissa, and Hope hug each other. "Silent Night" is sounding louder now, as the camera pulls back from the Steadman home and the episode ends.

The Christmas tree *and* the menorah suggest some sort of compromise and mutual respect for traditions. But, in light of Michael's earlier declaration that he believes only in his wife and nothing specifically connected with Judiasm, you have to wonder what exactly it might mean. Hope, at least, is willing to link her carols and Christmas trees to "heaven, angels and harps" under cross-examination by Michael. That is to say, her holiday symbols are linked to a theology. Michael's menorah has no reason for being there except possibly to keep him from feeling alienated and being so gloomy.

Melissa's presence in that scene is important, too, because she is the link to Michael's Jewish childhood in Chicago. Melissa, a single, freelance photographer, is one of the seven ensemble characters in the series and is always there whenever Michael's Jewishness comes up. Her character is featured in a secondary story line in "I'll Be Home for Christmas" that involves her and Michael in a bitter argument—which also lends meaning to the final scene of reconciliation. Her first scene in the episode shows her decorating a Christmas tree in her warehouse apartment. Gary, Michael's best friend and Melissa's sometime boyfriend, walks in just as she is putting a Barbie Doll atop her tree and calling it "the crowning touch."

"Isn't Barbie a WASP?" says Gary, who is not Jewish.

"Yeah, it's nondenominational. Meet Lauren, Barbie's Jewish Princess friend. Help me out here, Gar," she says, searching for a punch line. "She comes with her own dream house—no kitchen, no bedroom."

They both laugh uproariously and then give each other high-fives to celebrate Melissa's wit. While it might seem like a harmless little comic moment to some, Melissa is reproducing in that quip the Jewish Princess stereotype, a representation many Jewish women find offensive. Two of the key aspects of the stereotype are that Jewish women neither cook nor have sex with their husbands, thus "no kitchen, no bedroom" in Lauren's dream house.[6]

Even though she is not a major character, Melissa warrants discussion in the same way that Buddy Sorrell does in *The Dick Van Dyke Show* and Rhoda does in *The Mary Tyler Moore Show*. In serving as a foil for Hope, she is part of an overall construction within *thirtysomething* of the Jewish woman as inferior to her gentile counterpart. In the "I'll Be Home for Christmas" episode, Melissa has a flashback memory of Michael's bar mitzvah and how he had to pay a friend of his to dance with her. Later, during an argument with Michael about him taking her for granted and calling her at the last moment to do freelance photography for his agency, she says, "You look at me and you see this pathetic little red-haired *schlump*. No friends, no boys. You gotta pay people to dance with me. Poor Melissa, if Mikey's not going to be nice to her, who is?"

One major reference book on prime-time television describes Melissa as "Michael's sex-starved, want-it-all single cousin (an aging JAP) . . . a photographer."[7] A more enlightened assessment is found in *Tikkun*, where Melissa is characterized as a "photographer living a bohemian, but ultimately lonely existence."[8]

"What Melissa lacks, of course," the *Tikkun* article goes on to say, "is a husband and a baby; in their place is a therapist." Melissa is always taking pictures of Hope and Hope's life, as if she wants to experience it or possess it somehow through her lens. Melissa seems to be especially obsessed with continually snapping pictures of Hope and Janey. It is the same with the second child for Hope and Michael, a son, Leo. "I want him," Melissa says, articulating the palpable desire behind the camera for the first time. Echoes of Rhoda telling Mary she wants her life as she looks through Mary's photo album (see p. 175) are unmistakable.

"MIKE VAN DYKE"

Melissa is again featured in an almost identical role in the *thirtysomething* Christmas episode from the second season, "Mike Van Dyke." With its intricate story lines and black-and-white segments in which Michael imagines himself as Dick Van Dyke playing out scenes from *The Dick Van Dyke Show*, it is a brilliant and memorable episode on a number of levels. Given the history of how Reiner's Jewish *Head of the Family* was "re-packaged" as the WASP *Dick Van Dyke Show*, re-imagining it again with Michael in the lead is already quite a statement about Jewish identity by the producers. But virtually the entire episode is about Jewish identity.

Picking up the ongoing Christmas/Hanukkah argument between Hope and Michael from last year's Christmas episode, the producers this time give Michael some theological traction.

"Okay, we get a tree and a menorah. Are we talking lights on the outside of the house?" Michael says.

"Are we talking going to synagogue?" Hope parries.

"Okay, okay, theology. You want to know if I accept December twenty-fifth as the birth of Jesus."

"Michael!"

"Okay, okay, I accept it. Now you want to know if I accept that a star led three wise men to a manger where a lady who claimed she hadn't had sex just had a baby who is the son of God?"

"And I'm supposed to believe that a tiny drop of oil lasted eight days, and six men with bows and arrows defeated all the Roman legions?" Hope responds.

"Syrians. Okay, okay, I'll give you the star and three wise men, if you agree to no lights outside, presents and at least two nights of Hanukkah, and a 50 percent reduction in medium range missiles," Michael wisecracks.

"Listen, Michael, I just want this all to be all right, because last year you were so sad and obnoxious, because and because and because," she begins.

"Because it's Christmas," he says, finishing the sentence.

The argument goes on and on, but the most compelling story line involves Melissa trying to get Michael to join her for a Friday night young person's service at a synagogue. She said a friend got her to go last week, and she experienced "kind of a warm feeling." To which he cynically replies, "Yeah, and there's single men." The discussion takes place in Michael's car, which is parked in front of a Christmas tree lot. He is going to buy a tree before dropping Melissa at the synagogue.

"It's not like Hebrew School any more. There were people there like us, people who don't go to synagogue. And this guy, Markowitz, the rabbi, he's really sweet," Melissa says.

"And cute," Michael adds. "Okay, okay. Last time I was in a synagogue beside when my dad died, I think it was 1967 when Nate, the janitor, caught Alan Wuss and I slugging down Manischewitz. I don't know. I mean, Hebrew School and all that. What did that have to do with Little League and the Beatles and getting girls to go to second? I don't know, it's more than that. It's just not making sense."

"Do you believe in God?" Melissa asks, repeating what Hope asked Michael last Christmas.

"I think we better get this done," Michael says, ending the conversation.

They go in and buy a tree, and the next scene shows them pulling up in front of a sleek, modern synagogue with lots of stained glass and outdoor lighting.

"Last chance to see Rabbi Markowitz," Melissa says, opening the car door.

"No thanks," Michael replies.

As Melissa gets out of the car, she looks at the tree strapped to roof and says, "This is God's revenge for the time you planted a tree in Israel for Alfred E. Neuman."

The camera then gives us Michael's point of view as he watches Melissa walk into the synagogue. Just as he was an outsider to the world Hope and Janey shared as they watched snow through the window last year, so he is again as he watches Melissa walk toward the building that looks so warm and inviting compared to the cold, dark night in which he sits watching.

A few scenes later, Michael tells us what he was thinking as he sat outside the synagogue. He and Elliot are kidding about Jewish women whom Elliot has dated when Michael suddenly grows serious and says,

"I swear, I'm outside this synagogue last night, and I might as well have heard voices: 'Michael, why'd you do it? Why'd you marry a shiksa?'" To which Elliot replies, "Hope isn't Jewish?"

The joking between the two includes one of the more controversial moments in the series' history. Michael says, "So you have a history of consorting with Jews?" To which Elliot replies, "Oh, yeah. I have a lot of admiration for the Jewish race. They're warm, and there's their infinite faith in the face of adversity ... Of course, they've also killed our Lord. But I've forgiven them for that."

The synagogue story line is picked up a few scenes later when Michael finds himself back outside the building one night after running an errand. This time he goes into the lobby area, but not the sanctuary. As he studies the In Memoriam board and a glass case full of religious artifacts, a happy couple walks out of the rabbi's office. The rabbi himself, played by Jack Gilford, whose acting roots go back to the Yiddish theater, follows. Michael introduces himself as Melissa's cousin. "What can I do for you?" the rabbi asks. "Nothing," Michael replies, "I'm just skulking by. It's just been a lot of years. I just wanted to see how the old place is doing." The rabbi smiles and says, "We're doing fine." Handel's Hallelujah chorus is playing very loudly on the soundtrack as the scene ends.

The main story line in the episode is not "Michael goes to synagogue." The hour's drama centers on Hope getting into an auto accident with Janey in the car. Hope is badly shaken and, perhaps, seriously injured. The doctors say there is no way to gauge possible internal and head injuries except to look for certain symptoms in coming days. After a few days, Hope appears to be seriously ill. In fact, Michael fears she is going to die. But then, in the last act, the doctors discover the source of her dizziness, nausea, and various other ailments: she's pregnant. The next-to-last scene finds Michael and Melissa in front of the Christmas tree after getting the good news. Michael answers the question Melissa asked earlier at the Christmas tree lot about God.

"The problem is I believe in God," he says. "I didn't think I did, but I do. My father, he believed in God. He didn't have a problem. But then he didn't marry a non-Jew."

Melissa interrupts, "And he got divorced, Michael. What are you saying? That because you didn't marry into your religion, you can't believe in God?"

"No, no, no, no, no," Michael replies. "But which God, who God, where God? I mean, it's like almost losing Hope, it makes me want to."

"Want to what?" Melissa interrupts.

And the scene abruptly shifts to the synagogue, with Michael standing outside the open door to Rabbi Markowitz's office. He knocks just as a young rabbi comes out of the inner bathroom. It's not Jack Gilford, and Michael is clearly surprised. He starts to explain his confusion, but the young rabbi says he is Rabbi Markowitz, and there could not have been any other rabbi in this office. Michael gives up trying to explain, puts on his yarmulke and walks into the sanctuary where a service is underway. The cantor says, "We, who come in the faith that links one generation to another, let us rise and testify." The cantor then starts to chant in Hebrew. When he is finished, Michael bows his head and says "amen," which is where the episode ends.

The presence of the rabbi played by Gilford is never explained, but it is not supposed to be. The producers seem to want it to play as a mystery. Gilford also appeared in the black-and-white Dick Van Dyke scenes in the episode as Santa Claus. Thus, the same smiling, benign, aged face of Santa Claus is also that of this mysterious rabbi who tells Michael that Judaism is doing just fine. While there is at least one message about faith and religious belief encoded in the encounter, I believe that the synagogue scenes are also an attempt by Herskovitz and Zwick to symbolically forge a synthesis between the Jewish and Christian holidays or assimilate one into the other.

This may be purely subjective, but the manner in which Gilford played the mysterious rabbi reminded me of Clarence Oddbody, the angel in Frank Capra's *It's a Wonderful Life*. Gilford's rabbi certainly had at the very least an otherworldy air about him. And, just as the angel in *It's a Wonderful Life* led George Bailey back into his community, so did this one lead Michael back into his. If you think the analysis is farfetched, consider this: Zwick and Herskovitz named their production company Bedford Falls, which is the town in which Bailey lives. Their company logo is the Bailey house with snow gently falling around it. This entire episode is an attempt to reconcile Judaism with the mainstream Christian holidays—to finally find a way for Michael to connect "Hebrew School and all that" to "Little League and the Beatles and getting girls to go to second."

In the end, I do not think Zwick and Herskovitz succeed, but it is a brilliant effort, and the hour absolutely crackles with the intensity of their desire to synthesize the two traditions in a way that allows them to honor both. Just like Hope, Herskovitz and Zwick seem to want angels, too, but without losing their sense of what it means to be a Jew.

"PRELUDE TO A *BRIS*"

Repeating a pattern we have seen with other series, the most Jewish episode in the series' history came in its last season with "Prelude to a *Bris*" on September 19, 1990, at the start of the Jewish holy days of Rosh Hashanah and Yom Kippur that year. Here is how Michael Lerner, editor of *Tikkun*, described one of the episode's story lines in an editorial about the hour (the program inspired passionate editorials in *Tikkun* as well as other Jewish publications):

> In the fall premiere of *thirtysomething*, the show's hero, up-and-coming advertising mogul Michael Steadman, a mostly assimilated Jew, and his non-Jewish wife Hope must decide whether to have a *brit milah* (circumcision) for their newborn son. While Michael does his best to avoid the issue, Hope insists that if their child is going to be raised as a Jew both father and son should know what that means. Michael vacillates, but eventually opts for a ritual ceremony on the grounds that he doesn't want to break the chain of generations linking father to son from time immemorial.[9]

There is a second story line in the hour that runs parallel. It involves the visit of Michael's mother and a new man in her life, Dr. Ben Tietleman, an opthalmologist played by Alan King. Michael's mother, Barbara, is clearly in love with the man, but Michael takes an immediate dislike to him. Since the topic is Judaism, Melissa also plays a major role in the hour. In fact, the opening sequence includes her shooting pictures of Hope with Leo, the newborn son, in her arms. As Melissa and Michael leave Hope and Leo in the bedroom and move downstairs, it is Melissa who sets things in motion with the question, "So, Michael, did you find a *mohel* yet?" (Pronounced "moy-el" to rhyme with boil, the *mohel* is the person who performs the circumcision).

"A *mohel*?" Michael asks.

"Yeah, for the *bris*."

"The *bris?*"

"Everyone has a *bris*, Michael. Roots are in. Don't you know that?"

"Melissa, Hope who lives upstairs? She's not Jewish."

"She's not?" Melissa asks, repeating what has become a running joke among the characters, because it is impossible to know Michael and Hope without knowing that fact, so much is it discussed. Comic relief is provided throughout the episode by Melissa popping in at the times when Michael seems most stressed and asking, "So, Michael, have you found a *mohel* yet?"

Following the opening scene with Melissa, Michael's mother arrives with Ben, who congratulates Michael on the birth of Leo and goes on to explain what the name means in Hebrew. Before Michael has a chance to respond, Ben follows by asking Michael how much he paid for his house. And that is followed by the start of Ben's nonstop string of jokes. For example: "A *mohel* calls his lawyer. 'I'm getting worried, my hand's starting to shake. I think I need a little insurance.' Lawyer says, 'I'll check it out.' He calls back, says, 'I got good news and bad news. I can get you coverage for 300 a year.' 'So, what's the bad news?' the *mohel* asks. 'There's a two inch deductible.' "

"This is a nightmare," Michael groans to Melissa. "My mother's in love with Rodney Dangerfield." But, as Ben starts pushing Michael on the *bris*, explaining it as a covenant with God and wondering why Michael is waffling, Michael starts getting overtly hostile to him. At which point Hope pulls him aside and says he should be nicer to Ben. "You know," she says, "maybe he's a little . . ."

"Loud," Michael says.

"And," Hope replies, "a little . . ."

"Obnoxious," Michael interrupts.

"Maybe, but he's an okay guy, Michael."

"Look, Hope, I want to talk about this *bris*," Michael says, changing the subject. "Are we having it or not?"

"I don't know, are we?" she responds.

"I sort of assumed," he says.

"Oh, right, because of how religious you are."

"Well, no, no. But it feels like something I'm supposed to do . . ."

The argument continues until Hope says, "I'm not attacking you. I just want you to explain it to me [why they should have the *bris*], because you're the Jew in the house. Just explain it to me."

"I don't know if I can," Michael says.

The two story lines, which at first seem only parallel, now start to merge, as in the preceding scene and two others that take up the complicated issue of Jews being anti-Semitic. The set-up scene features Michael complaining to Gary about his boss, losing clients, and his mother's boyfriend.

"And, now I have this *bris*," Michael continues, "and I don't know if I really want this *bris*... It just seems a little, like, next thing I know I'm five two, in a sixty-eight Lincoln, driving four miles an hour, shouting "Goyim!" out the window."

To which Gary, a non-Jew, replies, "How come you Jews can say stuff like that? If I said something like that, you'd kill me."

The big scene comes after Michael rudely tells Ben he was out of line to invite a rabbi to Michael's home to talk about a *bris* for Leo.

"What's wrong with Ben?" Hope demands of Michael angrily.

"I don't even know this guy, Hope."

"Yeah, I think you do," Hope says.

"Well, he's a real pushy guy, I'll tell you that," Michael says.

"He's a pushy Jew, that's what you mean," Hope says.

"What? Hey, wait a minute. What are you, nuts? Wait, whoa, let me get this straight: you think I don't like Ben because he's Jewish, like I'm anti-Semitic or something?"

"Oh, no, not you. You married a nice Jewish girl, you observe the holidays, you keep a kosher home."

"You want to keep a kosher home now, Hope? I didn't even grow up in a kosher home. This is insane. I really think you're insane. How can I be anti-Semitic? You know how important this is to me, this religious thing."

"Oh, really," Hope says. "Janey might argue with that. Janey is four."

"I know how old she is, and I happen to have had a bar mitzvah, which is sort of a big deal."

"Don't take that tone, that dumb shiksa tone with me. Don't talk to me like that," she says and storms out of the room.

One of the more interesting aspects of how Jewish identity is depicted in that exchange involves the notion that there is more than one way to be Jewish, and that some Jews are made uncomfortable by others. *Tikkun*'s Lerner saw evidence of "ambivalence and internalized anti-Semitism" on the part of Michael in scenes like that. Prime-time network television had never dealt with such nuanced issues of Jewishness, which is not surprising, of course, when you remember it had hardly started acknowledging Jewish identity in leading characters before *thirtysomething.*

Michael does ultimately reconcile with Ben, telling him he was "right about the *bris,*" as well as sending the rabbi and "paying for the *mohel.*" Michael tries to explain why he acted the way he did by saying, "It's just that you locked me into it. I mean, my son, he's going to be a Jew, but what does that mean? I mean, am I Jew? I can talk like an old Jewish guy. I can tell a great Jewish joke. But do I really feel like a Jew? What is a Jew supposed to feel like?"

"You're asking me?" Ben says. "How the hell do I know? You're a Jew just like me. Maybe we lived it differently. Maybe I had rocks thrown at me when I was a kid. Maybe you didn't. Does that make me more of a Jew than you? No. Don't look up to me, kid, I'm not looking down on you. I'm next to you.

"My father used to tell a story about the chain, that golden chain that links us all together—you, your dead old man, his old man, et cetera. Get the point? The wonderful thing about the chain: nobody says we gotta keep it going. But do you presume to break it? That's your big-time question. Mull it over. Fools rush in."

During the ceremony, held in the Steadman living room, just as the rabbi says, "Blessed is he who comes in God's name," in walks Ben, who is late. In front of everyone, Michael asks Ben to be part of his family and says, "it would be an honor" if Ben would hold Leo. Ben does, and, as the rabbi says, "We rejoice, a child has come into the world," the producers cut to an image of Michael as a boy with his father. The episode closes on the image of a room full of friends as the rabbi says, "May his name be called in Israel, Leo, son of Michael. *Mazel tov.*"

The scene is a lovely one that can leave you with the same kind of "warm feeling" Melisssa found at Friday night temple, but the producers' answer about what it means to be Jew—the metaphor of a great chain— is a problematic one. As described by Ben, Jewish identity is something you are initially born into. So that would make it genetic; Jewish ethnicity is a matter of genes. But then certain religious actions must be taken on your behalf by someone else. Ben tells Michael he is a Jew because his father gave him a *bris* and bar mitzvah. Even though Michael has not gone to synagogue since his father left him and his mother when Michael was fifteen, he is still a Jew. But if Michael doesn't give Leo a *bris* and bar mitzvah, Leo will not be a Jew. As Ben says, "Do you presume to break it? That's your big-time question."

Another problem: as defined by Ben, being a Jew is essentially a passive act. The parent does everything for you, and, when you become parent, you repeat the pattern mainly out of fear of breaking with what has gone before. Not that fear has not been used by other groups to try and guarantee the passage of culture from one generation to the next. But there are other problems, too. For example, how do girls fit into the chain? Hope seems justified in asking, as she does of Michael's mother, "Is this baby [Leo] a Jew? And what does that mean? And where am I and Janey in all this?"

One of the biggest shortcomings of the episode is that some of the information is technically not correct. This is mainly the result of the producers not making the distinction between Jewishness as a religion (Judaism) and Jewishness as an ethnic identity. They are not one and the same. In Jewish religious law, it is the mother that determines the child's tie to Jewishness. If a child's mother is Jewish, he or she is automatically considered Jewish. Therefore, since Michael's mother was Jewish, he was born Jewish. But his son Leo was not. Actions either on the part of the parents or the child when he becomes an adult are needed for him to become a Jew. But that is a Jew defined by religion, i.e. Judaism.

Tikkun's Lerner admits his own ambivalence in not wanting to criticize a series he so admires yet feeling the need to show "how empty Steadman's reasoning turned out to be." As Lerner puts it:

> We have yet to see a single portrayal on national television of a Jew who has a good reason other than family tradition for holding on to Judaism. In a key scene, Steadman has an edifying fantasy that his son chooses football over a thirteenth birthday party; he recognizes that something has been lost by missing bar mitzvah. But what, exactly, he can't say ... What is the *content* and *meaning* of being Jewish? It apparently never occurred to the writers of *thirtysomething* that generations of martyrs died to keep Judaism alive because there was "a there there," a message and a meaning.[10]

Ultimately, the producers give us a collection of feel-good Kodak moments rather than sound answers on the meaning of Judaism in "Prelude to a *Bris*." But no one before or since wrestled as mightily or as skillfully in a prime-time series with the question of what it means to be a Jew as did Herskovitz and Zwick. Their greatest accomplishment might have been the character of Michael Steadman, who was presented with enough texture and dimensions to be the first leading Jewish character to remind us that identity is not monolithic—that someone is not just a Jew, a Catholic, or a Muslim. Jewishness is just part of the mosaic of identities that is the character.

When asked if Steadman was a "Jewish hero" or a "hero who happened to be Jewish," Herskovitz said, "He embodied so much of how we [Herskovitz and Zwick] saw the world, how we saw human beings. The fact that he was Jewish was inseparable from that, but it didn't form the center of it. No, it came in second, third, fourth, maybe fifth."[11]

As for Steadman being married to a non-Jew, Herskovitz said, "There were two issues to that. First, we were dealing with many personal incidents from our lives. We both were married to non-Jews. And this is very hard to understand when you are outside the process of creating stories, but when you are involved in that process, you look for the things that are dramatically interesting. And we felt it was much more interesting to talk about a mixed marriage. There were endless things to talk about . . . And we got a lot of wonderful drama out of the conflict of those two things, because after all conflict is what drama's all about."[12]

In terms of his Jewish identity, Steadman plowed new prime-time ground. As brought to life in the person of Ken Olin, he was in almost no way feminized—or, at least, demasculinized—as so many Jewish male characters were and continue to be. He was a large, strong, handsome, leading-man type. In fact, Olin was brought to Hollywood by Steven Bochco, producer of such police dramas as *Hill Street Blues*, to play an Italian-American detective, Harry Garibaldi, in that series. He also played an Italian-American baseball player, Rocky Padillo, in Bochco's short-lived NBC series *Bay City Blues*. The pattern of Jewish actors playing Italian characters was a well-established one starting in the earliest days of network TV and extending into the late 1980s.[13]

Olin described what he sees as his place within that weird loop of ethnic substitutions by saying "There simply were no Jewish characters. Italians apparently were ethnically okay but not Jews to the Jews running the networks . . . Thinking back, it's funny now, today, because if there's a role of a Jewish man, I'm him. I think who I am, the way I look, and the nature of the kind of actor I am made it probably more palatable to a lot of networks or whatever, the idea of casting me as a leading man whether or not I said I was Jewish. Like I said, up until *thirtysomething,* I had never played Jews . . ."[14]

In agreeing with the analysis that most male Jewish characters before the late 1980s were not particularly masculine in the traditional American television sense of that word, which emphasizes physical strength, decisive action, few words, and lots of aggressiveness, Olin said, "I think Michael Steadman to some extent was an evolution of a certain way that Jewish men were generally portrayed in the media in that he was prone to self-examination. He was certainly prone to self-effacement. I mean, people called it whining, but he was always within the throes of some kind of anxiety . . ."

At the time of his interview with me—September 1997—Olin was a playing a character named Abe Ringel in a made-for-TV movie titled *The Advocate's Devil.* Ringel was a no-nonsense, hardball attorney. He explained:

> I liked the idea of developing a character who I perceived to be a very tough Jew. I cut my hair very short. These are guys that I know— very, very tough Jewish men who come from tough neighborhoods who are fighters in both senses of the word. And that's not something that you often see even today on television in terms of Jews. I mean, these guys are tough. They're tough in every sense of the word. They're tough intellectually and they're tough physically, and their bearing is combative. But I think maybe you couldn't have gotten to that kind of tough Jew today without going through the stage of Michael Steadman ten years ago. That's what I mean when I say he was evolutionary to some extent.

Historically, television's toughest Jew was probably the supporting character Detective Mick Belker (Bruce Weitz) in the NBC police drama *Hill Street Blues*—an unshaven, hard-nosed undercover cop in a stocking cap who often posed as a homeless person on stakeouts. Belker also had a habit of barking like a dog at stray dogs and biting suspects who resisted his efforts to subdue or arrest them. Fierce as Belker was when he was on the job, calling suspects "scumbags and dirtballs," he was pure marshmallow in the hands of his mother, who often called him at home or at the office. We are talking here, though, about a character who could be called one-and-a-half-dimensional at best.

DR. FLEISCHMAN AND THE CAPTIVITY NARRATIVE

In 1990, as *thirtysomething* was starting its last season, the evolution of leading characters toward a multidimensional, more complex and resonant sense of Jewish identity continued with the arrival of Dr. Joel Fleischman (Rob Morrow) of CBS's *Northern Exposure*. Co-creators Joshua Brand and John Falsey often described their series as a "fish out of water show."[15]

Fleischman, who grew up in Queens and went to school in Manhattan, was the fish. The new pond he now found himself in was Cicely, Alaska, a strange and isolated town of 215 founded by two lesbians at the turn of the twentieth century. Fleischman is its most reluctant resident, forced to work for four years as town doctor under the terms of his medical school scholarship. His new employer is Maurice Minnifield (Barry Corbin), a former Mercury astronaut for NASA who now runs the town. Minnifield is a "man's man," and he and Fleischman take an immediate dislike to each other.

Audiences were flagged to Fleischman's Jewishness from the very first round of publicity materials sent to newspapers and magazines to promote the series by CBS. In all but one series of publicity photos, Fleischman is shown holding a bagel. One photo, for example, shows him in shirt, tie, slacks, and loafers, sitting on a rock at the edge of a lake with a snow-capped mountain behind him. His blazer is covering the rock, and his suitcase is in front of him, as if he just stopped to rest . . . and to nosh, since he is holding an onion bagel. The one series of photos that did not include a bagel pictured Fleischman in jacket, shirt, and tie, nose to nose with a moose.

The episode most often cited in connection with Jewish identity is one titled "Yom Kippur," which begins with Fleischman behaving in a manner even more dismissive and superior than usual to several townsfolk including his assistant, Marilyn, whom he fires. His day ends with an act of coldhearted indifference to one of his patients who now finds himself homeless after a fire. All of this happens on the eve of Yom Kippur.

In the manner of Dickens's *A Christmas Carol*, Fleischman is visited on the night of Yom Kippur by his childhood rabbi, who shows him his trespasses and takes him on a journey that includes stops at Yom Kippur Past, Present, and Future. While there is a good deal of infor-

Rob Morrow as Dr. Joel Fleischman in the CBS series *Northern Exposure*. The premise for this comic captivity narrative about a recent Columbia University Medical School graduate forced to practice in the remote Alaskan town of Cicely echoes back to a turn of the century vaudeville song, "Moshe from Nova Scotia," about another Jew in an unusual place. Photo by Tony Esparza. CBS Photo Archive mation about Yom Kippur and what an observant Jew's relationship to it should be, like *thirtysomething*'s "Mike Van Dyke" episode, the hour seems more an effort to synthesize a Jewish holy day into the literature of a Christian one than an examination of Jewish identity itself.

The episode of *Northern Exposure* that most clearly deals with Jewish identity is "Kaddish for Uncle Manny," which like "Yom Kippur" was written by Jeff Melvoin. It begins with Fleischman getting the news that his Uncle Manny has died in Florida. Sitting in The Brick, the Cicely bar and restaurant where everyone gathers, Fleischman explains to Ed, an Eskimo in training to be a shaman, that he was very close to Manny: "We used to spend Sundays together listening to Yankee games and playing gin rummy." He also tells Ed that he promised his Aunt Helen that he would say Kaddish for Manny.

"What's a Kaddish?" Ed asks.

"A Kaddish is the Jewish prayer for the dead. Only problem is you need a minyan to say it."

"What's a minyan?"

"It's ten Jewish males thirteen or older. Well, actually, in most places now, it can be women, but I'm not exactly sure how Uncle Manny would feel about that; he was raised Orthodox.

"Why do you need a minyan?'

"I don't know, you need nine guys on a field in baseball and ten Jews in a room to say Kaddish. I don't know where I'm going to find a minyan."

A subsequent scene finds O'Connell (Janine Turner), a professional pilot and non-Jewish love interest for Fleischman, knocking on his door late at night. She says she heard about the death of Manny and came by to see how Fleischman is doing. He shows her pictures of him and Manny "in front of Yankee Stadium" and the two of them standing arm in arm at Fleischman's bar mitzvah. There is a clarinet noodling in a minor key on the soundtrack as Fleischman says this, a signal that we are entering heavily Jewish territory, just as the clarinet and violin music did in *Bridget Loves Bernie* whenever we returned to the Lower East Side.

"What's this?" O'Connell asks, pointing to a tallis and yarmulke.

"This was the stuff I wore at my bar mitzvah. This is a tallis, it's a prayer shawl. Beautiful, isn't it?"

"It is beautiful."

"This is a yarmulke. You wear it on your head, obviously. He brought this stuff back from Israel for me. He helped me memorize my Torah portion. So, yeah, we spent quite a few hours together. I don't remember any of it."

The next scene features Minnifield chairing a meeting of a dozen or so of the town regulars. Minnifield says he called the meeting to discuss the death of Fleischman's "Uncle Morty."

"Uncle Manny, I believe it was Uncle Manny," O'Connell says.

"Whatever," Minnifield responds. "Anyway, Fleischman wants to say the traditional mourner's prayer, but he can't do it without nine more Jews."

"Why not?" someone asks.

"How should I know, do I look like Tevye?" Minnifield snaps, as another member of the group explains the reference to *Fiddler on the Roof*.

Then another resident explains that the "minyan thing is so that the mourner doesn't go it alone, you know, in the time of grief."

"Yeah, yeah, yeah," Minnifield interrupts, "the bottom line is Fleischman needs nine more Hebrews on his team." He then lays out a plan he has devised in which he will pay $100 and expenses "for any bona fide member of the Jewish faith who will come here and pray with Fleischman." Minnifield enlists the town members to search Alaska "sector by sector" to find the Jews via maps and various guides he has provided for each in sealed envelopes.

"But how do we know if someone's Jewish?" Minnifield is asked.

"Now that's a very good question. Does anyone here know the answer? Well, then, let me explain. The tip of the penis used to be a good pretty accurate yardstick, but with the proliferation of circumcision, it's no longer a valid form of ID," Minnifield says.

He then points to a picture on an easel of men in long beards, fur-lined hats, and long black coats crowded around a table, saying, "Now, right here I have a picture of what used to be considered your typical Jewish person. But, if that stereotype was ever valid, you can see that it no longer is. So, say hi to Iser Danilovich."

As he says this, he removes the first picture and replaces it with a portrait of Kirk Douglas as Spartacus.

"Wow, Hercules was Jewish," one woman says.

"Actually that's Spartacus," Ed says, "well, really Kirk Douglas."

There is silence for a few seconds as everyone ponders the portrait of a very tough Jew, and then O'Connell asks, "Maurice, what about last names? You know, Schwartz, Cohn, Levine?"

"Seinfeld?" someone adds.

"Well, last names will be your primary clue, and I've compiled a list of them. Of course, it's not comprehensive by any means," Maurice responds.

"Where are we going to find these names, Maurice, outside of the telephone book?" he is asked.

"Well, your Jewish people are a lot like your Chinese people—only with a sense of humor," Maurice says. "They value family, tradition, education. They tend to go toward the professions. When I blasted off into space, I was very happy to have a lot of Goldfarbs and Finklesteins at the button, although none of them got into a Mercury capsule."

The intended humor of the remark about the Mercury capsule plays off a stereotype of Jews as being physical cowards and not particularly patriotic, though it is undercut by the fact that Minnifield is the one saying it. In the context of the series as a whole, Minnifield is treated in much the same satirical manner as the super-patriotic Air Force general played by George C. Scott in the 1964 film classic *Dr. Strangelove: Or, How I Learned to Stop Worrying and Love the Bomb*. In fact, much of the episode is spent taking on such stereotypes.

Ed is the first to find a Jew for Manny's minyan. He knocks on Fleischman's door at night with the good news. "Where did you find him?" Fleischman asks.

"Hitching by the road," Ed responds.

"Impossible," Fleischman says, "Jews don't hitch."

"Would you like to meet him? He's right outside," Ed says, as he turns and calls, "Come on in, Buck."

"Buck?" Fleischman asks.

In walks a very large man—large enough to be a lineman in the National Football League. He has long hair and a beard. He is wearing a flannel shirt and red suspenders.

"Buck Schoen, I'd like you to meet Dr. Joel Fleischman," Ed says.

"Hey," Buck says.

"Schoen?" Fleischman says, shaking his hand. "That's kind of unusual, isn't it?"

"It's German, S-c-h-o-e-n," Buck replies.

"Buck's a lumberjack when he's working," Ed says.

"Would you excuse us for just a moment," Fleischman says to Buck as he walks Ed over to the other side of the room.

"Ed, I hate to look a gift horse in the mouth," he whispers urgently, "but someone's pulling your leg. That man is definitely not a Jew. Look at him. Jews don't wear red suspenders, they don't slobber tobacco in their beards, they don't hitch, and they definitely don't have names like Buck."

"Oh, his real name is Leon," Ed replies.

"Oh really, we'll let's see about that," Fleischman says, walking back over to Buck and asking him to recite a certain prayer in Hebrew. Buck recites the prayer without hesitation, and Fleischman is impressed.

"So, where'd you grow up?" Fleischman asks.

"Cleveland. Well, er, Shaker actually."

"Oh, Shaker Heights," Fleischman says, referring to an upscale Cleveland suburb with a large Jewish population. "I had a lab partner from there. He said it was like a Midwest version of Scarsdale."

"Not my bag," Buck says, ending the conversation by asking when he gets his money.

As the roster of Jews grows, so do Fleischman's doubts. When Marilyn, an Eskimo, announces that she found an Eskimo-convert-to-Judaism who is on his way by kayak, Fleischman confesses his uncertainty. "Why am I praying with these guys?"

"Because you're Jewish," Marilyn says.

"But what does that mean?" Fleischman replies. "We hold certain theological, ethical precepts in common, we know a smattering of Hebrew, years ago our ancestors schlepped around the Negev? Intellectually, I appreciate it. But, emotionally, I just don't know."

Fleischman's uncertainty is played out in a dream sequence straight out of Mel Brooks's feature film *Blazing Saddles*, in which he is dressed as the mousy city doctor, walking out onto a dusty main street in the Old West when up ride eight heavily armed cowboys and one Indian chief. Getting down from his horse, the leader introduces them as the Minyan Rangers. "Have Torah, will travel," another explains. The leader tells Fleischman to climb up on his horse so they can go and "set things right." But Fleischman hesitates. "Come on, we're packing strudel, son, but it won't keep," the lead rider says, as he yanks Fleischman onto the saddle and they thunder out of town.

The next day, Fleischman goes to Minnifield and tells him he wants him to call off the "hunt for Jews." His explanation, "I don't feel like I can say Kaddish with a bunch of hired guns."

"These are your people, Fleischman," Maurice says.

"I know, they're Jews. But I don't know them, and they don't know me."

"What, you don't like the Jews I got you? What do you need, New Yorkers or what?"

"No, the way I feel about my uncle is a very private thing. So, I don't feel like I can open up to a bunch of people I don't know, especially if you're paying them to be here."

The episode ends in the town's white wooden church with its Protestant steeple. Fleischman, wearing a yarmulke, is standing at a podium speaking to the townsfolk gathered before him in the pews. After thanking them for trying to get him a minyan and acknowledging that he "pulled the plug" on the campaign, he says, "I'm no rabbi, but it seems to me that the purpose of saying Kaddish is to be with your community. And I realized this week that you're my community. So, if you'll just bear with me."

As he kisses the tallis and puts it over his shoulders, Ed asks, "You want we should all wear beenies?"

"No, it's not necessary. I'll just say the prayer, and then we can all head over to The Brick for a nosh."

Fleischman invites the congregation to pray along "in your own way," and while some make the sign of the cross, others hold hands as he starts to pray in Hebrew for Manny. As the camera scans the faces of the congregation, Native American music starts to play, the music that has come to signal moments of spirituality in a series remarkable for its spirituality, according to television historian Robert J. Thompson. In his book *Television's Second Golden Age*, Thompson explains the spirituality in terms of a "natural religion" posited by the producers:

> The real cornerstone of *Northern Exposure*, the glue that kept it all together . . . was its spirituality . . . Although a variety of organized religions were explored in the series, especially Joel's reluctant brand of Judaism, the entire populace was guided by a natural religion that the awesome scenery, mighty climate, and diurnal irregularities seemed to force upon them . . . An inclusion of the spiritual and the sacred was very unusual for a prime-time series at the time . . .[16]

Andrew Schneider, one of the producers of *Northern Exposure*, says "We took some flak from rabbis" for the statement by Fleischman that the people of Cicely are his community, not the Jewish people. Schneider defends the statement by adding, "But the community of Cicely was the spirit behind the minyan."[17]

Melvoin said: "I got letters from rabbis. I have copies of sermons that rabbis have written about that episode because of the question of assimilation and things like that. So, it provoked a lot of discussion."[18]

Northern Exposure was consistent in its approach to Judaism. When discussing Jewishness as religion, the strategy (as shown in the discussion of "Kaddish") is first to explain. The scene in The Brick with Fleischman explaining Kaddish to Ed is a virtual carbon copy of a scene in "Yom Kippur" in which Ed asks, "What's Yom Kippur?" as Fleischman sits down for a huge dinner at The Brick in an attempt to "carb up" for his Yom Kippur fast.

As Yom Kippur is explained in Fleischman's straightforward, secular way, it becomes demystified. It is hard to think of Judaism as strange, exotic, or especially otherly after the little chats between Ed and Fleischman. And, once Judaism is cast as just another religion, it is then eventually merged into that larger pantheistic religion that Thompson described. This religion is presented as an *Ur* religion and is often linked to the elements of universal myth described by Joseph Campbell in *The Hero with a Thousand Faces*.[19] So, in this sense, at least, Jews were not depicted as "the other" in *Northern Exposure*, as they had been in other series. In fact, the attempt was to mainstream Judaism and make Fleischman into just another member of the community, more defined by geography than religion or genetics. In that sense, *Northern Exposure*'s central narrative is one of assimilation. Actually, it starts as a kind of comic captivity narrative, with Fleischman held captive as it were by these people he considers strange and threatening. But eventually he assimilates and becomes so much a part of the community that he feels closer to residents of Cicely than to any fellow Jews.

A MAN FROM NEW YORK

But there is another way that Fleischman's Jewish identity is depicted, a decidedly secular way that centers on his identity as a New Yorker. There is even an episode titled "Joel Misses New York." After two years in

Cicely, Fleischman starts to fear he has lost his identity as a New Yorker. As he puts it to O'Connell, "I'm losing it, O'Connell. I may have lost it already: New York... Yesterday, I couldn't remember whether the subway stopped at Washington Square or Canal Street... This is a serious personality meltdown. I'm Joel Fleischman, Jewish doctor from New York. You take that away, and who am I, what am I?"

To compensate, he places a special order at the general store: "Zabar's blend coffee, two pounds; corned beef, pastrami, lox, five pounds each; bagels—poppy, onion, sesame." But he continues to feel his "New York identity" is slipping away, until he gets in a silly fight with the owner of the fix-it shop over repairs done to his VCR. As Fleischman gets more and more unreasonable and upset, his speech patterns change. In explaining to O'Connell how he is going to "nail the bastard" in court, Fleischman says, "What a schmuck! What does he think I am, some greenhorn right off the boat, that he can jerk me around like some Chaim Yonkel? You should have seen the look on his face when he offered to fix it for free and I said no."

O'Connell tries to summarize: "So instead of a VCR that works, you have one that's useless and a pending lawsuit. And this makes you happy?"

"Yeah, I feel great."

"See, Fleischman, you didn't have anything to worry about. All this moaning, 'Who am I? What am I?' Please. A little shrillness, a little hostility, and you're back in the pink. All this talk about Zabar's, Rockefeller Center. That's not what this is about. Misery, that's the missing ingredient. A little heartburn with the Orange Julius, and the world's a beautiful place."

"You got it," Fleischman says.

While this conversation has been going on, a dog has been barking incessantly outside the open window of Fleischman's office. Fleischman has already yelled out the window for someone to quiet the dog, but now he jumps up from his desk and screams out the window, "What are you, deaf? The dog, muzzle it."

In the course of interviews for this study, several Jewish writers and producers spoke of "writing Jewish" or "using Jewish rhythms." Most talked about it as if it were a sensibility, a "vibe" or a feeling—like playing jazz. But a few were able to be more specific, and one of the key descriptions they offered for "writing Jewish" is to put the object of the sentence at the start rather than the end. As one writer explained it, "I am going to have a character tell the audience he loves apple pie. If it is a non-Jewish character, he says, 'I love apple pie.' But to signal that it is a Jewish character, you have him say, 'Apple pie, I love it.'" That is the syntax Fleischman reverts to when he regains his identity as a New Yorker and screams, "The dog, muzzle it." Thus, Jewishness and New York are linked without overtly stating so. Of course, the abrasiveness and love of misery that O'Connell identifies are also then linked to being Jewish.

The ultimate description of Jewish identity in terms of New York comes in Rob Morrow's final episode of the show, in which the producers put Fleischman and O'Connell on a classic hero quest searching for the mythical Keewaa Aani, the Emerald City. After much wandering in the wilderness and a few battles along the way, they see the city through the fog, and it is Manhattan. Fleischman asks O'Connell to come with him.

"New York City is the thing you dream about—the one sustaining constant in your life. That's for you. It's your place, not mine. This is my place," she says, referring to the Alaskan wilderness on which they are still supposed to be standing.

"I gotta do this," he says and walks off into the mist toward Manhattan.

Fleischman is returning to the community he first left on his singular hero quest. The mythic loop appears to be complete. Is he returning to his tribe, those "people from New York"—the very people that CBS research claimed American viewers did not want to see?

One Jewish publication wrote of the finale:

Dr. Fleischman's was not the first story of a Jew discovering God among alien peoples. The *real* first Jew—the patriarch Abraham—found God among the Canaanites . . . Abraham bought land, negotiated deals and became comfortable with foreign rulers and peoples. But he always maintained his devotion to God and family. Joel Fleischman didn't arrive in Cicely with family and many possessions. But he did have gray matter and sinew somehow imbedded with Jewish knowledge, customs and traditions. He had to confront his most ingrained beliefs, predilections and habits during his Cicelian journey, emerging more Jewishly aware than when he started.[20]

What is remarkable about Fleischman's final moment is the symbolism of the Jewish leading man abandoning the non-Jewish woman to return to New York. And the writers clearly understood the larger, metaphorical implications of that act in terms of intermarriage and assimilation, with O'Connell saying, "It's your place, not mine."

This was a profound, singular, and definitive moment in American popular culture, cutting against an unrelenting pattern in television, film, theater, and popular literature of Jewish leading men rushing to embrace the "higher" assimilated status promised by a relationship with a non-Jewish woman. Never did *Northern Exposure* shine as brilliantly as it did with Fleischman's departure. Nor has any one scene in a drama ever dealt as wisely with Jewish identity as Fleischman's farewell.

"AND WHAT ABOUT YOUR RESPONSIBILITIES AS A JEW?"

There was one other prime-time drama with a leading Jewish character, *Relativity*, a short-lived ABC drama that ran for part of the 1996–97 TV season. Zwick and Herskovitz were also the creators and executive producers of this story about a Jewish man, Leo, and a gentile woman, Isabel, both in their twenties, who meet in Rome and fall madly in love. Zwick and Herskovitz, though, did not write any episodes beyond the pilot, and their producer titles came as a result of the series being made by their Bedford Falls production company. Jan Oxenberg, the hands-on producer for the series, identified one of the goals in terms of Jewish identity:

> In creating Jewish characters who were a little bit more working class, you know, not prosperous, which is the stereotype . . . The father, in fact, was perennially unemployed . . . It was a different take on the Jewish family, a different style of neurosis, which I don't think we had seen before in Jewish families on TV. But, again, it was the Jewish man with the non-Jewish girlfriend. We actually got complaints about that from, I guess, from Jewish women who thought Jewish men should be portrayed as seeing Jewish women as desirable.[21]

Once the couple returned to the United States, Isabel broke off her engagement to a young man of whom her parents approved and moved in with Leo. What was interesting about this is that opposition to Leo by Isabel's family was not based on his being Jewish. If there was any friction, it was mainly class based, as Oxenberg suggests. Following a pattern we have seen before, the one episode that dealt with ethnic differences between the two lovers was the Christmas episode, "Unsilent Night," in which Isabel sets up a small Christmas tree in the apartment she and Leo share. When Leo and his older sister, Rhonda, see it, they both look surprised.

"What, you guys weren't one of those Jewish families that celebrated Christmas?" Isabel asks.

"We grew up with our Grandma Fanny," Rhonda says. "And Grandma Fanny used to say Jews celebrating Christmas, you know, assimilating that way were basically finishing Hitler's work for him."

"Rhonda!" Leo yells.

"Look, it's just this visceral thing," Rhonda replies.

"Is it a visceral thing for you, too?" Isabel asks Leo. "I mean, you can tell me. Be honest."

"I don't know. I mean, I like the tree. It looks nice, it smells great," Leo says, and the tree stays.

That is as Jewish as the show ever got. Perhaps the producers didn't have time to explore it further with such a quick cancellation. And I should explain that Rhonda was often given to overstatement, so within the context of the series her remarks don't seem quite as out-of-left-field as they might appear when excerpted.

Like Melissa Steadman, there are other supporting players from prime-time dramas that probably should also be mentioned. Most supporting Jewish characters fit comfortably into certain clearly identifiable patterns. For example, Stuart Markowitz, an attorney on the NBC legal drama *L.A. Law*, which ran from 1986 to 1994, is a clear example of the feminized Jewish male. Markowitz is married to another attorney, Ann Kelsey, and their relationship is described as follows by Thompson: "The relationship between Kelsey and Stuart Markowitz reversed gender roles . . . Kelsey was the ambitious, aggressive lawyer who often initiated the passion of the relationship . . . Markowitz was the more passive and liked to cook."[22]

Another lawyer as supporting Jewish character of note is Douglas Wambaugh, played by Fyvush Finkel on *Picket Fences*, a quirky, smalltown drama created by David E. Kelley that ran on CBS from 1992 to 1997. Wambaugh has been described in the Jewish press as "a loud, aggressive defense attorney," an image that was addressed in a 1994 episode of the series, titled "Squatter's Rights."[23] In the episode, Wambaugh is thrown out of his synagogue for telling a distasteful joke at a friend's funeral and calls a *beit din* (Jewish court) in an effort to win readmittance. But his overall image within the town quickly becomes the focus of the trial, with one of the *beit din* judges saying to Wambaugh, "Like Rabbi Levin says, the ambulance-chasing shyster is a negative stereotype that has plagued us. My father was a Jewish attorney; he was victimized by that caricature."

"My father was in Poland; he died in an oven. You want to compare hardships?" Wambaugh says.

"And what about your responsibilities, your responsibilities as a Jew to act in a manner that does not perpetuate the prejudice that you know is out there?" another judge asks.

"I suppose I could wake up every day and assume like you suggest that the world is full of anti-Semites, but that would make me a bigot," Wambaugh says. "I prefer to presume that the people are enlightened and not prejudiced . . . Integrity has never been mine to sell. I have it. I know in my own mind that I have it. But to get by, I became Douglas Wambaugh, the character, the opportunist, the winner."

"And you can live with that?" one of the judges asks.

"I can survive with that," he answers.

"Your actions may help you survive personally, but they endanger our culture," one judge says.

"There's another old saying," a second judge adds, "the future of the Jewish people is in your hands."

"I remember reading that standing at the urinal," Wambaugh says, as the three judges all look away in embarrassment at him making another questionable joke. But he continues, "You see, I'm a character. I embarrass myself. But I would never embarrass my God or my faith. If I have done so, I am nothing."

The problem with this logic: Wambaugh's answer speaks to religion, while his accusers are questioning his secular behavior in connection with cultural stereotypes. It is not a very good defense, but this is after all entertainment, and Wambaugh wins his right to return to the congregation.

When asked if Wambaugh was an offensive or a beloved character in terms of Jewish identity, Melvoin, who became executive producer for *Picket Fences* after *Northern Exposure*, pointed out that Wambaugh was created by Kelley, who is not Jewish. As to the question of offensive or beloved, he said:

> I suppose that depends on the eye of the beholder. David Kelley has a particular gift for developing confrontation in his drama. Often his characters are conceived to promote weekly confrontation on issues, and the challenge is to give those issues a human face. So, my answer is that his intent was both. But I think the first rule was to outrage and then he sucks you in with the outrage and then he tries to get under it and show you the humanity as with that scene [the one described from "Squatter's Rights"]. It is offensive in some ways, but there's a point... A lot of this is just different sensitivities... David wrote that episode, and I took over *Picket Fences* after it aired. I think David's non-Jewishness allows him to write that character and do things that I can't... Personally, I thought there were things that Wambaugh did in the early going that were offensive to me. But it was good drama.[24]

Once the gatekeepers left and the gates were allowed to open far enough to allow writers like Marshall Herskovitz and Joshua Brand to bring characters like Michael Steadman and Joel Fleischman onto the prime-time stage, network dramas like *thirtysomething* and *Northern Exposure* did start to reflect Jewish life in America. That is to say, a more normal relationship between television and social reality was able finally to kick in.

Problems of "successful" assimilation, movement away from Jewish neighborhoods, intermarriage, and related child-raising questions that Jews had been grappling with in their own lives since the 1950s and before finally started playing out symbolically on American television each week, as the producers of the series tried to define a space that allowed their characters to assimilate into mainstream America but also retain a core sense of Jewish identity—to have Christmas and Hanukkah too. Or, perhaps, in the case of Steadman and Fleischman, it is more a sense of trying to recover some core sense of Jewish identity within themselves in the wake of their parents' "successful" assimilation amid all the new possibilities in postwar America for Jews. The important thing is that we finally had fully realized characters whom we could count on being there week in and week out—characters that Jews and non-Jews in the television audience could come to know and care about as a result of the sense of familiarity that comes with connections forged through the ritual of weekly viewing.

The producers who created these television narratives are for the most part third-generation Jews with immigrant grandparents and, in many cases, parents who threw themselves headlong into assimilation and all that often came with it from suburbia to private schools for their children. In *The Problem of the Third Generation Immigrant*, sociologist Marcus Lee Hansen says that most immigrant groups by the third generation feel comfortable enough in American society to try and recover some of the ethnicity that their parents rejected in their efforts to assimilate.[25] That is what was happening in the lives of many baby boomer American Jews in the 1980s and 1990s. For the first time, starting in 1987, almost a quarter of a century after feature films, network television offered them what Melvoin called "good drama"—characters and narratives that resonated with their lives.

And then came the sitcoms, another story altogether . . .

Intermarriage II (Shiksa Goddesses Transforming Jewish Guys) – *Anything But Love, Flying Blind, Mad About You, Brooklyn Bridge,* and More

The thing is Hollywood is run by Jewish men. We all know the Jewish
syndrome in high school. The Jewish boys don't like the Jewish girls . . .
They really want the goddesses and Michelle Pfeiffers.
Actress Jennifer Grey on her decision to have plastic surgery on her nose[1]

One is a recently wed documentary filmmaker living in Manhattan with a woman he is absolutely mad about. Another is a recent college graduate working on his first job and his first relationship with a woman who makes him sexually crazed. The third is a dour newspaper columnist who has fallen "madly in lust" with a woman named Wally.

What Paul Buchman (Paul Reiser) of *Mad About You*, Neil Barish (Corey Parker) of *Flying Blind*, and Jack Stein (Jay Thomas) of *Love and War* have in common is that they are all Jewish male sitcom characters that were in relationships with non-Jewish female sitcom characters at the start of the 1992 television season. As such they are representative of a pattern so dominant during the 1990s as to include all but a handful of the many sitcoms with leading Jewish characters that came through the door opened by the sale of the networks and the success of *thirtysomething* during the previous decade.

This Jewish man/gentile woman pattern not only offers a way to survey most of the decade's sitcoms, it also serves as another striking instance of Jewish identity being defined on prime-time network television as much by what is not there as by what is. It was not just that Jewish female characters were depicted as inferior in some ways to their non-Jewish counterparts—the way Rhoda Morgenstern was to Mary Richards in *The Mary Tyler Moore Show*—they were instead all but invisible by the early 1990s. At the very moment that Jewish men arrived as leading characters, Jewish women virtually disappeared.

That near invisibility, while non-Jewish women were being worshipped as objects of desire in series like *Mad About You*, is one of the most powerful depictions of Jewish identity on television in the five decades this book covers. The worship of non-Jewish women in these series, in fact, goes beyond just depicting them as objects of desire. The series imbue them with an almost magical power to transform their Jewish boyfriends and husbands from nervous, guilt-ridden, sexually frustrated, anxious outsiders to confident, sexually fulfilled, fully vested participants in American life.

Lynn Roth, a Hollywood producer and former studio executive at 20th Century Fox, described this relentless pattern:

> Anyone calling the shots—the network executives—this is somehow their fantasy. And it's just perpetuated. This is the bad part. It's almost a tradeoff. If you get a Jewish character, they either have to be married to or lusting after a gentile. It's in every single show. With the man, it's the Woody Allen syndrome—the Jewish guy who's portrayed as kind of angst-ridden and funny, instead of the guy who can pick up a Toyota and throw it across the room. And he's always completely in love with the blond, shiksa goddess again. And it's odd, because there are so many [Jewish] women involved in the decision making process now and they're just continuing the stereotype. I don't think they are making any difference.[2]

ANYTHING BUT LOVE

Anything But Love—which debuted on the ABC network on March 7, 1989—was the decade's first Jewish man/gentile woman sitcom. It starred Richard Lewis, whose standup comedy career is built on a super-neurotic, Woody Allen–like persona. In the series, Lewis played Marty Gold, a hot-shot investigative reporter working for a Chicago city magazine. Like Lewis's standup persona, Gold also is a bundle of neuroses, buried in layer upon layer of guilt and depression.

His love interest in the sitcom is Hannah Miller, played by Jamie Lee

Richard Lewis and Jamie Lee Curtis from the 1989–1991 ABC series *Anything But Love*.
The neurotic Jewish male meets the non-Jewish beauty in one of the earliest versions
of a funny Jewish guy being dazzled by a non-Jewish woman.
Photo: Dallas Times Herald

Curtis. She is an aspiring writer looking for a magazine job. Despite her name, which could be taken for Jewish, it is quickly established that she is not, as the pilot episode goes about setting up their relationship as one of opposites. In fact, the attraction of opposites is the premise on which the series is based.

In the pilot, Marty and Hannah meet on a plane. He is deathly afraid of flying and starts freaking out before the plane leaves the ground. She winds up seated next to him and has enough calm and composure for both of them. By the end of the flight, he is infatuated with her and willing to do anything, including getting her a job at his magazine as a researcher, in the hopes of getting the chance to act on his intense attraction. While he is more successful professionally, she is the object of desire and clearly the stronger of the two. It should be noted, though, that Gold's incredibly neurotic makeup does not feminize him the way, say, Stuart Markowitz's neuroses did in his relationship to the gentile Ann Kelsey on *L.A. Law*. Here Gold is more the adolescent boy than the feminized male.

While *Anything But Love* was not officially cancelled until June 1992, it never got off the ground in the ratings. It never enjoyed even one full season in the ABC lineup, often airing in the summer while regular series were in rerun or being used as backup in midseason to replace regular series that were cancelled. Lewis would reappear near the end of the decade playing a similarly neurotic role in another ABC sitcom, *Hiller and Diller*, about a sitcom writing team. The series, which lasted only a few weeks, was doomed before the pilot ever aired when Jamie Tarses, then president of the entertainment division of ABC, expressed her concern that the sitcom might be "too ethnic, too Jewish" in a *New York Times* interview on the eve of the new season.[3]

Writer-producer Peter Mehlman, who wrote the acclaimed *Seinfeld* episode titled "The Yada, Yada," pointed to *Anything But Love* as an example of the superficial and, in his opinion, unfunny way that some sitcoms exploited rather than explored Jewish identity through the relationships of their central characters.

Before I ever got into writing for TV, I remember seeing the beginning of an episode of *Anything But Love* . . . And the cold opening [the start of the episode straight from commercial before opening credits] is them sitting in a restaurant and, you know, talking about cream cheese and how cream cheese on a bagel is called a schmeer. And the Jamie Lee Curtis character couldn't, you know, pronounce it. And then finally she learns to pronounce it and says something like, "This is so much fun. We're really doing stick here." And I just cringed. I just utterly cringed. I thought it was a) horrible writing, and b) almost condescending.[4]

CHICKEN SOUP

One of the strangest Jewish man/non-Jewish woman couplings came in *Chicken Soup*, an ABC sitcom that debuted a few months after *Anything But Love*, on September 12, 1989. *Chicken Soup* starred Jackie Mason as Jackie Fisher, a short, fifty-two-year-old former pajama salesman. Fisher lives with his mother, a "stereotypical nagging Jewish mother" in the words of one reference book.[5] His co-star and love interest is Maddie Peerce, played by the tall English actress Lynn Redgrave. After meeting her, Fisher quits his job in sales and becomes a volunteer at a community center where Maddie works—such was the power of her attraction.

Maddie, who is Irish Catholic, lives next door and owns the house Jackie lives in—another form of power and control that clearly establishes her as the stronger of the two. Not that it took much to establish that in viewers' minds, given the height disparity between the two actors and the fact that Fisher is fifty-two and living with his mother, who also dominates him.

The series was cancelled after only eight episodes. With an audience of some sixteen million homes—which meant it ranked thirteenth highest among the 110 or so shows in prime time that year—it was the second highest rated series in history to be cancelled. That fact requires some context, though. *Chicken Soup* followed *Roseanne* on the ABC schedule at a time when *Roseanne* was the second most popular series on TV behind *The Cosby Show*. *Chicken Soup* was made by the same producers—Marcy Carsey and Tom Werner—as *Roseanne*, which is how it got the choice piece of scheduling real estate after *Roseanne*. ABC said that while the ratings were high, they were not high enough; it was losing too many of the viewers (six million households) who tuned into ABC for *Roseanne*.

The highest-rated series ever to be cancelled is *Bridget Loves Bernie*, and the similarities between it and *Chicken Soup* in that regard are noteworthy.

Jackie Mason and Lynn Redgrave from the short-lived 1989 ABC series *Chicken Soup*. This is another version of the Jewish man/non-Jewish woman sitcom in which she has the power to transform him. Photo: Dallas Times Herald

The premise of *Chicken Soup* was the same as *Bridget Loves Bernie*: a New York Jewish man falls in love with an Irish Catholic woman to the intense disapproval of their families. Like the 1972 sitcom, *Chicken Soup* also met with protest from Jewish groups, though here it was limited to a minority within the Jewish community: the Jewish Defense League, which wanted an all-Jewish cast or for Maddie to convert.[6] Furthermore, while *Bridget Loves Bernie* legitimately captured some sense of the generational conflict in post-1960s America, *Chicken Soup* seemed to be nothing more than a failed attempt to cash in on the success Mason was enjoying with a one-man show on Broadway and an industry trend of sitcoms built around the onstage persona of standup comics like Roseanne and Bill Cosby.

THE MARSHALL CHRONICLES

ABC introduced another Jewish leading man that season by launching *The Marshall Chronicles*, a sitcom set in a Manhattan high school and starring Joshua Rifkin as a teen Woody Allen type. As one reviewer put it, "This half-hour sitcom could have been titled Woody Allen Goes to High School."[7]

The central character was seventeen-year-old Marshall Brightman (Rifkin), who was indeed a bright young man, sharing his observations on life with the camera in what was then a fairly innovative way to break the fourth wall and take us inside the mind of this teenager. The series debuted on April 4, 1990, and was cancelled after only five episodes on May 2, getting the hook quicker than even *Chicken Soup*. But it is a culturally important series for several reasons.

First, it was the only series of that period in which the female object of desire, Melissa Sandler (Nile Lanning), was Jewish, though that was never overtly stated. I label Melissa as Jewish based on her name and the stated intention of creator Richard Rosenstock.[8] But Rosenstock acknowledges that viewers could have easily seen Melissa as gentile and offers an anecdote involving acclaimed sitcom director James Burrows, who directed the pilot and several other episodes, that suggests even Burrows read the character as gentile:

> In my mind, Melissa was Jewish—in my mind when I was writing. But, in the casting, we wound up with someone who didn't look

Jewish. For me, the ideal is not blonde, she is brunette, say Katherine Ross, or Ali McGraw in *Goodbye, Columbus*. That is what was in my mind as we were casting . . . Anyway, Jimmy [Burrows] did the pilot, and then when it was picked up as a series, he agreed to direct some more. As I was bringing him up to date on everyone, he said, "And the shiksa [Melissa], how's she doing?"

Rosenstock is very clear about what he was trying to do on network television during the 1989–90 season: in part, bring to the small screen the sensibility and some of the depictions of Jewish-American life that readers had been offered in Roth's 1959 novella *Goodbye, Columbus* and moviegoers had seen in the 1969 film version—two works that he says had an enormous impact on him. The film featured McGraw in the role of Brenda Patimkin, the Jewish object of desire. Rosenstock, who first saw the film when in high school, said he has since viewed it "thirty or forty times" and has yet "to recover from the first close-up of McGraw."

The most direct example of Roth's influence on Rosenstock and *The Marshall Chronicles* is the episode titled "Night of the Chopped Liver," in which Marshall winds up (against his fervent wish to be at a New York Knicks basketball game) at a suburban Jewish wedding in Long Island as the date of a classmate, Leslie Barish (Meredith Scott Lynn). The wedding is that of Leslie's older sister, Brenda. Rosenstock says the scene is his "homage" to the suburban Jewish wedding scene in *Goodbye, Columbus*.

In contrast to the tall, slender, long and straight-haired Melissa, Leslie is short, plump, and has very curly hair. Whereas Melissa is an ethereal figure that inspires Marshall to quote Shakespeare, Leslie is a comic figure designed to provoke laughter with her over-the-top intensity. Her right leg, for example, bounces uncontrollably as she pleads with Marshall to accompany her to the wedding. Even her father admits to Marshall, "Let's face it, you and I both know my Leslie is not the easiest person in the world to get along with."

On one level, the episode defines Jewish identity through food and language as we have seen before in other sitcoms with Jewish characters. In terms of food, for example, two guests join Marshall and Leslie at their table, and he offers to get them something to eat, saying: "Well, I know I can't get enough of that chopped sturgeon in the shape of Uncle Harry. Can I get anyone else some? I think there's still an ear left." In trying to convince Marshall to accompany her, Leslie had promised "herring from four different lands."

As for language, the bandleader, Ray Weinstein (Alan Blumenfeld) of the Dance-Stein Orchestra, peppers his patter with Yiddish throughout the reception. "The place is posh, so let's nosh," he says into the microphone as the band is about to take a break. "*Oy*, am I *schvitzing*," he moans to Marshall, wiping his face with a handkerchief as he walks off the stage. During the family photo session, Leslie urges Marshall to stage next to *"Bubbie* Barish," the matriarch of the family.

But what is most interesting is both the more and less that Marshall offers in relation to what came before with Jewish identity on television. In terms of less, the series never depicts Jewish identity in a religious sense, even though we have a wedding between a Jewish man and Jewish woman in "Night of the Chopped Liver." Rosenstock said the decision to not use religion anywhere in the series was a conscious one: "I was interested in a secular Jewish identity, again like Roth, concerned with social class differences and suburban Jewish life versus urban, New York Jews like Marshall and his family."

In that sense *The Marshall Chronicles* is noteworthy for not using the yarmulkes or prayer shawls or religious articles that virtually every other television series had used at some point to identify characters as Jewish. As for the depiction of secular, suburban Jewish identity, Rosenstock's sitcom is kinder than Roth's novella or director Larry Peerce's film. A sense of excess and, perhaps, lack of taste among the suburban set is certainly suggested by the "herring from four lands" and "sturgeon in the shape of Uncle Harry." But there is none of the feeding-at-the-trough sense of truly gross and garish behavior by the wedding guests that Peerce emphasized in his film version.

Rosenstock's sitcom is one of the first to depict Jewish identity openly and mainly through preferences of taste and cultural references, much as Woody Allen did in film. For example, in an aside to the audience, Marshall explains the relationship between him and Leslie by saying, "She's been chasing after me since the seventh grade." He admits liking the fact that "She calls me whenever *Funny Girl* is on *The Million Dollar Movie*, or to argue which is better, chocolate pinwheels or mallomars, or even when another Nazi war criminal is discovered running a grocery store in Cleveland." After delivering the Nazi war criminal line, Marshall starts to walk off camera. Then he stops, turns, and, facing the camera again in a form of direct address to the viewer, says, "What? It's just something we did." At another point in the episode, a friend mocks Marshall for feeling guilty about initially turning Leslie down on the wedding. The friend tells Marshall that he has been guilt-ridden since "you made your mother's water break at the matinee of *Fiddler.*"

At the end of the episode, the audience is cued to the fact that Marshall and Leslie have reconstituted their friendship after a serious fight by Marshall saying, "Hey, did you hear they caught another Nazi war criminal yesterday?"

"Cleveland?" Leslie asks.

"Buffalo," Marshall says.

"Buffalo, wow!" Leslie responds.

The Marshall Chronicles seemed more comfortable with its Jewishness than any sitcom that came before. No one in prime time made jokes about Nazi war criminals in Cleveland, let alone admitting a certain interest, if not satisfaction, on the part of its leading character when one is caught. But, in terms of the history of Jewish identity on television, the short-lived series also gives a sense of how much resistance there still was in network television in 1990 to certain depictions of Jewish identity, despite the work done on *thirtysomething* and *Northern Exposure*.

This is thirty years after the book *Portnoy's Complaint*, and twenty years after the film *Goodbye, Columbus*, which speaks directly to this book's central argument about how the gatekeepers of network television kept social reality at bay when it came to Jewish identity. By his own admission, Rosenstock was not trying to break new ground; he was merely trying to do on television what had been done decades earlier in popular literature and film.

Coming into the 1989–90 television season, there were actually two new series with the word "chronicles" in the title—*The Marshall Chronicles* at ABC and *The Seinfeld Chronicles* at NBC. The hotter of the two and the first to get a spot in the weekly prime-time lineup was *The Marshall Chronicles*, which is why *The Seinfeld Chronicles* was to become known simply as *Seinfeld* when it finally debuted as a series on May 31, 1990. Why was *The Marshall Chronicles* pulled so swiftly, before it had a chance to find an audience? Rosenstock thinks he knows one of the reasons:

They never use the word. They start out using all the bizarre euphemisms. "It's too urban. It's too ethnic." The feeling at the time was it was impossible to set a show in New York, because of what it said about the ethnicity of the characters: they were Jewish. It was a kind of shorthand: New York equals Jews. Then, after [the NBC sitcom] *Friends* hit [in 1994], every show *had to be set* in New York. That's the way it is with networks. But, after all the euphemisms and all the evasions, someone from the production company came back to me and said that the head of development at ABC had finally admitted the truth: *The Marshall Chronicles* was too Jewish. The network thought it was too Jewish, and they believed it wouldn't work because it was too Jewish. And, as hurt and upset as I was about it getting cancelled, I felt better after they admitted they thought it was too Jewish. At least, someone finally spoke the truth.

Ten years after its cancellation, *The Marshall Chronicles*—five episodes in all—remains a cult favorite among some Jewish viewers, especially those who are college age, even though its only circulation comes from copies taped off the air by viewers in 1990. At the mention of the series during our interview (16 July 2000), Michael Elkin, entertainment editor of the *Jewish Exponent* and winner of the prestigious Smolar Award in 1985 for a series exploring Jewish identity on television, said, "Did you see the one with the conga line?" It is a reference to "The Night of the Chopped Liver" episode that ends with Marshall joining Leslie on a conga line, an act he vowed never to do.

"I love that show," Elkin said. "But I have to tell you that many people at the time, and these are Jews, you know what they said? They said, 'It's too Jewish. It's just too Jewish.'"

Rosenstock's reaction when told of the reaction reported by Elkin: "It's the classic Jackie Mason routine: the gentiles are laughing, and the Jews are walking away going, 'No, no, no. It's too Jewish.' [It's] what [Alan] Dershowitz calls a *schande* (a public embarassment or shaming) before the goyim. 'I'm ashamed, I'm ashamed.' But, in that same season, *Seinfeld* and its pilot heard the same stuff about being too Jewish, so what can I say?"

FLYING BLIND

Following the arrival of *Seinfeld* in May 1990 and *Brooklyn Bridge* in September 1991, the three Jewish man/non-Jewish woman series mentioned at the start of this chapter all debuted during a two-week period in September 1992. The first to appear, *Flying Blind*, was also a Rosenstock production. This one lasted a full season on the Fox network, and this time the object of obsession (it was beyond desire) for the young Jewish male was decidedly gentile. In fact, Tea Leoni as Alicia seems in several ways to be the very embodiment of television's depiction in the 1990s of the shiksa goddess as forbidden fruit holding all the promise of glamor, excitement, and healthy, guilt-free sex so noticeably absent in the life of the Jewish protagonist. A poster from the show offers a pose that perfectly captures the nature of the relationship between Alicia and Neil Barash. The pose was also featured in on-screen television advertisements for the series.[9]

In the poster, Alicia and Neil are standing side by side—she on the right, he on the left (if you are facing them). She is slightly taller than him. He is wearing a blue blazer, blue button-down collar shirt, maroon and white floral print tie, Bass Weejun loafers, and argyle socks: the schoolboy. She is wearing a gauzy, strapless, black chiffon evening gown that is see-through everywhere except at her breasts and pelvic area. There the material is not see-through but looks like Victoria's Secret underwear worn outside in the style popularized at the time by Madonna. The dress features a pointed cone over each breast. Aside from the gown, Alicia is wearing elbow-high leopard-skin gloves, fishnet stockings, and black high heels. Her hair has a wild, windblown look to it, and she is wearing bright red lipstick.

She stands tall, with her left hand clenched into a fist resting on her left hip. Her right arm is raised and bent upward at the elbow in the pose of someone flexing to show off her/his bicep—except her right fist is not closed. She has a smirk on her face as she looks straight at the camera.

Neil, meanwhile, stands with head tilted to the side and resting on her right arm in the curve between her shoulder and bicep. His head is pressed down into the curve by her gloved hand and the inside of her right arm, which completely frame his face. The look on his face is one of wide-eyed wonderment, as if there should be a bubble over his head encircling the expression "Holy cow!" The headline text on the poster says "Mild Meets Wild!" She is the wild woman; he the tamed boy. Her dominance and his submission are unmistakable.

And, yet, they are supposed to be the same age—mid-twenties, as he

Tea Leoni and Corey Parker in the 1991 Fox series *Flying Blind*. The Fox advertising campaign billed this sitcom as "Mild Meets Wild." It was the story of the nebbish utterly overwhelmed and transformed by the uninhibited, non-Jewish woman depicted in this series as a sex goddess. Photo: Dallas Times Herald is a recent college graduate. The premise was described this way in one guide to prime-time series:

> *Flying Blind* was about a rather dull young man whose life was turned upside down by an unlikely affair with a beautiful, free-spirited woman. Neil was a marketing assistant at Hochman Foods, the company where his neurotic father, Jeremy, was a senior executive. Neil's life was about as interesting as yesterday's dishwater until one night at a party he ran into Alicia, an incredibly sexy and uninhibited woman ... Neil, who still lived at home, spent his days trying to look good at work and his nights having a torrid and exhausting affair with the insatiable Alicia.[10]

What is most important about this series is how perfectly it embodies the concept of transformation for Jewish men involved in relationships with gentile women. As that show summary suggests, Neil's life is transformed ("turned upside down") from dull-as-dishwater to glamorous and sexy via his relationship with Alicia. This narrative of Jewish men being magically transformed—like a frog getting kissed by a princess—pre-relationship versus post-relationship is an especially potent one within the flow of prime-time network television programming. American television is built on the concept of transformation as much as it is anything else. Just as European-based fairytales, folklore, and myth once taught children about transformation through stories like "The Frog Prince," so does children's television—whether it was Popeye eating his spinach for baby boomers or the teenage heroines of *VR Troopers* turned into brave and graceful fighting machines through magic pendants that they rub. Such transformation is also at the core of American TV advertising, of course, which features an endless stream of ads promising that you can transform your life by purchasing various products.

In *Flying Blind* and, in fact, in most of the other sitcoms featuring such relationships, the non-Jewish woman is the very agent of such transformation, and that is some powerful allure. I do not think it is an accident, in that regard, that the term "shiksa goddess" is often used to describe such characters, as there is something magical or otherwordly—goddesslike—about their power to effect such change. Furthermore, I don't think it is coincidence that metaphors of madness are used to describe the response of the Jewish man in the face of such transforming power, as in *Mad About You*.

Transformation for the Jewish male through his relationship with the gentile woman in television sitcoms almost always involves movement away from being Jewish (in whatever way that might be characterized in a particular series). Again, the publicity photographs distributed by the Fox television network to promote *Flying Blind* offer a textbook symbolic depiction. One such photograph features Leoni, Parker, and Michael Tucci, who plays Jeremy Barash, Neil's father. The elder Barash is short, timid, and incredibly repressed—a little man in constant fear of losing his job. This is one of the central ways that Jewish male identity is constructed in the series, and it harks all the way back to Uncle David of *The Goldbergs* and Menasha Skulnik of *Menasha the Magnificent*.

The picture shows Jeremy and Alicia standing on either side of Neil, each leaning on a shoulder in a classic good-angel/bad-angel pose. Alicia has her hands cupped on Neil's right shoulder, with her chin resting on her hands. She is again looking at the camera in a pose of calm, cool control, with a slight, knowing smile on her lips. Jeremy, meanwhile, who is standing slightly behind Neil's other shoulder, is wagging his finger and looking highly agitated. His mouth is open as if whispering in Neil's ear. But Neil is leaning toward Alicia. In fact, their heads are touching, and he has a slight smile on his face, too, as if he and Alicia have entered another space not populated by sweaty, anxious little people like his father.

MAD ABOUT YOU

The neurotic, urban, young Jewish male and the beautiful gentile object of his desire is also the central dynamic of *Mad About You*, starring Paul Reiser as newlywed Paul Buchman and Helen Hunt as his wife, Jamie. The idea of his intoxication with her—a kind of love-as-madness that might be found in Shakespeare, in fact—is clearly suggested in the title. In case anyone did not catch it there, though, the primary story line of the pilot involves Paul and Jamie inviting some of his relatives over for dinner in their new apartment and then making love to each other on the butcher block table in their tiny kitchen while the relatives in the next room wait for them to return with dinner.

In the early days of this series, just as it was with Neil and Alicia, sex was always in the air—and almost always in terms of his inability to keep his hands off of her, though she, too, is depicted as having a healthy enjoyment of sex. That is, in fact, another important aspect of gentile female identity on network television that establishes the non-Jewish woman as superior to her Jewish counterpart. And, just as in *Flying Blind*, Paul's intense attraction to Jamie and the actions he takes in response to it in the kitchen literally pull him away from his Jewish relatives, who are waiting in the living room.

In 1992, when *Mad About You* debuted, co-creator Danny Jacobson explained the arrival of Jewish leading men in sitcoms to me by saying it was a matter of industry trends, with Jewish identity mostly a byproduct. From Bill Cosby to Roseanne and Tim Allen, television had been having great success packaging big-name stand-up comedians in sitcoms, Jacobson said. Many of those comedians happen to be Jewish and come with a pre-sold persona that involves their Jewishness. You can't suddenly ignore that Jewishness when a character moves into a sitcom, Jacobson said. As he put it: "Television has always been an industry of trends that way. When you get one success, you then get multiples of it ... That's part of what's happening here ... Look, Paul Reiser and me are both Jewish, we're both from New York, we're both married. We said, 'Hey, let's do a show about that' ... We just happened to be Jewish"[11]

At its debut, Jacobson promised a show that would be comfortable with the Jewish identity of its star, saying, "When I started to break into television in the late 1970s, you always heard, "Don't make him [any character] Jewish." And, being Jewish and knowing that Jewish is funny, it seemed stupid to me. It seemed like, "Okay, you can do a martial arts show, but no Asians."

Jacobson said when he went to work on the ABC sitcom *Soap* in 1979, executive producer Susan Harris told him, "None of our characters are Jews, but we write them all Jewish." He said in 1992 that he thought we were long past the days of Jews as non-Jews on television.

But, ironically, that is exactly what he and Reiser created over the seven-year run of *Mad About You*—a character in Paul Buchman who was almost as silent about his Jewishness as Jack Benny (Benjamin Kubelsky) and George Burns (Nathan Birnbaum) had been in *The Jack Benny Show* (1950 to 1965) and *George Burns and Gracie Allen* (1950 to 1957)— the template for the Jew as crypto-Jew in television sitcoms.

The lack of self-identification by Buchman as a Jew in more than 160 episodes for *Mad About You* from 1992 to 1999 is astonishing. Downright mind-boggling is the absence of discussion between these two highly talkative, introspective characters—Jamie and Paul—about ethnic differences between them. Even after they have a child, there is no discussion about their differences in backgrounds or how the child should be raised.

Instead, like series from earlier times when networks allowed little or no discussion of Jewish identity, Reiser and Jacobson relied on signifiers that demanded decoding by viewers and allowed for ambiguous readings. For example, Paul's father, Burt, is played by Louis Zorich, who played the heavily accented, immigrant, Russian-Jewish grandfather on *Brooklyn Bridge*. In *Mad About You*, he speaks without an accent. Paul's Uncle Phil is played in two guest appearances by Mel Brooks, whose entire career— from writing for Sid Caesar's *Your Show of Shows* through the landmark comedy LP *The 2000 Year Old Man* to such films as *The Producers*—has been associated with exploring Jewish identity. Uncle Phil speaks with the same Yiddish accent as does Brooks's 2000 Year Old Man. In the episode titled "The Penis," Paul and Jamie visit Uncle Phil in the hospital, and the scene opens with an establishing shot of the hospital focusing on the sign, Beth Israel Medical Center.

But there is a big difference between using such signifiers to suggest Jewishness and self-identifying, and a bigger one still between self-identifying and then going on to explore issues of Jewish life as *thirty-something* or *Northern Exposure* did. The reluctance of Reiser to have Buchman self-identify in a straightforward way is one of the more peculiar aspects of the series and has not gone unnoticed by some of his colleagues.

Elon Gold, who played a very Jewish character in the short-lived 1998 sitcom on the WB (Warner Brothers) network *You're the One*, said he felt we would not even be seeing Jewish leading men in sitcoms at the end of the century were it not for Jerry Seinfeld's success as a standup comedian and star of the sitcom *Seinfeld*. And then Gold added: "Paul Reiser has helped, too, but unlike Seinfeld, he never mentions he's Jewish on *Mad About You*. Maybe he's afraid to, but it bothers me that he's so obviously Jewish and it's just so glossed over."[12]

LOVE AND WAR

Debuting with *Mad About You* and *Flying Blind* that same season was another nervous Jewish male involved in a relationship with a gentile woman, Jack Stein (Jay Thomas) in the CBS sitcom *Love and War*. Perhaps the most distinctive aspect of this series involves its creator. While most members of the network and creative communities attribute the Jewish man/gentile woman pattern to the tastes and interests of male Jewish writers and producers, *Love and War* was created by a non-Jewish woman, Diane English. She is, however, married to a Jewish producer, Joel Shukovsky, who is also her business partner. So we are operating within the same cultural realm of production to some extent.

Here is how one directory describes the show:[13]

Jack was a cynical rather insecure columnist for the *New York Post*. Opinionated and aggressive, he was a regular at the seedy Blue Shamrock, a restaurant/bar where he hung out with his buddies and let off steam. Into his life walked Wally, recently divorced . . . a classy, uptown woman with champagne tastes. After exchanging heated words with Jack and downing one too many vodkas, Wally impulsively bought a share of the bar . . . and declared she would turn the "joint" into a chic restaurant. Jack was both aghast and excited.[14]

What is not clear in the description is that Wallis (Wally) Porter stops in the bar on her way home from the hearing at which her divorce was granted, so she is in a highly agitated state. That is episode one. By the second episode, Wally (Susan Dey) and Jack are sleeping together. There are two aspects worth noting here. One is the emphasis on social class. The name Wallis itself suggests the upper classes, but, in case the implications of the name are lost on anyone, much of the humor in the pilot is based on the clash between Stein's seedy world and her "classy, champagne tastes." She is better educated, better dressed, far more cultured and refined, and affluent enough to just buy a bar on a whim.

She is, in short, of a higher social class than Stein, who sounds like a Damon Runyan character the minute he opens his mouth to speak to her. The depiction of the Jew as a cruder, lower-class character was last seen this overtly in *Bridget Loves Bernie*. What the two shows, like *Abie's Irish Rose*, share are gentile creators and producers. I don't want to make too much of this observation, since two shows do not a pattern make, and both *Bridget* and *Love and War* also had Jewish producers involved in week-to-week production of the series. Still, this emphasis on social class is not something regularly seen in series created and produced by Jews, with the exception of *Relativity*. The Jew as cruder, lower-class character will surface again later in the decade in another series created by a gentile writer-producer team, *George and Leo*, on CBS starring Bob Newhart and Judd Hirsch.

There is one other notable difference between *Love and War* and most of the other Jewish man/gentile woman sitcoms of the decade. Unlike Neil Barash in *Flying Blind*, who defines the Jewish man as nice boy, and Paul Buchman in *Mad About You*, who epitomizes the Jewish man as hopeless neurotic, Stein is neither nice nor especially neurotic. "Opinionated and aggressive" is one way of describing him. But, sitting at the bar where much of the action takes place, he sometimes comes off as a belligerent know-it-all, which some viewers might just read as the "pushy Jew."

There was some of that in Joel Fleischman on *Northern Exposure*, but it was much subdued and usually carefully balanced by some good deed from Joel or a putdown of him from another character. There was also the Alan King character in *thirtysomething*'s "Prelude to a Bris," but there it was directly discussed and addressed by the characters, with the writers throwing up red flags left and right that essentially said "We're doing this intentionally, because we want to explore the possibility of internalized anti-Semitism on the part of Michael Steadman. We do not think the Alan King character is a pushy Jew." Both series were dramas, which are, of course, more capable of such explorations of sensitive subjects. *Love and War*, a sitcom, mainly left Stein out there in all his opinionated aggressiveness for viewers to make of him what they would.

GEORGE AND LEO

On paper, *George and Leo* might seem like it would be groundbreaking in terms of the Jewish man/gentile woman dynamic. The young couple about to be married in the pilot that debuted on CBS in the fall of 1997 featured a Jewish woman, Casey Wagonman (Bess Meyer), and a non-Jewish man, Ted Stoody (Jason Bateman). But the series was not about them; it was about their parents, Leo Wagonman (Judd Hirsch) and George Stoody (Bob Newhart). They are the odd couple who wind up living together in this short-lived series.

With gentile producers, an upper versus lower social class dynamic, and the depiction of an "obnoxious" Jew as one of the lead characters,

George and Leo is best understood in connection with *Love and War* and the observation linking it to *Bridget Loves Bernie*.

Stoody is a bookstore owner on Martha's Vineyard, Wagonman is a low-rent con man, part-time magician, and bag man for the mob in Las Vegas. The pilot opens with Stoody locking up the bookstore for the night—with the "closed" sign already on the door—when a stranger waltzes in.

The first thing you notice is the difference in clothing. Stoody is in a blue blazer, blue button-down collar shirt, khaki slacks, and black loafers. Wagonman is in a garish gold blazer with a black-and-white polka dot shirt open at the chest and showing hair.

Wagonman's entrance is accompanied by the same kind of fiddle music used in *Bridget Loves Bernie* whenever the show traveled to the Lower East Side and the Steinberg Deli—an audio cue to Jewishness. In this case, it sounds even more like gypsy music and, thus, has an even stronger suggestion of the exotic other. The next most obvious difference between the two: Stoody is polite, while Wagonman is rude.

"I'm sorry, sir, we're closed for the night," Stoody says.

"Not yet," Wagonman says, walking past him and picking up a book. Wagonman says he is in a hurry and wants a gift book. Stoody suggests a Martha's Vineyard picture book.

"All right, how much is it?" says Wagonman.

"Eighty dollars," says Stoody.

"I'll give you fifty," Wagonman replies to laughtrack laughter.

"This isn't a flea market," Stoody shoots back to more laughter.

Wagonman is cheap, too, we now know. As he starts to write a check drawn on a Las Vegas bank, Stoody dials a check verification service.

"Whoa, whoa, whoa, what're ya doing?" Wagonman yells. When Stoody says he is dialing Compu-check, Wagonman says, "Oh, interesting, interesting. First it's, 'We're closed, we're closed.' Now, all of a sudden, we've got time to hassle the Jewish guy."

"I resent that. I am not a bigot. The bank told us we have to verify every check. They had a seminar at the Sheraton and everything . . ." Stoody stammers.

"Yeah, yeah, yeah. Come on, come on, come on. This has nothing to do with seminars or Sheratons, and you know it. This is about two thousand years of hate and oppression," Wagonman says.

In the next scene, the audience finds out that these two are going to be in-laws. The marriage of the children is the ostensible reason for Wagonman's visit to the island—that and the fact that he is running from the mob after having messed up as a bag man. But Casey does not want him at her wedding, because he abandoned her and her mother twenty years ago. In fact, she is greatly distressed by his arrival and the fact that her future husband invited him without telling her. But Leo is oblivious to all the misery he is causing and proceeds to wolf down food that had been laid out for a family dinner at the restaurant owned by Casey and Ted. Stoody tells Wagonman to his face that he is obnoxious, and Wagonman agrees.

Rob Long, co-creator of the series, acknowledged that Wagonman is loud and manipulative, but said he is not a Jewish stereotype. "He is a lovable rascal. And Hirsch is our litmus test . . ."[15]

Long said that he and partner Dan Staley did not necessarily go into the project looking for a Jew to play opposite Newhart. As he put it, "What we wanted is Bob Newhart, who is incredibly white and Catholic, surrounded by people who aren't that . . . We saw a lot of people. Some were Jewish, some weren't. So a lot of the Jewishness is what Judd brought with him. The actor being Jewish made a difference."[16]

Neither Long nor Staley is Jewish. Long said that he and Staley relied heavily on Hirsch to tell them if the words and actions they wrote for Wagonman were acceptable or not. My interview with Long about the way in which he and his partner tried to think about and depict Jewish identity took place halfway through the show's one season on CBS, and Long said the greatest number of complaints from viewers at that point had involved Wagonman using Yiddish expressions.

"I use Yiddish expressions myself. It's a great colorful language," he said, dismissing the complaints. Long also said that he and Staley had "not yet decided how religious Leo is going to be." He added, "We'd like to have him be bar mitzvahed."

That did not happen. Wagonman was depicted only in a secular sense and primarily in opposition to Newhart. While Long described Newhart as "incredibly white and Catholic," onscreen Newhart's character was more WASP, with Wagonman as the obnoxious and gauche other. This is a series that might have been semirelevant in the early 1970s as the larger culture started to refocus on ethnic differences. There was no reason for it to be on the air in 1997, and it was mercifully cancelled before the year ended.

LATELINE

Lateline, an NBC sitcom set in a fictional late-night network news program much like ABC's *Nightline*, was groundbreaking in that it was one of the only series of the decade to break from the Jewish man/gentile woman formula for its leading character. But, even in this savvy sitcom from Al Franken, the Jewish woman is still made invisible in an important and fundamental way.

Franken, the co-creator and executive producer, played the series's leading character, Al Freundlich, who is described in press materials from Paramount (the production company that made the show) and NBC (the network that distributed it) as an "overly earnest, yet totally oblivious news correspondent." In one episode of the short-lived series, he is described by a co-worker as "not good looking, bad on camera, and America doesn't like him." The humor comes from the fact that Freundlich fails to see himself as others do. As another press release says, "Al believes he continues Edward R. Murrow's journalistic legacy."[17]

So, he is a self-important fool, but he is on the side of journalistic virtue. In a press conference to promote the show, Franken jokingly referred to Freundlich as "the foolish Jew," saying, "By the way, when we syndicate the show in Germany, the title there is going to be *Der Narishe Jud*, which means The Foolish Jew."[18]

Franken said he didn't consciously set out to make Freundlich openly Jewish: "I didn't deliberately go in saying, 'OK, this is going to be an openly Jewish guy.' But I also didn't fight it. When I thought it was funny for him, for example, to talk about his *zayde* [grandfather], I had him do it. I mean, I have Freundlich talking about his grandfather, Isadore P. Freundlich, in one episode, talking about him organizing garment workers on the Lower East Side, and it just felt right. I mean, I just felt like this guy, Freundlich, was Jewish."[19]

Another episode features Freundlich booking the WASP anchorman of the *Lateline* newscast to speak at a benefit that Freundlich's wife is organizing at the couple's synagogue. Conflict occurs when the anchorman, a notorious womanizer, tries to cancel the speaking engagement because he has a "hot" date that night. Part of the humor centers on Freundlich's fear of his wife and the abuse she will direct toward him if he doesn't get the anchorman to appear. As Franken described it:

> Freundlich is very afraid of his wife in this situation. It's interesting. We have Caroline Aarons playing my wife in the show. I should say the voice of my wife, because you never see her in the series, you only hear her [mostly on the phone]. And my wife is a bit of a *baleboosteh* [a bossy woman].[20] Anyway, Caroline was invited to lunch one day by a rabbi in Los Angeles who does seminars on movies and stuff. He was doing one on the movie *Crimes and Misdemeanors*, which she had been in, which is why he invited her to lunch. So, when Caroline told me about the upcoming lunch, I told her to ask the rabbi how he's going to feel about us depicting this Jewish woman this way—you know, the idea of having this *baleboosteh* on the phone. And Caroline came back from lunch and said the rabbi felt that as long as Freundlich's married to a Jewish woman, no one's going to mind. "We're so sick of Jewish guys marrying gentiles on TV, the fact that she's Jewish is enough," the rabbi told her.

The comparison of the anchorman as a ladies' man with Freundlich as a henpecked husband is one way Jewish masculinity in *Lateline* is constructed along a continuum that stretches all the way back to the second Jake Goldberg. But the most significant aspect of *Lateline* might be the strange, offscreen narrative straightjacket created for Freundlich's wife. We can hear her but never see her. And what she has to say is generally unpleasant.

As compared with invisibility, I guess the presence of any voice for a Jewish woman could be seen as progress, if you want to call it that. What is of special interest, though, in terms of the pattern of Jewish men and gentile women, is that the Jewish woman is still missing, even where the narrative clearly seems to have space for her.

BROOKLYN BRIDGE

There was a Jewish woman near the center of the CBS series *Brooklyn Bridge* in the person of Sophie Berger, matriarch with a capital "M," played by the same Marion Ross who had played Gertrude Berg's daughter in *Mrs. G Goes to College* thirty years earlier. But even in this loving and brilliantly crafted elegy to growing up Jewish in Brooklyn in the 1950s, the female object of desire was gentile, a fourteen-year-old Irish-Catholic girl named Katie Monahan (Jenny Lewis). The context within which these two female characters appeared, serving as opposing poles of influence in the life of Sophie's grandson, fourteen-year-old Alan Silver (Danny Gerard), is central to the way Jewishness was depicted in this series, which ran from 1991 to 1993.

Brooklyn Bridge was called a sitcom, but it played more like a "dramady"—an industry term for a hybrid drama-comedy that is less punch-line and more character oriented. Dramadies do not use laughtracks. Creator Gary David Goldberg, who was already an acclaimed writer-producer for his *Family Ties* series when he started *Brooklyn Bridge* in 1990, says, "I went into it saying this is not going to be a sitcom. We're going to make a twenty-one-minute movie each week, and I think we did that."[21]

Alan Silver was at the very center of the series, set in 1956, when the Dodgers still played at Ebbets Field and candy was a penny at Elgart's soda shop down the block from Alan's apartment building. Alan lived in a lower-middle-class family with his father, a postal worker; his mom, who worked in an insurance office, and a nine-year-old brother, Nathaniel. The Silver family extended to an apartment on the next floor down in the building, which housed Sophie and Jules Berger, Alan's maternal grandparents. Jules immigrated from Russia, Sophie from Poland. Their old-country roots were an important part of the show's dynamic. Sophie ruled everyone and everything in the family—and much of the surrounding neighborhood, for that matter.

Publicity photographs for the series often pictured Sophie looking out an open apartment window just like Gertrude Berg's Molly Goldberg forty years earlier, and on the same network as *The Goldbergs*. With her Eastern European accent and overpowering personality, comparisons between Sophie and Molly Goldberg are inevitable. For his part, Goldberg says:

I watched *The Goldbergs* as a boy and happened to love that show. But it wasn't a conscious influence . . . *Brooklyn Bridge* was highly autobiographical . . . I watched *The Goldbergs* in my grandmother's apartment because she was the first person to have a television set in the whole neighborhood. The interesting thing about my grandmother, as she

Sophie Berger (Marion Ross, center) and grandsons, Alan (Danny Gerard, left) and
Natie (Matthew Siegel), in the 1991 CBS series *Brooklyn Bridge*. Leaning out her
apartment window just like Molly Goldberg, Sophie Berger represented the ethnic past
and its pull on Alan in this nostalgic look at coming of age in the 1950s.
Photo by Geraldine Overton. CBS Photo Archive

was portrayed in *Brooklyn Bridge*, she did not read a word of English but she instinctively understood how to control power, so that all entertainment, all communication and all mobility was hers. In other words, grandma owned a car, but she didn't drive . . . She had a telephone; we didn't have a telephone. So, if I got any phone calls, I had to come downstairs and take it in grandma's living room in the parlor there. And the phone had one of those short, little, brown rope chords, and she would sit there while you were on the phone. And, if you said, "You know, grandma, could I have some privacy here?" she'd say, "What, do you have secrets from the family? What are you, Julius and Ethel Rosenberg?" It wasn't enough to be just one of them. It was such a heinous thing to want privacy on the phone that you had to be both of them.

During the interview, Goldberg chuckled at such recollections, and that sense of an affectionately remembered past suffuses both the series and the way in which Sophie Berger is generally portrayed. There does not seem to have been any effort on the part of Goldberg to de-ethnicize the milieu of his youth. As Goldberg puts it:

When we went in to sell the show to CBS, I said, "I don't want to do the Andersons [the upper-middle-class WASP family in the *Father Knows Best* sitcom]." You know what I mean? This is a Jewish family. There's Italian people, there's Irish people, there's Polish people. I want to be able to have people speak Yiddish without subtitles. I want them to be reading Yiddish papers. "And, if you want to do the Andersons," I told CBS, "I don't want to do this show, because that would be way too hard for me." And they said, "Fine."

Indeed, even though only thirty-five half-hour episodes were made, *Brooklyn Bridge* is as Jewish-rich a television landscape as can be found. I wish I could explore all thirty-five in this book. But the focus here needs to be on the structural dynamic that drove the series and ultimately sounded its loudest and most resonant statement about being Jewish and male in post–World War II America. At the center of this dynamic is Alan. On one pole, pulling him back are his grandmother, his relatives from the Old Country, and Judaism, especially as it is manifested in Hebrew-language religious rites. This pole consists of the past and most things Jewish.

The opposite pole is the present and the future. It is all things American, best symbolized by the Brooklyn Dodgers and their all-star first baseman, Gil Hodges, whom Alan worships. It includes all sports, the radio in his bedroom that brings him accounts from across the country of his beloved baseball games, and, most of all, Katie Monahan, the girl he adores. In some ways, it is similar to the pattern described in *Bridget Loves Bernie*, with old-fashioned and Jewish being one pole, and modern and American the other. But this structure is far more complicated, and Jewishness is more closely bound to other matters of identity, particularly masculinity.[22] Ultimately, *Brooklyn Bridge* is about assimilation more than anything else, as Goldberg himself suggested:

> There are a couple of things, which are interesting in terms of my relationship to the show. Obviously, as a kid, I was brought up in a very close and loving family. That's for sure. But I was a little bit embarrassed by the Jewishness, by the Old-Worldness, you know, because my brother and me were athletes and we wanted to be tough guys. My wife always says to me, "Your whole life is dedicated to proving Jewish guys are as tough as Italian guys." I've given up that. But we were very physical, and then there was my grandfather—very learned, davening every day, the sweetest man in the world . . . And when we sold the show I said, "We've learned a lot of things in this multicultural society, which is really true. And we learned basically that Jewish families and Italian families are exactly the same, except in the Italian families the men are allowed to speak." That was the major difference as far as I could tell, because in my family, the men were not [allowed to speak]. My grandfather and father were both the sweetest guys in the world, but they were not making the decisions.

Sophie is the one who makes the decisions in *Brooklyn Bridge*. Her dominance of Jules is even more total than that of Molly over the second Jake. Most of the time, all it takes is a harsh glance from Sophie and Jules falls silent. Such a moment occurs at the very start of the episode titled "A Death in Brooklyn," which opens with Sophie getting the news that her Cousin Ira has died.

Neither Jules nor Alan's parents, Phyllis and George Silver, notice how deeply affected Sophie is by the news. And so, sitting around the dining room table in the Berger apartment, the three joke about Ira, pointing out all the feuds he had been embroiled in with family members, many of which resulted in him not speaking to some of them for years. There were also the matters of him being a gangster and tremendously overweight, all of which is recalled in a joking manner.

Sophie, who has been lost in thought, suddenly erupts when the disparaging words from the three penetrate her consciousness. "What are you now, Jules the big joker?" she says, glaring at her husband. "Ira was family. Enough with this talk." Jules lowers his eyes and instantly falls silent, along with Sophie's son-in-law and daughter.

This episode, which Goldberg identified as "so Jewish" in our interview, also articulates the central dynamic and tension in the series between the Old and New Worlds better than any other. For some reason that is incomprehensible to any of the other family members, Sophie, who has not spoken to Ira for many years herself, decides to make all funeral arrangements and bring "the entire family together" at the Berger apartment for Ira's funeral on Sunday. As usual, everyone goes along with her plan—such is the strength of her will. Everyone, that is, except Alan, who suddenly realizes he has a major conflict: he has two tickets for the Dodgers game on Sunday, a game in which the Dodgers can clinch the pennant. Furthermore, he has a date to take Katie to the game.

Alan tries to do the right thing, going over to Katie's Catholic high school to tell her the date is off because he has to go to Ira's funeral. But when he sees her looking adorable in her white blouse, plaid skirt, knee-high stockings, and schoolgirl field hockey gear, he is a goner. He starts to explain, but as she looks deeply into his eyes, he loses his resolve and reconfirms their date. But now he has to tell Sophie that he won't be attending the funeral. Alan procrastinates until the day of the funeral, and then springs it on her just as the family is leaving for the cemetery. Sophie is furious. She pulls him into a room, slams the door, and says through clenched teeth, "When they take everything away from you and you have nothing in the world, do you know what the only thing that you have left is?"

"That's a tricky question," Alan says.

"Family, that's what," she hisses, ignoring his sarcasm.

"But I didn't even know Uncle Ira. I don't even know half the people in that living room," Alan protests.

"Come, I'll introduce you to them," Sophie says.

"This isn't fair. Nobody liked Ira . . . Everybody's in there remembering someone they can't wait to forget. It doesn't make sense," Alan replies, going for the jugular, thinking maybe he can end it by throwing the truth in her face.

But Sophie doesn't buckle that easily. "That's what family is," she says, "people who don't really like each other getting together to do things they don't really want to do."

"That's family? That's nuts," Alan says, as Sophie walks away thinking the matter settled.

Alan's parents leave it up to him to decide what he should do. But, on his way out, Alan's father informs him that they are one man short for a minion to say prayers for Ira after the graveside services. Alan's presence would give them a minion. The ante of guilt has just been upped.

Just as Herskovitz and Zwick always managed to forge some sort of synthesis that at least felt like resolution out of the competing forces pulling at their Michael Steadman in *thirtysomething*, so Goldberg does here ultimately. Alan gives the tickets to his friend, Warren, making Warren first promise to spend the game telling Katie what a wonderful guy Alan is. Alan then returns home as the family is coming back from the funeral service. He is just in time to hear Sophie reading a letter that she had written to Ira many years ago when she was still a young woman living in Poland. Ira's mistress had given it to Sophie at the funeral. Ira kept it all these years. In the letter, Sophie thanks Ira for the $25 he sent her. As she finishes reading to the family, she wipes her eyes and says, "That was the first $25. He sent me plenty more. Ira wanted everybody to come to America. He was the first you know. He helped all of us."

The next shot shows the men saying the minion prayers. Alan is among them, chanting and davening. And then the camera cuts to the street, where Alan's little brother Nathaniel is standing with a group of friends around the ice cream man's cart listening to a transistor radio with the voice of Vin Scully delivering the play by play of the Dodgers game just as Gil Hodges, the epitome of American masculinity in the calculus of *Brooklyn Bridge*, homers in the eighth to put his team ahead ahead 3 to 1. Nathaniel races back to the Berger apartment, rushes into the center of the prayer circle and whispers into Alan's ear. Alan turns to his father, who is standing next to him, and chants in cadence with the Hebrew words that the men are saying, "Dodgers 3, Braves 1, Hodges homers in the eighth."

That final brilliant scene from "A Death in Brooklyn" was also autobiographical, Goldberg said: "That was my job, like Natie, always during Yom Kippur or whenever, I had to bring the score of the games . . . That last shot of them davening was just so Jewish. But there is also my rebellion against it, the archaic nature of it, in what Alan says to Sophie about everyone disliking Ira and being hypocritical about it now that he is dead."

That final shot is the very embodiment of the tension at the heart of this show: Alan davening and speaking in the rhythm of the Hebrew prayer but saying English words announcing the very American message that the Dodgers are likely headed for the World Series.

Goldberg says the only thing that was made up in *Brooklyn Bridge* was Katie Monahan: "The Irish girl, Katie, she was made up. My wife is Irish now. But that's the only thing [that was invented]. It would have been hard for my family to accept that relationship between Alan and Katie, or to accept it as easily as the family did in the show, I think. But, you know what? This is a memory, not a documentary. There are deeper truths than what was true."

At its deepest, *Brooklyn Bridge* stands shoulder to shoulder with *thirtysomething* and *Northern Exposure* as television's most serious, conscientious, and eloquent treatments of postwar Jewish masculinity on the journey of assimilation. But you can't help wondering how the larger pattern it played into with Jewish men and non-Jewish women affected viewers.

In 1997 and 1998, the Morning Star Commission, a group funded by Hadassah Southern California and made up of artists, writers, scholars, actresses and media, and advertising industry executives, tried to determine such effects. The commission started by trying to define the depiction of Jewish women in American popular culture and then demonstrate the impact of those depictions on viewers.

One of the commission's primary working hypotheses was that "media images, like literary and dramatic images, affect the social construction of reality." That is to say, "Media images are absorbed into the interpretive frameworks of American Jews and non-Jews, and have a clear impact on the way in which Jews are perceived and 'Jewishness' is interpreted."[23] In other words, media images of Jews, no matter how off-base and fabricated they might be, have real-life consequences in shaping both the ways Jews think of themselves and the manner in which non-Jews see Jews—another kind of "deeper truth" than what is true, to paraphrase Goldberg.

In general, almost no one today disputes that there is a link between media images and the social construction of reality. However, there is still great disagreement about how to determine and assess that relationship. The Morning Star Commission chose focus group research, a qualitative strategy favored by the entertainment industry as well as some media and cultural studies scholars under strictures aimed at helping the interviewers see the world through the eyes of focus group members. The commission convened eight focus groups "of women and men, both Jewish and non-Jewish, of varying ages and levels of religious affiliation."[24]

Among the findings: the overwhelming majority of Jewish women saw the non-Jewish woman the way they wanted to be viewed, at least physically—"tall, thin, blond." The non-Jewish woman was also perceived by Jewish women as being "athletic and very fun loving, someone who knows how to have a good time."

As for how Jewish women saw themselves, Hadassah's Sarah Kirscher summarized the findings by saying, "Jewish women perceived themselves to be well-educated, intelligent, very giving and supportive of others, not, however, beautiful or even attractive, [and] never sensuous, playful or fun loving... And, thus, [they] feel insignificant, passed over. The high incidence of intermarriages depicted in programs like *Mad About You* reinforce such feeling."

A few other important, related findings of the Morning Star study:

Non-Jewish men and women saw the typical Jewish woman in a predominantly negative light. "Jewish women can be spotted most obviously by their prominent noses and also their dark, Middle Eastern complexions and inclinations to be overweight," respondents said.

Jewish women, meanwhile, described the typical Jewish woman depicted in film and television as "pushy, controlling, selfish, unattractive, materialistic, high maintenance, shallow and domineering..."

All respondents—male and female, Jewish and non-Jewish—said Fran Drescher, who played Fran Fine on the CBS sitcom *The Nanny,* best fit these "negative attributes."[25]

Along with Jerry Seinfeld of *Seinfeld,* Drescher's Fran Fine was the most prominent depiction of Jewish identity on television in the 1990s. What neither the Morning Star Commission nor any of the papers written in connection with its findings explored is the fact that Fran Fine is primarily the creation of a woman. This is one female image that could not be blamed on a male author.

Intermarriage III (Some Jewish Women Get Gentile Guys) – *Rhoda, The Nanny, Dharma & Greg, Friends, Will & Grace*

> In certain ways, we shied away from things with Rhoda in terms of her Jewishness. We really didn't embrace it as much as we should have.
>
> Allan Burns, co-creator of *Rhoda*[1]

> People can say what they want about the series, but we never tried to hide from anything Jewish . . . The whole history of the show has never done anything except call a spade a spade. The whole MO of us is we are what we are what we are.
>
> Fran Drescher star of *The Nanny*[2]

Against the pattern of missing Jewish women in 1990s sitcoms, the arrival in 1993 of *The Nanny*, a CBS sitcom featuring Fran Drescher as a lower-middle-class woman from Queens who comes to work for a wealthy Broadway producer in Manhattan, might strike some as progress. At least it featured a female Jewish character in the leading role. Furthermore, unlike *Rhoda*, where ethnicity was rarely mentioned, Drescher's Fran Fine character regularly referred to hers.

But almost no one who has examined those references ever wound up characterizing the series as progressive in terms of the way it depicted Jewish identity.[3] The series ran five years, just as *Rhoda* did, and is remarkably consistent in its depiction of Jewish identity from the pilot in 1993, when Fine arrives on the doorstep of producer Maxwell Sheffield's Manhattan townhouse selling cosmetics, to the final episodes in 1998 that include her marrying Sheffield and then giving birth to twins.

Forget about whether Fran Fine made you cringe with her gauche ways. The particulars of that marriage, as well as the fact that the Jewish character involved in it was the creation of a female author, make *The Nanny*, like *Rhoda*, a landmark series whether you liked it or not.

Along with *The Goldbergs*, *Rhoda* and *The Nanny* are the only series featuring a leading female Jewish character that can claim female authorship. More importantly, they are the only two series in which the Jewish woman got the non-Jewish guy, reversing the dominant pattern of not only network television but also American popular culture when it comes to intermarriage.

There is one other landmark aspect of *Rhoda*: it introduced a new kind of Jewish mother to prime-time series television in 1970. Not the good-hearted and wise Yiddishe-Mama-in-transition as seen in Molly Goldberg but rather a neurotic, smothering Jewish mother more like the one seen in Philip Roth's *Portnoy's Compaint*. The character type would grow to monstrous comic proportions—becoming a near-permanent attachment to her adult daughter's life—in *The Nanny* a quarter of a century later.

RHODA AND MARY

Television viewers already knew the character Rhoda Morgenstern (played by Valerie Harper) by the time her series debuted at the start of the 1974–75 television season; Rhoda had been a supporting character on *The Mary Tyler Moore Show* since its beginning in 1970. But, while any discussion of the character must start in 1970, there is an important distinction to be made between Rhoda, the sidekick to Mary Richards, and Rhoda, the leading lady in her own sitcom.

Viewers first met Rhoda in the pilot for *The Mary Tyler Moore Show*, a pilot even better than *Bridget Loves Bernie* in terms of defining relationships, sounding themes, and introducing viewers to a world they would want to revisit each week. In establishing Mary's domestic space, the producers have her calling on an old friend of hers named Phyllis—the only contact Mary has in Minneapolis—who has an apartment to rent in the large Victorian home that she and her husband own. Here is how one historian describes the introduction of Rhoda:

As she begins showing Mary the room she'll be renting, Phyllis whips back the curtains . . . and is appalled by an apparition of plump, dowdy,

Semitic womanhood outside washing the windows. Phyllis calls her "that dumb awful girl who lives upstairs," but she is, in fact, the sardonic, brash, eternally frustrated Rhoda Morgenstern, who left New York because she couldn't find an apartment, ended up in Minneapolis, and now intends to take over the apartment that Phyllis is saving for Mary. With urban cheek Rhoda intimidates the too polite Mary into agreeing to switch rooms with her. But then, taking pity on this poor *goyische* waif, she proves she's a good girl and gives in.[4]

It is noteworthy how closely that reading seems to match the intent of the writer-producers Allan Burns, who is not Jewish, and Jim Brooks, who is Jewish, in their creation of the Rhoda character. According to Burns, Rhoda was not even in the original pilot for the series, the one that led to the meeting with CBS executives and the big lie about CBS's research. But, in trying to make up for what might be lost in terms of compromise on Mary not being divorced, Burns and Brooks added the television newsroom workplace and the character of Rhoda in their rewrite. Rhoda was "based on a woman Jim knew from New York, a friend named Rose Golden who worked in a brassiere factory, I think," Burns said. As he further explained the process: "Jim would tell me stories about Rose, and we developed the Rhoda character from that. And, then, we thought we'd never be able to cast it. And, then at the eleventh hour Ethel Winant [legendary Hollywood casting director] found Valerie [Valerie Harper who played Rhoda]. It was like a miracle . . ."[5]

Central to the creation of Rhoda was the notion of her in comparison and opposition to Mary. Describing Harper's appearance at the casting session, Burns said, "She was almost too attractive for the part, but her type was so perfect. The fact that she was a little overweight helped. She worked very hard at being *schlumpy*. We wanted an urban and an ethnic type from a big city to play against Mary's character—which was small-town, white, Anglo-Saxon Protestant. We wanted there to be some tension between them."[6]

The stock figure Rhoda played in *The Mary Tyler Moore Show* is often described as a sidekick to Mary, but that notion of inferior status only starts to describe what is going on with the relationship in a cultural sense. This is the Jew as Other—Rhoda constructed in her "Semitic womanhood" as an ethnic foil to Mary, who represents the dominant culture. As Peggy Herz put it in her book *All About Rhoda,* "They were a perfect pair—Mary slim, beautiful, calm, together; Rhoda a laughing, lovable clown who got all the rotten blind dates in town."[7]

It is worth noting how much of the difference is depicted in terms of dark versus light and slim versus heavy body image, just as it was done with the women in *Bridget Loves Bernie*. Harper explained her casting in terms of body: "I got the part of Rhoda because I was a little out of shape . . . Rhoda is the type who wears jeans and big shirts around the house. We try to keep her real. During the first season of the show, I weighed 145 to 150 pounds. I didn't show it in A-line dresses—nobody knew I was filling them out. It was Mary who said, 'Why don't you lose weight, Val? You don't always want to be my sidekick.' I wouldn't mind being her sidekick for the next five years but she was right about the weight! I'm about 130 pounds at this point, but I should be 120 pounds to really look like the Pepsi Generation."[8]

Furthermore, just as Buddy, the male sidekick in *The Dick Van Dyke Show*, was constructed not only as a physical foil for the star (short and plump versus tall and slim) but also shown as being immature in comparison, so is Rhoda. Again, as Harper put it, "We've found that young viewers respond to Rhoda because Rhoda says the unsay-able. Rhoda says the things that other people don't say either because of maturity or whatever. Rhoda's kind of free and open. Her opinion of herself is not solid. It's not secure."[9]

Episodes of *The Mary Tyler Moore Show* are loaded with Rhoda-as-foil-to-Mary. After looking through Mary's photo album, Rhoda asks, "Could I have it? I'd like to leave it in my apartment and have people think it was my life." And just as Mary Tyler Moore confronted Valerie Harper, the Italian-American actress playing Rhoda, about being her sidekick forever, so does Mary Richards confront Rhoda on-screen, telling her to quit putting herself down all the time.

"I don't say that I am nothing," Mary says to Rhoda.

"Sure, but you don't have to worry about someone beating you to it," Rhoda replies.

Rhoda, who was always dieting, once picked up a piece of candy off Mary's desk and, just as she was about to eat it, said, "I don't know why I'm putting this in my mouth, I should just apply it directly to my hips."

In response to learning that Mary was Gamma Gamma Delta in college, Rhoda says she was a Sharkette—"the ladies auxiliary of the sharks"—while growing up in the Bronx.

It is important to note the way Rhoda, the character, defines herself as inferior to Mary—just in case anyone wasn't clear as to what they were seeing with their eyes and hearing other characters say about Rhoda versus Mary. As one writer put it in a 1995 article for *Hadassah*, remembering her viewing of *The Mary Tyler Moore Show* as a child:

> In my childhood memory, Mary's wisecracking sidekick is fat and ugly. But now, as an adult, I see that she was neither fat nor ugly—she was simply a Jewish woman in Minnesota. She had dark hair, her clothes were funky and she had hips. That's all. The most unattractive thing about Rhoda was her self-deprecation, the way she constantly told us how unattractive she was, making us laugh at her own expense. Eventually, what she told us became reality, even if it wasn't in fact the visual image on the screen.[10]

The initial viewer response to the character of Rhoda was not good, according to CBS research that the network shared with the producers. As Grant Tinker, the founder of MTM, the celebrated production company that created both *Mary* and *Rhoda*, recalls, "CBS tested all its shows, and our pilot tested poorly ... And we were advised to tone down Rhoda—Valerie Harper—or get rid of her, because she came off as too New Yorky and brassy (read: Jewish)."[11]

Burns recalls the memo from CBS in much the same way but says the wording on Rhoda was that she was "too abrasive." Remember, though, this CBS "research" saying Rhoda was too Jewish might be no more a reality than that which was supposed to have said American viewers did not want to see Jews on television. But again, to this day there are those who accept it as fact.

And how did viewers know Rhoda was Jewish? As the quote at the start of the chapter states, the producers were very careful about depicting Rhoda's Jewishness. In fact, Burns says he can remember only one such mention of it during the first season of *Mary*. It came, not surprisingly, in the Christmas episode titled "Christmas and the Hard Luck Kid," which centered on Mary having to work Christmas. During the episode, Phyllis, who has become Rhoda's nemesis in the series, wishes Rhoda a Happy Hanukkah. In her pronunciation, Phyllis tries to roll the "h" of Hanukkah from the back of throat as if it were the Hebrew "kh" sound: khon-eh-keh. To which Rhoda replies that Phyllis should have a Merry Christmas, rolling the "ch" to sound like the "kh" in Hanukkah. In response to a question asking how the producers went about trying to let viewers know Rhoda was Jewish, Burns said, "Well, you have the name, Rhoda Morgenstern, which is not likely to be mistaken for gentile."

There is one other episode from that first year of *Mary* that is important to the depiction of Jewish identity on prime-time television, the episode titled "Support Your Local Mother," which introduced Nancy Walker, as Ida Morgenstern, Rhoda's mother from the Bronx. In the episode, Ida comes to visit, but Rhoda wants nothing to do with her. She doesn't even want her staying with her since she knows they will fight. Ida winds up staying with Mary, who serves as go-between in the mother-daughter war. There is an important backstage story connected with this episode. In his autobiography, Tinker quotes Burns as to how the network flatly forbade MTM from shooting the episode after reading the script. In Tinker's book, the primary reason for the network saying no to the episode is a scene in which Ida walks in on Mary as the younger woman is beating a table with a chain in an attempt to "distress" it—make it look antique. "Whatever makes you happy, dear," Ida says in a failed attempt at hiding how incredibly weird Mary seems to her. When Mary sees herself through Ida's eyes, she collapses into a giggling fit. The scene is one of the funniest in the distinguished history of the series. Tinker quotes Burns as saying that the CBS executive who served as network liaison to the show forbade them from filming the episode.[12]

But, according to Burns, the CBS executive who served as network liaison to the series forbade them from filming the episode, saying: " 'Look, you can't do this, you have sado-masochism here.' And I said, 'What?' And, he said, 'You have Mary beating on this table with a chain.' And, I said, 'Boy, that's in your brain.' "

Burns said he explained "distressing" to the executive and offered to take him to a furniture factory to see for himself. But Burns said that he quickly found out there was another problem, and this one seemed to be the real reason that CBS was taking such a strong stand in forbidding the episode: "The executive said, 'Look, we can't have a major character in a new series turning her back on her mother this way, and all these other attendant issues . . .' And, because it was Rhoda's mother, it became here's this harridan who is Jewish, and we can't have that. And, so, they said, 'We're going to forbid you to shoot this show.' "

CBS did, of course, relent, and, as a result of what would be an eight-year combined run on *Mary* and *Rhoda*, Ida Morgenstern is easily the most widely known Jewish Mother in prime-time network television history. To borrow Burns's description, she started out as a "harridan," and the caricature became more and more exaggerated as the two series ran on. A generic description of the media stereotype is offered in Charlotte Baum's *The Jewish Woman in America*:

> The stereotypical Jewish mother overdoes her job. We are told she hovers over her children, preventing them from achieving autonomy by interfering, cajoling, advising and manipulating. Whether she is actually holding the spoon and urging them to take "just one more bite," or operating through guilt, . . . she is seen an ubiquitous and eternal from the first diaper change through the last word on the doctoral thesis . . . Her children's achievements belong to her, for she has lived her life for—and through—her children. They succeed not to please themselves but to satisfy her, the fear of her displeasure intensifying their own anxieties about failing. Her domination extends over her husband as well . . . Although there are scattered references to the particular type of Jewish mothering over the entire range of Jewish American literature, the full blown negative stereotype does not appear until the sixties . . . [13]

Television picked up the ball with Ida Morgenstern in 1970 and Sophie Steinberg in 1972 and ran with it straight through most of the decade, as Ida moved to center stage on *Rhoda*.

RHODA

When Rhoda Morgenstern left Minneapolis to return to New York and her own series in 1974, the first words viewers heard were these said in voiceover:

> My name is Rhoda Morgenstern. I was born in the Bronx, New York, in December of 1941. I've always felt responsible for World War II. The first thing that I remember liking that liked me back was food. I had a bad puberty; it lasted 17 years. I'm a high school graduate. I went to art school. My entrance exam was on a book of matches. I decided to move out of the house when I was twenty-four. My mother still refers to this as the time I ran away from home. Even-

tually I ran to Minneapolis where it's cold and I figured I'd keep better. Now I'm back in Manhattan. New York, this is your last chance.

There are a number of things worth noting in the way that opening defines Rhoda. There is irrational guilt in the World War II joke. Food, image, and self-worth problems are suggested by the next joke. Then it is on to unresolved adolescent conflicts with her mother.

What is easy to overlook today in that opening is the way the female voice is so overtly privileged, which is unusual for network television of the time. The creators and producers set up Rhoda as a female character who could talk directly to us in a way no other woman had done on prime-time network television since the last time Molly Goldberg leaned out her apartment window on the DuMont network in 1954. And, borrowing a voice from a number of Jewish women's novels in the 1970s, Rhoda was going to talk back to some of the depictions of Jewish women being presented elsewhere in the culture in a way Molly would never dream of doing.

One of the most important things to know about *Rhoda* is that its authorship is more complicated than most historians have understood or acknowledged. While it is often noted that two men, Burns and Brooks, created the character, I have yet to find anyone detailing the role of Charlotte Brown in shaping *Rhoda*. Brown wrote more episodes of the series, thirty-six, than any other writer including Burns and Brooks. She started as executive script consultant, moved up to producer, and took over near total control of the show as executive producer during its last two years. Burns himself cites Brown as the single most important person in terms of authorship of the character of Rhoda Morgenstern as she appeared in her series during its five-year run.

For her part, Brown says Rhoda's Jewishness was *not* the most important thing about the character and resists discussing her solely in those terms. As she puts it:

The ethnicity was flavoring. It was just spicing. It didn't drive the bus ... Rhoda involved self-exploration, but it wasn't about my Judaism. I mean, it was part of self-exploration, because it's part of who I am. But I never went looking for Jewish stories. It was about my experiences as a woman. I was single then. It was about my relationship with my mother, with my father. You know, my view of the world, my relationships with my friends and those experiences. It wasn't so

Rhoda (Valerie Harper, left) and her sister Brenda (Julie Kavner) with their television mother (Nancy Walker) in *Rhoda*. The sidekick, the ugly duckling and the Jewish mother as harridan—and, yet, this series was landmark especially in the way it tried to transform Rhoda from sidekick to object of desire. Copyright CBS-TV.
Photo courtesy The Kobal Collection

much my Jewishness . . . The legacy of Mary and Rhoda may not be about the overt ethnicity of Rhoda. With Mary and Rhoda, we created positive female role models, women who a) could star in their own shows, and b) who had careers and were not desperate to be married. That was the first time you saw that, and that was the more positive effect Rhoda had if you look at characters who came later like Murphy Brown. Rhoda was the first woman in prime time to have sarcastic, self-deprecating humor—that razor sharp wit. It was the first time that a lead female character was allowed to be negative. That's what it was about much more so than the Jewishness.[14]

A careful viewing of the series supports Brown's contention about ethnicity. Despite cultural historians who claim that the series showcased "Rhoda's Jewishness,"[15] the episodes themselves tell another story. In fact, during the first season, I could find only one direct mention of Rhoda as Jew. It came in the eighth episode, the most famous and watched episode of the series' five-year run, "Rhoda's Wedding," which was seen by about fifty million viewers, according to Nielsen Media Research.

The mention of Jewishness comes at a dinner in the Bronx apartment of Rhoda's parents on the eve of her wedding. The old Minneapolis gang is there, including Rhoda's nemesis, Phyllis. "Oh, I'm having fun," Phyllis announces during dinner, followed by the non-sequitor "I just love Jewish food." To which Ida replies, "Funny, we never thought of steak as Jewish."

The wedding suggests better than any other moment in the series how greatly any sense of Jewishness was downplayed in *Rhoda*. The wedding takes place at the apartment of Rhoda's parents. She is marrying a Roman Catholic, Joe Gerard (played by David Groh). But CBS was not going to make the same mistake it made with *Bridget Loves Bernie*: this wedding was strictly civil and over before you knew what happened.

The brilliant, comic part of the episode involves Phyllis forgetting to pick Rhoda up, so the bride in full wedding gown has to take a subway from the apartment she shares with her sister, Brenda (Julie Kavner), in Greenwich Village all the way to the Bronx. But, in terms of a ceremony, once Rhoda arrives, all you have is the justice of the peace saying, "When two people love each other, they want to share each others' lives." Rhoda follows that up with, "Joe, whatever I've got to give, you got." And then they are man and wife.

In looking back at the episode and the series, Burns said, "We didn't really embrace her Jewishness as much as we should have. I remember we would do Christmas shows and she would be celebrating . . . And, you know, when she was married, it didn't seem like any kind of religious service. And when I look back at it now, I sort of regret that we didn't embrace it a little more. But we weren't trying to be controversial or groundbreaking."

As for Rhoda marrying a non-Jew instead of a Jew, Burns explained it in the following manner: "I don't think we made a conscious decision to make him Italian. It seemed more like we wanted a volatile guy for her to bounce off of. Volatility was the key."

But non-Jewish masculinity is depicted as superior to Jewish masculinity in the series. In the pilot of *Rhoda*, on her first day back in New York, a man calls her out of the blue. His name is Steven Schlossberg. All we hear is Rhoda's end of the conversation, but it is clear that she intimidates the caller and is not the least bit interested in him. It turns out Ida, playing matchmaker, put him up to making the call. "I know a lot of Steven Schlossbergs," Rhoda says, hanging up the phone, "which gives you some idea of the kind of life I've had."

"Don't be so choosy, young lady," Ida says. "If I was as choosy as you, you'd only be three years old."

But this Rhoda can afford to be choosy, because she has been physically transformed since leaving Mary and the gang in Minneapolis. And, in the end, this transformation might be the most significant aspect of Rhoda in connection with her Jewishness, even though the connection is not overtly stated in the show. In terms of the physical transformation, it should be noted that Harper joined Weight Watchers and started dropping pounds during her last two seasons with *Mary*. So there was already some change in Rhoda's physical appearance. But, with *Rhoda*, from the opening montage to the first words said, she is defined not just as thinner, but as glamorous.

Her sister Brenda's first words in the pilot are "You look so gorgeous, I can't believe it." A few moments later, "Oh, I wish I could be as thin as you. One bite of a Sarah Lee [cake], and I inflate like a rubber raft." In case anyone in the audience misses the point that Brenda is playing Rhoda to Rhoda-as-Mary, Rhoda says, "Why do I get the feeling I'm looking in an old mirror, when I look at you?" The major message of the pilot: Rhoda has been transformed from *schlumpy* to glamorous. With that much talk in the pilot about Rhoda's body and its transformation, you can't help but think it might have some deeper meaning.

Anthropologist Riv-Ellen Prell, in her essay "Cinderellas Who (Almost) Never Become Princesses: Subversive Representations of Jewish Women in Postwar Popular Novels," looks at a series of novels "about unmarried Jewish women in search of love" that were written between 1973 and 1976 by Jewish women. Prell argues that the women authors created the literary characters in reaction and opposition to the character Marjorie Morningstar (the English translation of Morgenstern) of the novel of the same name by Herman Wouk, and Brenda Patimkin of Philip Roth's *Goodbye Columbus*, and the other "Jewish-American princesses" who came in their wake:

> The novels written in the 1970s elaborated images constructing Jewish women in one way in order to challenge their basic representation in popular culture. They shared an aesthetic in which women "talked back" . . . The novels, which are all funny and poignant, are familiar Jewish writing. Their young woman is a female version of the classic *schlemiel*—the loser. However, just like the small heroes of Woody Allen or Sholem Aleichem, they subvert the meaning of winning and losing and power and powerlessness. This talk back style was closely linked to each novel's dependence on the central character's "grotesque" body. Each protagonist experienced part or all of her body as misshapen and transgressing socially acceptable norms.[16]

The concept Prell uses for "the grotesque body" comes from Mikhail Bakhtin's *Rabelais and His World*. Prell describes that body as "one that is protruding, unrestrained and never complete." In each of the novels, to be deemed acceptable the woman must lose weight, have plastic surgery performed on her nose, or reduce the size of her breasts: "But Bakhtin's insight on the grotesque body asks us to look further. Why must the Jewish woman shed her features to be reconstituted as desirable? . . . The Jew in the Jewish women, unconfined by the demands of American culture, is what is symbolized by the grotesque body."[17]

Prell argues that those Jewish heroines who resist the transformation "appropriate and reformulate the loser/outsider as a woman bursting out of cultural restraints." As she explains it, " 'Grotesque bodies' keep women from love but also reveal their independence, autonomy and the possibility of pleasure. As classic 'losers,' these women are funny; their voices control the novels, providing commentary on contemporary Jewish life, the family and the impossible dilemmas that beset women . . . These women not only talk back to Philip Roth and others, they appropriate their writing."[18]

Prell never mentions *Rhoda* in her discussion of such works as *The Launching of Barbara Fabrikant*, *Fat Emily*, and *Cousin Suzanne*. She is dealing with the popular novel, not television. But the novels and *Rhoda* existed in the same time and sphere of popular culture, and the parallels seem obvious to me. *Rhoda* lasted five years, which is a highly respectable run for network television. And yet it is often described as a failure. As one historian puts it: "Whatever happened to Rhoda Morgenstern? This is one of the most confusing sitcom mysteries of all time. Why did Rhoda the Soaring [of *The Mary Tyler Moore Show*] turn into Rhoda the Boring [of *Rhoda*]? She went from being that nice Jewish girl to *That Girl*."[19]

The consensus among those in the industry is that the producers rushed Rhoda into marriage too fast. They did it for ratings reasons at the behest of Silverman, who wanted a huge audience in November when advertising rates are set based on viewership, and even Silverman acknowledges that it was a mistake.[20] So, two seasons later, they had Rhoda and Joe separate. But the series still never realized the promise with which it started.

The instant marriage was part of what went wrong with *Rhoda*, but I believe there is a deeper reason for the show's ultimate failure, and it is connected to the transformation of Rhoda's body. Joe, the hunky gentile, was Rhoda's reward for transforming herself so completely from the funny, back-talking "loser" who challenged cultural expectations for Jewish women of her generation. There is a line in that famous wedding episode that resonates with Rhoda's desire to conform to the Midwestern, small-town, Anglo-Saxon notion of physical beauty represented by Mary. Rhoda goes to the airport on the night before her wedding to greet Mary and the rest of her old friends from Minneapolis, but Mary's plane is delayed for several hours. When it finally lands, Mary embarks, looking disheveled. "I hate to gloat, but for the first time in my life, I think I look better than you," Rhoda says to Mary.

Rhoda was right; she did look better even by Mary standards. But that is also when she lost her comic soul. That is when she stopped being a comic heroine and became just another sitcom wife—as the Jewishness was transformed all but right out of her.

As with *The Goldbergs* and *Bridget Loves Bernie*, I have gone into considerable depth with *Rhoda* for two reasons. First, as the oldest series with leading Jewish characters, they are in the greatest danger of being lost—especially in the sense of researchers not being able to talk to the writers and network executives involved in their production and distribution. Second, too much of what we do have on these shows is either falsely remembered or simply incorrect, especially regarding the simple facts of their production.[21]

THE NANNY

Fran Fine was the standard bearer of female Jewish identity not just in the series but in all of network television through most of the 1990s, and she is loud, nasal, crass, gauche, whining, materialistic, manipulative, addicted to food and shopping, and endlessly scheming toward her grand goal of getting Maxwell Sheffield to marry her. Furthermore, despite her employment as a nanny to Sheffield's children, she really does not do anything that could be called work. In fact, her lack of labor is regularly referred to as a central source of humor in the series. Such consumption of material culture and lack of productive labor are at the core of the negative stereotype of the "Jewish-American Princess."[22]

And yet she is the sexually attractive one whom the male lead wants, which in the language of prime-time television makes her the feminine ideal of the series. In that sense, Fran Fine could be seen as progressive—the next step in the evolution of female Jewish characters started by Rhoda from *schlumpy* sidekick to object of desire in prime-time network television.

Furthermore, whereas minor Jewish female characters are regularly depicted in sitcoms as neurotic-brittle-icy (Lilith Stern on *Cheers* and *Frasier*) or lesbian (Debbie Buchman on *Mad About You*), Fran has a "healthy" heterosexual appetite.[23] In that regard, she is more like Jamie Buchman (Helen Hunt), the idealized, non-Jewish female lead in *Mad About You* who so dazzles the Jewish male lead.

Even more important, unlike Melissa Steadman in *thirtysomething*, who can only witness motherhood through her camera lens as she endlessly photographs the tableau of gentile mom and child, Fran has her own twins practically the instant she and her gentile prize of a husband get married.

While many would dismiss Fran Fine as just another regressive image of Jewish womanhood, in the end that is a mistake. If Jewish male characters can lust after WASP women, Drescher went them one better with her female character lusting after the very prototype that the American WASP seeks to emulate—the wealthy Englishman. Culturally, that reversal matters, especially in terms of what it suggests about how male identity is depicted when Jewish women rather than men are writing the scripts.

In terms of the particulars of *The Nanny*, though, there is much to want to dismiss, even about that marriage. In the 1998 episode titled "The Wedding," the bride is late to make her entrance for the walk down the aisle. When Sheffield finds her, she is in a dressing room sobbing. The reason Fran is crying is that Sheffield's snooty sister, Jocelyn, had come by to extend her "well wishes" and went on to tell Fran that she was divorcing her husband, Lester, who had formerly been her chauffeur. Jocelyn explains that they had nothing in common except sex, and that "marrying beneath her" resulted in great unhappiness.

"Mummy was right about mixing the classes," Jocelyn says as she departs. When Sheffield asks Fran why she is crying, she tells him about Jocelyn's divorce and says, "Don't you see, it's all wrong. You're the smart, sophisticated, classy Jocelyn, and I'm Lester, the poor *schlub* who works for you."

Sheffield puts his hands on Fran's shoulders, looks deeply into her eyes, and says, "Oh, come on, darling. You never really worked."

The laugh is enormous. And it should be. The producers had been setting up such punchlines since the pilot, when, moments after being hired, Fran fills a plate with food off the breakfast sideboard and then sits down with the family to eat, despite the butler telling her the last nanny ate in the kitchen.

Fran is delighted moments later in the pilot when she finds out that Sheffield is throwing a party for potential backers of his next play that night. She tells Sheffield's fourteen-year-old daughter, Gracie, they have a lot of "work" to do to get ready for the party—even though neither she nor the children have been invited. "We have to go shopping, get our hair done, get a manicure . . . So, we'll go, we'll do, you'll love it."

The joke about what constituted Fran's idea of hard work was regu-

Fran Fine (Fran Drescher) and Maxwell Sheffield (Charles Shaughnessy) from *The Nanny*. The dominant pattern of Jewish guy/non-Jewish woman in 1990s sitcoms was reversed in this CBS series with the Jewish woman chasing a non-Jewish guy.
Photo courtesy The Kobal Collection

larly repeated throughout the run of the series, with the list of duties in a "hard day's work" growing longer as the years went on to include pedicures, lunches, and always more shopping. "I'm so proud of my work with Gracie," Fran says in another episode. "The other day we went shopping. She tried on every pair of shoes in the store and bought nothing. When she made the salesman cry, I knew she had a gift."[24]

But the negative depiction of the Jewish woman as a voracious consumer of material goods and adornments without performing the labor to produce anything in return goes beyond even the stereotype of the Jewish-American Princess. Both Fran and her mother, Sylvia (played by Renee Taylor), connect to food in a way that is every bit as coarse as that of the guests in the controversial wedding scene from the feature film *Goodbye, Columbus*. In fact, in the backstage-at-her-wedding scene already described, Fran delivers her "poor *schlub*" line through a mouthful of mallomars. Again, it was a moment that had been set up since the pilot.

Following her firing by Sheffield in the pilot—essentially for sexualizing Sheffield's teenage daughter with the hairstyle, manicure, and adult party dress—Fran returns home to the rent-controlled two-bedroom apartment in Queens where she lived with her mother and father. The first image we see of Fran back home is her lying on a plastic-covered couch, leafing through a fashion magazine, while Sylvia stands over her with a box of mallomars. It is a tableau of pure consumption.

"Fran, you need a mallomar?" Sylvia says.

"Oh, no, Ma, food's not the answer to everything."

"Meanwhile, your father and I have based our entire relationship around food. Passion goes, sex goes. Communication we never had. But food is forever."

"Okay," Fran says, reaching in the box for a mallomar.

"Morty, you want another mallomar?" Sylvia hollers through a mouthful of cookies to her husband in the next room. "Morty," she yells louder.

"Ma, Daddy can't hear you, he's watching the game. Why can't I find a man like him: deaf and on a pension?" Fran says, biting into her mallomar.

"You will, dear," her mother assures her.

In another episode, the running gag has Sylvia putting her hand to her chest repeatedly and saying, "*Oy*, all day I'm tasting pesto garlic coming up." From gag to gag, the only thing that changes is the food, as in, "*Oy*, I keep tasting the Kung Pow chicken, all day." And following each "*oy*," someone offers her more food and she wolfs it down. Meanwhile, the heavyset Sylvia is either wearing a garish muumuu or incredibly tight-fitting outfits that generally look to be bursting at the seams—a grotesque, cartoon version of an overweight woman.

In her autobiography *Enter Whining*, Drescher describes Taylor as Sylvia by saying "Not only is she [Taylor] a brilliant comedienne, but her voice tone has a similar nasal drone to mine and my mother's . . . There was Renee [onstage as Sylvia in the pilot], all dolled up in a loud, printed, brightly colored float (muumuu to anyone not from Queens), huge hair resembling a blond tidal wave, heavy makeup, jewelry and slippers."[25]

In *The Wit and Wisdom of The Nanny*, Fran describes Sylvia by saying "You should have see Ma's old nose. She could hook a marlin with it." *The Nanny* regularly suggests certain body types and physical characteristics for Jews, and they are often positioned as less desirable than those she projects for non-Jews.[26]

Beyond her "look," Sylvia's behavior is also grotesque. Here is a typical Sylvia moment, this one also from the wedding episode: as Fran is chatting in the dressing room with her bridesmaids prior to the ceremony, Sylvia comes barging through the door and says, "*Oy*, where's the can. I took a diuretic instead of Tylenol." Sylvia's diuretic becomes a running gag throughout the episode. An even more striking Sylvia moment comes just before Fran and Sheffield finally exchange wedding vows. Quiet descends over the room as Fran arrives in front of the minister and rabbi who are scheduled to perform the wedding ceremony together. Just as you expect the clergymen to begin, though, Sylvia grabs Fran's right hand, spins her around toward the guests and, holding out her daughter's hand to feature the wedding ring, exclaims, "Seven and a half carats!" Fran seems not at all embarrassed.

Only a few weeks earlier, there had been an entire episode devoted to Fran getting the ring. It opened with Sylvia urging her daughter to pressure Sheffield for a ring, saying "Darling, it's not a real engagement until I can take my daughter's hand and say, 'Stick these carats it your soup, Mrs. Glickman.' "

Fran responded by saying she wasn't concerned about not having a ring. "Mom, all that matters is that Sheffield and I love each other." To which Sylvia replies, "*Oy*, she's turning into a shiksa right before my eyes."

But not to worry, Fran wants the ring, and just at that point in walks Sheffield to announce that they are going to Cartier to buy Fran a ring. "Retail!" Fran and Sylvia shriek in harmony, with Sylvia explaining that Uncle Stanley would be terribly insulted if they didn't first visit his shop in the diamond district. Uncle Stanley (played by Drescher's real-life father, Morty) is dressed in a loud plaid sports coat, with his shirt open at the chest to show lots of hair (just like Judd Hirsch's Leo in *George and Leo*) and a Star of David necklace. Uncle Stanley shows them one of his "finest" pieces: a lion's head made out of four ounces of diamond chips. "We call it the quarter-pounder," he says proudly. "My God," Sheffield gasps, "That's the gaudiest thing I've ever seen." They ultimately wind up at Cartier.

So, the ring comes with more than a little history when Sylvia interrupts the marriage ceremony to waggle it in the guests' faces. But the ostentatious act just as the rabbi is about to open with a prayer takes Sylvia's crass behavior into another realm altogether. It links it not just to Jewishness in an ethnic sense—wherein the Jewish female is depicted in TV traditional terms of food, body image, and language—but Judaism as a set of religious beliefs and rituals.

One of the most pronounced examples of this pattern in the series came in a 1996 episode titled "The Cantor," which found Fran dating the young cantor from her mother's Synagogue.[27] When the star of Sheffield's Broadway musical becomes ill, Sheffield replaces him with the cantor at Fran's suggestion. The cantor is a hit and leaves the temple, which makes the congregation angry at Sylvia. One scene finds Sylvia and Fran in temple sitting in the very last row.

"We've been banished to Siberia," Fran says to her mother, who is busily unwrapping a bacon, lettuce, and tomato sandwich. "At temple?" Fran asks, looking at the sandwich. "Nobody can see us here," Sylvia replies. "I could throw a luau." The series often seemed to be going out of its way to showcase the love of non-kosher food on the part of both Sylvia and Fran, but the bacon sandwich in temple was a new benchmark in the way it violated accepted behavior in a sacred space.

For her part, Drescher, who created *The Nanny* along with then-husband Peter Jacobson, said she is proud of the way the series dealt with matters of Jewish identity, but that the series was more about social class than ethnic differences between her and Sheffield. "As much as you're asking about ethnicity, I really think this was much more about social class, blue-collar meets blue blood," Drescher said. "That's where the humor came from. And not just blue-collar meets blue blood, but blue-collar *gets* blue blood."[28]

As was suggested by the pre-wedding discussion between Fran and Sheffield's sister, social class did play a role in this series, but it was permanently coupled to issues of Jewish versus gentile identity just as it was in *Bridget Loves Bernie*. And the most important aspect of that dialectic involves male Jewish identity, with the gentile male being idealized here just as the gentile female was in series like *Bridget Loves Bernie*. Part of what makes this fact so important is that the depiction of male Jewish identity at the hands of female Jewish authors has been largely overlooked when it comes to television.

Feminist critics have written considerably about gender, Jewish identity, and cinema. Sylvia Barack Fishman, for example, explains "a cinematic tradition" of stereotyped Jews in part in terms of "grotesque images" created by anti-Semitism, which "Diaspora Jews internalized from Freud onward." As they aspired to a more assimilated status, Jewish men sometimes projected what they had internalized about Jewish identity onto women. As Fishman puts it, "Hollywood portrayals of Jewish women (which are usually created by Jewish men) are often reflections and vicarious re-enactments of American Jewish men's rejection of their alien status onto Jewish women, or at the very least their unresolved relationship with their own ethnic and religious identities."[29]

But what happens when Jewish women are the authors of on-screen images? How do they depict Jewish masculinity? That has not been so systematically studied, but the history of television told in this book finds Jewish women doing unto men just as the men did unto them.

This book finds three clear examples of female authorship of popular prime-time series in *The Goldbergs*, *Rhoda*, and *The Nanny*. Television authorship is always collaborative to some extent. Even in *The Goldbergs*, where there is no question that Gertrude Berg was the author in every sense of the word, you will find her son, Cherney Berg, listed as co-author on many scripts. But Gertrude Berg is clearly the *auteur*. And, while Jim Brooks and Allan Burns are the creators and executive producers of *Rhoda*, in part by nature of having created the character of Rhoda Morgenstern for *The Mary Tyler Moore Show*, Burns himself describes Charlotte Brown as the person exercising the greatest degree of authorship over *Rhoda*.

And so it was with *The Nanny*. While Drescher, Peter Jacobson, Pru Fraser, and Rob Sternin were all listed as executive producers, Drescher said she "broke" every story idea and "outlined" them with Fraser, in addition to "working on parts of this character all my life since high school."[30] No one can claim more authorship of *The Nanny* than Drescher.[31]

And what kind of gentile versus Jewish males did female Jewish authors create for television? It is not simply a case of Jewish men depicted in a negative way through such punchlines as Rhoda saying, "I've known a lot of Steven Schlossbergs, which gives you some idea of the kind of life I've had." Nor is it just a matter of Jewish women marrying gentile men in *Rhoda* and *The Nanny*, the way Jewish men married gentile women in *Bridget Loves Bernie* and practically all of the 1990s sitcoms. The depictions of Jewish masculinity and some of the implications of those depictions run much deeper and are far more destructive, starting with *The Goldbergs*.

Laying the groundwork for her feminist critique of cinematic images of Jewish women, Fishman says, "Many nineteenth-century Christians in sophisticated cities such as London and Vienna and the United States believed Jewishness to be essentially pathological . . . Jewish men were perceived as physically weak, hysterical beings unmanly in their physiologies and psychologies. Reputable works described Jews as having harsh and unmusical, whining voices, large and fleshy facial features, and unathletic feet and legs."[32] These are the kind of grotesque images she believes that Jews internalized, with men then projecting them onto female characters.

But doesn't the description of Jewish men as physically weak, hysterical, and unmanly beings describe Uncle David, the character created by Gertrude Berg? Nor is that the only depiction of male Jewish identity in such terms in *The Goldbergs*.

Sammy, Molly's son and the show's strongest depiction of masculinity in terms of mainstream 1950s values, disappeared from the series in 1955 after the marriage of the character. That void was filled by the arrival of actor Arnold Stang as Seymour, a shipping clerk at Jake's factory in Haverville. Seymour defined what at the time was often referred to as a ninety-eight-pound weakling. Short, frail, and incredibly nervous, his voice repeatedly cracked when he spoke—straight through his adenoids. With a pencil neck, protruding Adam's apple, oversized hornrimmed glasses, and a bow tie, he looked like a Jewish Barney Fife (of the CBS series *Andy of Mayberry*). Seymour came to Haverville in 1955 in an episode titled "The Seymour Story," arriving uninvited and asking Jake for a job. When Jake hires him, Seymour starts to cry.

Seymour's mother also appears in the episode. She is somewhere between nervous and hysterical, overbearing and obnoxious. We see her in split screen on the phone with Molly throughout the episode. "How does he look?" she asks Molly on the day of his departure from home. "Is he tired from the train trip? What do you mean he's not there yet? Has something happened?"

When Seymour does arrive at the Goldbergs, he complains that the "train was very stuffy." When Molly serves dinner, he rejects it, saying, "Chicken, I don't care for it." Molly insists. "Sorry, I just can't eat," he whines. "I'm too excited by the trip."

There are more phone calls from Seymour's mother during the episode. "What do you mean he's at work?" she demands of Molly. "What do you mean he doesn't take off in the middle of the week? When does he go to the clinic?"

Seymour is the weakest and most emotionally maimed of the men in *The Goldbergs*. His weakness is portrayed in part as being the result of his mother's excessive and obsessive behavior. But there is an even darker aspect to it—a suggestion that he is somehow physically defective, given to endless infections and ailments. Seymour's defectiveness is clearly defined in terms of the body, and here is a troubling connection between anti-Semitic "theory" and such depictions of the weak and feminized Jewish male in popular culture. As Maurice Berger put it in his discussion of Jewish masculinity, "It was precisely this desexualized, ambivalent body that underlay the understanding of the Jew in the arts and science of the late nineteenth and early twentieth centuries. Indeed, in almost all "legitimate" medical and biological discussions of pathology from 1880 to 1930, Jews represented the absolute negation of Aryan health and purity . . . Even Sigmund Freud's own understanding of the constructions of gender to some extent appropriated these paradigms of the feminized Jewish male body."[33]

And here it is reproduced for American television audiences in 1955 by Gertrude Berg.

The nearest we come to her sense of a male ideal in Berg's work is found in her 1961 autobiography as she gushes over the "impeccably mannered, perfect" Sir Cedric Hardwicke, her co-star in *Mrs. G Goes to College*. She offers this description in connection with saying how much she yearns to play a "British heroine, a Mrs. Miniver on the white cliffs of Dover," rather than a "Bronx mother."[34]

Thirty-five years later, the echoes of that sensibility can still be heard in Fran Drescher's autobiography as she sings the praises of Howard Stringer, the English-born president of CBS Entertainment in the 1990s, saying "Howard is an impressive man, with a large, imposing stature and Brooks Brothers Oxford tailoring...a king among kings"[35]

The ideal is most strikingly stated, though, in Drescher's description of the English actor Leigh Lawson, whom she describes as "the inspiration for Mr. Sheffield." Drescher said the idea for *The Nanny* came to her on a visit to England during which she stayed with Lawson, his wife, Twiggy, and their two children. Drescher knew Twiggy from the short-lived CBS sitcom *Princesses*, in which they co-starred. The series about three young women sharing a fabulous penthouse overlooking Central Park was mercifully cancelled after only a month on the air in 1991. Drescher's character, Melissa, is described as "an outspoken, stereotypical Jewish American who sold cosmetics at a department store."[36]

"And then there's Leigh, a talented actor unto himself," Drescher writes. "Can you believe before Twigs...he was married to Hayley (*The Parent Trap*) Mills? Isn't that wild? Two of the most famous English-women I grew up wanting to be...The longer I stayed with this wonderful British family...the more *shlubby* I became. I never felt so close to Flushing as when I stayed with them in London. Was I always so loud and crude?"[37] Jewish is "*shlubby*," loud, and crude in contrast to the WASP ideal.

The contrast is most clearly seen on-screen in *The Nanny* in the comparison between the suave Sheffield and Fran's gauche Uncle Stanley—with the loud plaid sports jacket, shirt open at the chest, and Star of David—trying to sell them the "quarter-pounder" diamond ring. This and Fran's dad, Morty, deaf and on a pension, are male Jewish identity according to *The Nanny*.

In the end, the most potent endorsement of gentile over Jewish identity is found in the way Fran Fine is transformed by her marriage to Sheffield from crude interloper to member of the magical kingdom of mainstream America. Rhoda did not find such transformation in her marriage to the Italian-Catholic Joe Gerard. But Fran did, and nowhere is this more apparent than in the birth of twins to the happy couple, as Fran moves from neurotic Jewish outsider caring for Sheffield's children as an employee to having two of her very own little Sheffields and becoming the center of their father's universe.

When you move beyond critique based solely on gender and see the pattern holding both ways—men to women *and* women to men—you can't help but recall the words of Lynn Roth, the former studio executive who asked in the introduction to this book, "So, where is the pride? Is there a lack a pride in the creators . . . ?" Roth was, of course, delicately raising the issue of self-hatred in connection with the creation of Jewish television characters.

THE FRIENDS

As the decade of the 1990s came to an end and *The Nanny* left the air, there emerged a new image of the Jewish woman on network television in three highly successful series, ABC's *Dharma & Greg* and NBC's *Friends* and *Will & Grace*. For the first time, female Jewish characters in leading roles were consistently being constructed as objects of desire. Given the twin patterns of missing Jewish women and Jewish-men-mad-about-Helen-Hunt, this might seem like a major development. But, as Norman Lear asked in response to my question about such characters, "Are they really Jewish? How can you tell?"[38]

On closer inspection, it does indeed seem that these characters might be more a throwback to some of the crypto-Jews of the 1970s than any sort of paradigm for Jewish identity in the new millennium. Among the six leading characters of the sitcom *Friends*, three are Jewish—or, perhaps, I should say, appear to be Jewish. They are Rachel Green (Jennifer Aniston), Monica Geller (Courteney Cox), and Ross Geller (David Schwimmer). Green was discussed earlier in connection with the Americanization of Molly Goldberg as she became Sarah Green in the short-lived *Mrs. G. Goes to College*. Green was also the Jew-not-a-Jew name for the leading character in the feature film *Gentleman's Agreement*.

Like *Mad About You*, *Friends* rarely directly referenced the characters' Jewish identity. Instead, viewers were forced to guess from the names and certain signifiers that could be read in different ways by different people. For example, Elliott Gould played the father of Ross and Monica. Gould was one of the most popular leading men of feature films in the 1960s and 1970s, playing a succession of Jewish characters. But younger viewers—and the six characters in *Friends* were all in their twenties—might not be familiar with that aspect of Gould's career.

Not only did the producers obscure the characters' Jewish identity on screen, they also were reluctant to discuss them as Jewish characters in interviews about the series. When asked whether or not the characters are Jewish, David Crane, co-creator of the series, said, for example, that Ross and Monica are "half Jewish because Elliott Gould is [their] father, but Christina Pickles [who plays their mother] certainly is not [Jewish]." Crane used the same peculiar logic of using the ethnicity of the actors playing the characters' parents to determine the ethnicity of the characters themselves in saying that Rachel also is "half-Jewish," because Ron Liebman, who plays her father, is Jewish, while Marlo Thomas, who plays her mother, is not. Crane acknowledged that the characters' Jewishness is "not an aspect we've done much with." An article in *Lilith* speculated that neither woman appeared to be Jewish because they are each "too thin, too sexy and too struggling in their nondescript professions to be considered Jewish."[39] Another critic more accurately suggested neither appears Jewish because they have absolutely no Jewish interests or affiliations.[40]

The Jewish identity of the characters on *Friends* is so obscured, Charlotte Brown, the former executive producer of *Rhoda*, said, "I don't think they really do play Jewish characters, do they? I mean, which two of the three are supposed to be Jewish? Lisa Kudrow in real life is Jewish, but I don't think she plays a Jewish character. But I guess the Courteney Cox character is supposed to be Jewish, but how do you know that? And with the Rachel Green character is it because she was supposed to marry this dentist named Barry? So, to answer your larger question [about change over time], I'm not sure how far we have come since the days of *Rhoda*."[41]

DHARMA FINKELSTEIN

Dharma Finkelstein (Jenna Elfman) of *Dharma & Greg* does self-identify as Jewish in the pilot. But as soon as she tells her future non-Jewish husband, Greg, in response to an inquiry from her future mother-in-law, that she is Jewish, she quickly starts to distance herself from it, saying, "but I wasn't raised Jewish." She explains that her father, Larry Finkelstein, a burned-out hippie from the 1960s, is Jewish but that he was non-observant. In fact, she says, "He started his own church, until the IRS got interested." That is the end of any discussion of Dharma's Jewishness onscreen. In an interview, Chuck Lorre, the creator of the series, talked with some reluctance about the "back story" of the characters—the history of the characters that the writers make up for themselves but never share with the audience: "Larry Finkelstein, like so many post-war, baby boomer Jews, went to San Francisco and went to Los Angeles, and ran from his faith. And he tried to re-create himself with a hodge-podge. I mean, that's what California's all about. It's a starting-over place," Lorre said. "As for Dharma, we asked ourselves how did she become this very un-neurotic person. And we decided she was home-schooled by her father, who broke from a very traditional Jewish background, and her mother, Abby O'Neill, who broke from a very traditional, Christian, Midwestern background.

"I don't want to throw a wrench into your thesis about Dharma being a Jewish character, but I think the character transcends religion. You can think of her as a Jewish character if you want, that's fine. And, I suppose, technically, she's half-Jewish. But, more importantly she's 100 percent human."[42]

In a 1998 focus-group study funded by the Jewish women's group Hadassah of Southern Californa, Dharma, who is thin and blond, was judged by Jewish men to be the only "positive" image of a Jewish woman on television. The men said it was her "non-Jewish appearance" that made them see Dharma in a positive light.[43]

GRACE ADLER

Grace Adler (Debra Messing), one of the two leading characters in *Will & Grace*, is attractive and sexy—and America seemed to like her just fine. The series, which debuted in 1998, was drawing an audience of about twenty million viewers a week by the fall of 2000. In its second season, *Will & Grace* won the Emmy Award as television's best comedy, with Messing nominated as best lead actress in a comedy series.

Being Jewish was just one part of Grace's identity, but it was treated with an ease and self-confidence not previously seen for any female character in a sitcom except Fran Fine. For example, the act that disrupts the world of *Will & Grace* in one episode is the theft of a music box off the mantle in Grace's apartment by a neighbor. The story line is primarily about the neighbor, but the way viewers are told that the box matters to Grace is her explanation to Will that the box was a bas mitzvah gift from her father. The implication of the remark is that the box is doubly important to her because of both the Jewish rite of passage it marks and the fact that it came from her father. Most sitcoms would have ignored such a signifier of Jewish identity, which could have been replaced by a dozen other objects of value in her apartment.

Perhaps more revealing, though, is the way this sitcom about the friendship between a gay man (Will) and a heterosexual woman (Grace) dealt with matchmaking on the part of Grace's mother, Bobbie Adler, a character played by Debbie Reynolds. A 1999 episode titled "Whose Mom Is It, Anyway?" opens with Grace entering Will's apartment and letting out a primal scream.

"One [phone] message from her and I am completely insane," Grace says, explaining that her mother left a phone message saying that she is coming to town to "fix Grace up" with Andy Felner, a former classmate of Grace's.

"Another one of her famous fix-ups. Can you believe her?" Grace moans.

"Well, maybe this one will be cute," Will says. "It's got to be better than the guy she found on NiceJewishChiropracters.com."

"I doubt it. I went to camp with Andy Felner," Grace says. "Three years in a row, we did the re-creation of Noah's Ark, and three years in a row he was Woodchuck Number Two."

Grace prevails upon Will to attend the luncheon with Andy and Mom, which Mrs. Adler has set up. At the luncheon, though, just as Grace launches into her speech about how her mother has to stop playing matchmaker, Mrs. Adler interrupts to say Andy is not there to meet Grace, he's there to meet Will.

What is most striking is how similar Grace's construction of Andy Felner as a loser was to Rhoda Morgenstern's reaction to the Jewish guy her mother tries to set her up with in the pilot of *Rhoda*. Except here instead of the main story line being Jewish-mother-making-daughter-nuts-with-Jewish-guys, it is just the set up for the humor of Andy being gay and Mrs. Adler matching him with Will. What happens in the episode—and elsewhere regularly in the series—is that Will's gay identity trumps Grace's Jewish identity so that, in comparison, Jewish is treated as "normal" or, at least, "more normal" than it is elsewhere in prime time.

Max Mutchnick, co-creator of series, suggested as much when he was asked why he thought the series seemed so comfortable with Grace's Jewish identity in comparison to all things Jewish about Rachel Green being ignored on *Friends*. "I don't know. We don't have any of the Jewish self-loathing. We limit that to my homosexuality," Mutchnick said. "I don't know, maybe Jerry Seinfeld and Paul Reiser, these guys who are playing clearly Jewish men on television, maybe they have issues about it and they didn't feel good about it. We just write to it [Grace's Jewishness] because she [Messing] plays it beautifully."[44]

David Kohan, co-creator of the series, added, "You know, it seems to me on TV there is a sort of archetypal character that's kind of Jewish but it's never mentioned. And our attitude is: you might as well mention it, you know. You might as well say, well, that's what she is and that's how she was raised, and that was really our thinking about it."

Messing agreed, explaining the relationship between herself and the character she plays by saying "On my Jewishness, there are a lot of Jews around on the set, and we have fun. And, I mean, yeah, I'm Jewish, and I think it's just a sensibility that they write and I recognize because it's part of my family and my history and my language. So, there's a rhythm to it that's familiar to me and fun to play...They've given me some really wonderful colors to play, and being Jewish is just one of them."

The relative lack of extreme self-consciousness and ambivalence about Jewish identity is progress. So, too, is the sense of Grace's Jewishness as just one part of her identity in keeping with the more postmodern sense of self.

But how different is the depiction of Grace's Jewish identity versus Will's homosexuality here from the way Bernie's Jewishness was defined in light of his friend Otis as an African-American in the pilot for *Bridget Loves Bernie* some thirty years ago? For both, Jewishness is only somehow better because it is less "other."

And, while Grace is attractive and playful, she is also incredibly neurotic. She defines brittle to a degree that exceeds even that of Dr. Lilith Sternin on *Cheers* and *Frasier*. And, whereas Lilith is generally in control of her emotions, Grace is perpetually on the brink of hysteria.

In the end, Grace is a character who seems incapable of a fulfilling relationship with either the homosexual leading man who offers her emotional and psychological ballast or any of the heterosexual boyfriends with whom she tries to find physical pleasure. Is this character really an advance over Fran Fine? Which might be the most succinct way of saying what a sorry history it continues to be in many ways for Jewish women on American television.

A "Too-Jewish"/Not-Jewish-Enough Jew for the '90s – *Seinfeld*

Looking back on it, with all the complaints about the gossipy rabbi or the shaky *mohel* ... and the doubts somebody like Brandon Tartikoff had about how it could succeed with this real Jewish vibe, in the end, I think Seinfeld was great for Jews. And it's kind of a funny paradox, because these were not good people.

Peter Mehlman, writer-producer of *Seinfeld*[1]

In the end, no series better embodies the paradox of "too-Jewish"/not-Jewish-enough than Seinfeld, the 1990s hit sitcom on NBC starring Jerry Seinfeld.

It almost failed to see the light of day because NBC programming czar Brandon Tartikoff thought it "too Jewish." Yet, as it rose to become the most-watched and most-talked-about network sitcom of the decade, much of the talk, especially among Jews, involved the purposefully murky ethnic and religious identity of supporting characters, as well as the decided lack of connection to things Jewish by the leading character. The not-Jewish-enough list ranged from Seinfeld's general disinterest in dating Jewish women to his ignorance of such Jewish religious rites as *bris*.

The talk grew so loud that it found its way into the mainstream press in April 1998, as *Seinfeld* was nearing the end of its remarkable nine-year run. "It's ironic that the late Brandon Tartikoff ... worried it would be too Jewish—because what the show turned out to be was too self-hatingly Jewish instead," Tom Shales, television critic for the *Washington Post*, said of the series in a column headlined "So Long, 'Seinfeld.' Let Me Show You to the Door."[2]

The vast difference of opinion on that matter of self-hatred and *Seinfeld* within the Jewish community itself is suggested by articles that ran a week apart in the Jewish press on the eve of the *Seinfeld* finale in May 1998. A headline in *The Jewish Bulletin of Northern California* said, "Critics call the show 'self-hating': Was 'Seinfeld' good for Jews?"[3] A week later, *The Jewish Journal* answered with an article that concluded by saying, "This is not Jewish self-hatred. It's something else: It's a new generation of Jewish humor . . . Jerry and company wore their Jewishness comfortably on their sleeves."[4]

Peter Mehlman, who co-wrote one of the episodes cited by Shales as evidence of the way in which the series was "mean and perverse" in its treatment of "Jews and Judaism"—an episode titled "The Hamptons" that dealt with kosher food laws—acknowledged such criticism. "You can't say that we at *Seinfeld* were ever very easy on Jews in certain ways. You know, we had that gossipy rabbi, and a lot of Jewish people were upset about that. Not to mention that Jerry dated a lot of girls who you would look at and say, 'Oh, she's not Jewish,' " explained Mehlman, who also wrote a celebrated episode titled "The Yada, Yada," which featured Jerry's conviction that his dentist converted to Judaism so that he could tell Jewish jokes.[5]

But, as his quote at the opening of this chapter suggests, Mehlman believes that ultimately *Seinfeld* offered a contemporary, sophisticated, and positive depiction of Jewish identity that was a watershed in a number of ways.

The watershed part is indisputable. *Seinfeld* was the first series in the history of the medium with a clearly identified leading Jewish character to become number one in the Nielsen ratings, making it the most popular series on all of television. That happened twice, once during the 1994–95 season and again during the 1997–98 season, when one out of every three American households with a television set in use Thursday nights at 9 had it tuned to *Seinfeld*.

If nothing else, that massive popularity exposed the lie told by all the network executives over the years who argued that Jewish identity had to be masked for economic reasons. With only six million or so Jews in the total U.S. population, the argument went, a show featuring a Jew could never find a large enough audience to be commercially viable.

But *Seinfeld* found the largest audience of any network series during the entire decade and made Thursday nights on NBC the most profitable evening in the history of network television at the peak of the show's

The four leading characters of *Seinfeld,* the most popular network series of the 1990s, all started out being Jewish, but a funny thing happened on the way to getting on NBC's schedule. (From L to R): Jason Alexander as George Costanza, Jerry Seinfeld as himself, Michael Richards as Cosmo Kramer, and Julia Louis-Dreyfus as Elaine Benes. Photo courtesy The Kobal Collection popularity. And, in terms of sociology, what about the profound relationship that many of the viewers in the twenty million or so households that tuned in to *Seinfeld* every week formed with this TV Jew and his New York friends?

It did not happen very often, but at its best moments, *Seinfeld* offered as informed an exploration of Jewish identity as any sitcom except *Brooklyn Bridge*. And, unlike *Brooklyn Bridge*, which in dealing with nostalgia and the fondly remembered past had less sociological relevance and potential impact, *Seinfeld* was offering its mass audience a look at a significant part of baby-boomer Jewish life as it was lived in 1990s America.

ETHNICITY MATTERS EVEN AMONG PARTNERS

Any responsible discussion of *Seinfeld* needs to start with setting the record straight on the oft-quoted story about Tartikoff thinking the show "too Jewish" and being reluctant to commit NBC to the series. Actually, there are two versions of that story, and the differences between them matter. As Tartikoff told it:

> Did I ever tell you my *Seinfeld* story? . . . I have to admit I really missed that one. I saw the pilot and I didn't like it. I thought it was too New York Jewish. So I passed. And then I ran into Rob Reiner [who co-founded Castle Rock Entertainment, which produces *Seinfeld*], who really reamed me a new asshole. He was yelling and screaming that I made the biggest mistake of my life. So I thought about it, and I decided to order the show. But I gave it the smallest order in TV history—four shows. It wasn't an immediate success, but you know, the rest is history.[6]

The other version comes from Rick Ludwin, who as head of late-night programming for NBC was one of Tartikoff's lieutenants. He says Tartikoff hated the pilot: "Brandon Tartikoff felt it was too Jewish, too New York . . . But, not being from New York and not being Jewish, it struck a chord with me."[7] So Ludwin ordered four episodes out of his budget for late-night variety specials, a huge gamble on his part, especially as he essentially overrode his boss to keep the series alive. That is why the order was so small; it was all that his budget allowed. As to whether four episodes is the smallest order in the history of television, that is debatable. But, in the words of Alan Horn, the co-founder of Castle Rock, "An order for six [episodes] is a slap in the face."[8]

The true version of events is Ludwin's, and what is important about it for this study is that the non-Jewish network executive saw it differently than the Jewish executive, which resulted in the series getting on the air. Tartikoff's reaction is a textbook example of the kind of self-censorship that helped keep Jewish leading characters in the shadows during the era when there were only three networks and all three were Jewish-owned—the "too Jewish" catchphrase still being sounded some four decades after it was first used to try and get Gertrude Berg to ditch Uncle David as *The Goldbergs* became *Molly* and moved to the suburbs. In fact, figure six decades if you go back to 1929 and the first time Berg said she heard it in connection with her radio show at David Sarnoff's NBC. Here with *Seinfeld* we have a case that shows a non-Jewish executive having a very different reaction than that of his Jewish boss to a Jewish leading character and citing the ethnic difference between them as the very reason for it.

Doing interviews for this book, I heard several such stories often involving Jewish and non-Jewish producing partners or network executives. The Jewish half of the team would not want to deal with Jewish subject matter, while the non-Jewish partner did.

Allan Burns recounted just such a difference of opinion between him and partner Jim Brooks on the episode titled "Some of My Best Friends Are Rhoda" on *The Mary Tyler Moore Show*. The episode involves Mary being invited by a woman friend to play tennis at a country club. When the woman arrives at Mary's apartment, she asks if Mary knows of anyone who might like to join them, since the fourth player for their scheduled doubles match cancelled. When Mary suggests Rhoda, the woman seems hesitant. After some back and forth, Mary finally realizes that the woman doesn't want Rhoda as the fourth because her club doesn't allow Jews. An angry and shocked Mary winds up showing the woman the door.

Burns said the idea came from him overhearing anti-Semitic remarks "by some of the pros" at a tennis club at which he played. He said he thought the episode was a great idea, but that Brooks was far less enthusiastic about doing it than he was. In retrospect, Burns said he thinks Brooks was right, because the episode came off as "preachy."[9] But it highlights the different sensibilities between the two—the Jewish Brooks and non-Jewish Burns—when it came to dealing with Jewish subject matter.

Jeff Melvoin also cited such a difference between him and David E. Kelley on *Picket Fences* over the character played by Fyvush Finkel, while Mike Burke had a decidedly different take on *Fiddler* than did his Jewish boss, William Paley, who felt it was "too Jewish" to risk investing in.

Tartikoff's reaction is also important because it shows how, even though the founders had left the scene and the networks were no longer Jewish-owned in 1990, the culture they inherited from the Hollywood film moguls and nurtured for four decades was still maintained by some of the executives whom they had groomed and who remained in power. A reminder that cultures and policies like the ones founded by Paley, Sarnoff, and Goldenson do not die overnight.

Tartikoff did, though, exact some compromise before allowing Ludwin to order the quartet of *Seinfeld* episodes: of the four characters, all of which were supposed to be Jewish, only Seinfeld would remain so. Furthermore, the producers would go out of their way to indicate to viewers that not all the characters were Jewish. Hence, the strange and utterly inexplicable Italian surname for Jason Alexander's George Costanza character.

Estelle Harris, who played George's mother, said the confusion over the ethnic identity of that character was intentional and carefully maintained by series co-creator and executive producer Larry David, on whom the character was based. "When I first started on my first one [episode of the series], I went over to Larry David and I said, 'You know, it would help my motivation to know what the Costanzas are. Are they Spanish? Are they Italian? Are they Jewish?' And he said, 'You don't have to know.' And that was the only answer I ever got, really," Harris said.[10]

As for Jerry Seinfeld, his decidedly Jewish name and comic persona as a standup comedian had already been established on network television. You could not now change the name to something less ethnic sounding, as George Burns and Jack Benny had done in an earlier era before they made their moves from vaudeville to the mass medium of radio.

But, to his credit, the leading character referenced his Jewishness from the very beginning. Mehlman says it wasn't always "that overt" at first, but it was there in that very first quartet of episodes ordered by NBC. Mehlman points to a moment with Seinfeld introducing Elaine to one of his relatives, whose last name is Levine. Jerry pronounces it "Le-veen" in making the introduction but is quickly corrected by his relative, who says, "It's La-vine." To which Jerry responds, "Yeah, and I'm Jerry Cougar Mellencamp."

"I mean, that's a Jewish joke," Mehlman said. "It's just not that overt . . . I don't think we shied away from talking about Jewish identity, but it did take a few years before we really dealt with it . . . But I think the show had a strong enough Jewish vibe to it from the beginning that we didn't want to hit it over the head. It had to be something that was really funny rather than a gratuitous mention.

"I think the characters, if you're familiar with Jewish people, are very Jewish. You know, a lot of the characters had Jewish names. I mean, I think they went out of their way not to have George sound Jewish by having his last name be Costanza, but who's thinking George isn't Jewish?"

Mehlman made several important distinctions in his discussion of *Seinfeld* and Jewish identity, starting with the difference between Jewish as an ethnic identity and Judaism as religion. The series came in for some of its harshest criticism when it took on the latter—Judaism as a religion or a set of rites.

One of the most controversial episodes centers on Elaine and Seinfeld asked to be godparents to an infant boy. One of their duties in that role is to find a *mohel* for the circumcision. Seinfeld does not even know what a *mohel* is, which gives you some sense of the character's connection or, perhaps, lack of connection to the religion. The punchline of the episode involves the incompetence of the *mohel*, who winds up cutting Seinfeld's finger.

By and large, the *bris* seems to be depicted as a foolish ritual in the episode. Whereas the *bris* was treated as a solemn and profound moment in *thirtysomething*, here it is played essentially for laughs. Despite the fact that we are dealing with a sitcom rather than a drama, some saw the ritual as being demeaned by the treatment *Seinfeld* gave it. One rabbi described the episode by saying "Yet the program sank to new depths when viewers met the *mohel* . . . a coarse, cold and uncaring, buffoon-like character. The entire . . . ceremony was presented this way with no nods to its meaning, importance or spirituality."[11]

Kosher food practices were also taken on in an episode that features Seinfeld's Jewish girlfriend—one of the few Jewish women he dated during the series—joining him and the gang for a weekend in the Hamptons. She keeps kosher and so declines when Kramer offers her lobster at dinner. But then, late at night, unable to stop thinking about how much everyone seemed to be enjoying the lobster at dinner, she is caught by Kramer sneaking into the kitchen trying to find some leftover lobster.

Then there is the rabbi in whom Elaine confides that she is undergoing an emotional crisis over the prospect of George getting married. The rabbi proceeds to violate the confidence and share what she said with the entire audience of a television talk show, to Elaine's great embarrassment. The rabbi is not just indiscreet, he is an insensitive fool.

Perhaps the most commented-upon Jewish moments in *Seinfeld* were those that referred, however obliquely, to the Holocaust. One involved the use of the term "Soup Nazi" for the owner of a soup stand who treated his customers with utter contempt. Another has Newman, Seinfeld's arch-enemy, catching Seinfeld and a girlfriend "making out" in a movie theater while *Schindler's List* played. A third has a character played by guest star Judge Reinhold doing a parody of Oskar Schindler's moving speech, which comes near the end of the film, in which Schindler laments that he did not do enough to save more Jews from the Nazis.

"The general *Seinfeld* philosophy of Larry David and Jerry Seinfeld [the co-creators of the series] was that if it's funny, that's all that matters," Mehlman said in response to a question about the way Judaism was treated in episodes like "The Hamptons," which he co-wrote with Carol Leifer. But, again, he acknowledged room for different readings.

"We did one episode, 'The *Mohel*,' which I thought was kind of funny. But a lot of people didn't like it—even, I think, some people related to the show. I'm pretty sure Jerry felt queasy about it. We got a ton of letters—stuff like that.

"I mean, the *mohel* thing, some people just didn't find it funny, and I think you could debate whether it was or not. But the gossipy rabbi was absolutely funny, no doubt about it. It's just the rule: if it's funny, it's good."

The kind of humor with which *Seinfeld* often treated Judaism can seem mean-spirited or, at least, needlessly coldhearted to some. But I think that we should be extremely careful in our use of the term "self-hating," and that the manner in which *Seinfeld* represented Jewish identity should be given context. First, *Seinfeld* was mean-spirited to many aspects of American life beyond Judaism. The series also mocked priests, Catholicism, dwarves, physically disabled persons, immigrants from any number of countries, and mentally disabled war veterans, to name just a few of its targets.

Furthermore, as regards the treatment of religion, *Seinfeld* can be placed in a longstanding tradition of Jewish humor. Moshe Waldoks, co-editor of *The Big Book of Jewish Humor*, says there is a certain style of Jewish humor that grew out of the cultural tension engendered by the birth of the *Haskalah*, the Jewish Enlightenment, in early nineteenth century Europe. Much of that style of humor involves urbane, modern, sophisticated Jews making fun of their "country-bumpkin" cousins, shtetl Jews, and the Hassidic rabbis they blindly followed. Waldoks says that *Seinfeld* is operating firmly within this tradition when he makes fun of *mohels* and rabbis.[12] In this stance, Jerry Seinfeld is the urban, New York, postmodern Jew standing outside the mainstream of middle-class Jewish propriety, making fun of religious practices that he considers archaic or, at least, worthy of satiric examination.

"THE YADA, YADA"

But *Seinfeld* doesn't need to be defended in terms of traditions and the past. What matters most about the series is the postmodern sensibility on Jewish identity that it brought to a mass audience, particularly in positioning Jewishness as just one of many identities for Seinfeld. The best example of this informed discourse on Jewish identity is found in Mehlman's "The Yada, Yada."

The episode opens with Seinfeld and George in a booth at their favorite restaurant when Tim Whatley, Jerry's dentist, walks in.

"Hey, George, you know Tim Whatley," Seinfeld says.

"Yeah, dentist to the stars," George says.

"What's up?" Seinfeld asks.

"I'll tell you what's up," Whatley says, "I'm a Jew."

"Excuse me?" Seinfeld says.

"I'm a Jew. I finished converting two days ago," Whatley responds.

"Oh, whoa, well, welcome aboard," Seinfeld says, taken aback a bit.

George notices the gym bag Whatley's carrying. "Hey, did you just work out?"

"Yeah," Whatley says.

"Huh, we must have just missed you," Seinfeld observes.

"Yeah, well, I didn't do much. I just sat in the sauna. It was more like a Jewish workout," Whatley says, chuckling and taking his leave as Seinfeld and George look at each other quizzically.

The next scene opens in Seinfeld's apartment, with Seinfeld complaining to Elaine, "I mean, the guy's Jewish only two days, and already he's making Jewish jokes."

"So what?" Elaine responds, "When someone turns twenty-one, they usually get drunk the first night."

"Booze is not a religion," Seinfeld says.

"Tell that to my father," Elaine replies.

In terms of Jewish identity, there are already several things to notice. Seinfeld's "welcome aboard" remark suggests that he sees Jewishness as something one would be happy to be have been allowed to join, a cause for celebration. This cuts directly against the self-hating hypothesis. Also, we see Seinfeld defining Jewishness totally as a religion—as Judaism. The depiction that appears negative comes from Whatley, whose joke about a "Jewish workout" relies on a stereotype of Jewish males as non-athletic for its attempted humor. Whatley's construction of Jewish identity has nothing to do with religion.

Whatley and Seinfeld are together again a few scenes later, when Seinfeld has a dental appointment. As Whatley holds Seinfeld's mouth open with a tongue depressor and a dental mirror, he says, "Which reminds me. Did you hear the one about the rabbi and the farmer's daughter?"

Seinfeld starts making noises of protest indicating he does not want to hear the joke, though he can't speak.

"Those aren't matzoh balls," Whatley says, ignoring him as he skips right to the punchline.

Seinfeld pushes Whatley's hands away from his mouth and says, "Tim, do you think you should be making jokes like that?"

"Why not?" the dentist asks, "I'm Jewish, remember?"

"I know, but . . ."

"Jerry, it's our sense of humor that sustained us as a people for three thousand years," Whatley says, cutting him off.

"Five thousand," Seinfeld says, exasperated.

"Five thousand, even better," Whatley says, as he goes back into Seinfeld's mouth with the mirror. Then, turning to his assistant, he says, "Chrissie, give me a *shtickle* of flouride, will ya?"

The next scene is back in Seinfeld's apartment with him again complaining to Elaine. "And then he asked the assistant for a *shtickle* of flouride," Seinfeld says.

"Why are you so concerned about this?" Elaine asks.

"I'll tell you why, because I believe Whatley converted to Judaism just for the jokes."

In Seinfeld's next visit to Whatley's office, he is waiting with a priest. As Whatley greets them, and the priest goes back to the chair, Whatley asks Seinfeld if he heard the one about "the pope and Raquel Welch in a lifeboat." The punchline plays off the size of Welch's breasts and a misunderstanding over what the pope meant when he said, "Hand me the buoys."

Again, Seinfeld expresses his outrage to Elaine: "So he says to me, 'I can make Catholic jokes, I used to be Catholic.' "

Elaine only makes Seinfeld madder when she says she thinks it is more a Raquel Welch joke than a pope joke.

"Don't you see what Whatley's after?" Seinfeld demands. "Total joke telling immunity. He's already got the big two religions covered. If he ever gets Polish citizenship, there'll be no stopping him."

Seinfeld decides to tell the priest he had met in Whatley's office about the dentist's pope jokes and does so by visiting the priest's confessional. The priest at first is pompous and officious, but then he laughs like a fool at the pope joke. What makes Seinfeld really angry, though, is that the priest does not laugh at a dentist joke Seinfeld follows it up with: "What's the difference between a dentist and a sadist? Newer magazines."

The next scene finds Seinfeld back in the dentist's chair and looking pained as Whatley pushes and pulls on his mouth.

"We about through?" Seinfeld asks.

"Oh, no, I'm just warming up," Whatley says. "Because I'm just a sadist with newer magazines." The remark makes it clear that the priest also violated the confidentiality of the confessional, which makes him as awful a character as any rabbi in the series.

"Father Curtis told me your little joke. I really didn't appreciate it," Whatley says.

"Well, what about all your Jewish jokes?" Seinfeld demands.

"I'm Jewish. You're not a dentist. You have no idea what my people have been through."

"The Jews?"

"No, the dentists. You know we have the highest suicide rate of any profession?"

"Is that why it's so hard to get an appointment?"

This time, it's Kramer whom Seinfeld meets up with at his apartment. "You have no idea what just happened with Whatley. It got back to him that I made this dentist joke, and he got all offended. Those people."

"Those people?" Kramer says. "Listen to yourself."

"What?" Seinfeld asks.

After comparing dentists to immigrants in search of a better life, Kramer tells Seinfeld, "You are an anti-dentite." And then he screams it: "You are a rabid anti-dentite. Oh, it starts with a few jokes and few slurs, 'Hey, denti!' Then next thing you're saying they should have their own schools."

"They do have their own schools," Seinfeld screams back at Kramer, who takes Seinfeld's remark as absolute confirmation that Seinfeld is an anti-dentite and runs screaming from the apartment.

The final scene takes place in a church, with all the cast members there for a wedding. Seinfeld is in attendance with a new girlfriend who enjoys his dentist jokes. After an exchange with a man in the pew in front of theirs, who calls Seinfeld "an anti-dentite bastard" and threatens to knock out his teeth, Seinfeld's girlfriend asks, "What was that all about?"

"Oh, I said something about a dentist and it got blown all out of proportion," Seinfeld says.

"Hey," she whispers, "what do you call a doctor who failed out of med school?"

"What?" Seinfeld says.

"A dentist."

"Hey, now that's a good one," Seinfeld says, smiling broadly. "Dentists."

"Yeah, dentists, who needs them?" the girlfriend says. "Not to mention the blacks and the Jews."

The episode ends on a freeze frame of Seinfeld's face just as his smile turns to a grimace.

As a series, *Seinfeld* was clearly conflicted about its Jewish identity—especially in the matter of George and Elaine. But we should not overlook episodes like "The Yada, Yada" that feature Seinfeld clearly self-identifying in a positive way as a Jew and then go on to explore Jewish identity with considerable depth for a sitcom. The first few encounters between Seinfeld and Whatley establish a humorous dialogue that lays the groundwork for a very sophisticated discourse on Jewish identity. While Seinfeld is thinking of Jewishness totally as a religion—which is something to which you can convert—Whatley is appropriating Jewish cultural identity (via the use of Yiddish language) and ethnic identity (with such remarks as the one about three thousand years of suffering). The tension among the meanings of "Jewish" is at the very heart of the humor in the episode and begs such questions in the thoughtful viewer's mind as, What part of Jewish identity can the convert lay claim to? Who is a Jew? What is a Jew? Is ethnic identity in general determined by heredity (descent) or choice (consent)?[13]

I would further argue that we have a fairly informed notion of identity—that each person's identity is made up of many identities—at work in the way that Seinfeld defines himself as a comedian first and a Jew second, as he lets his friends in on his theory that Whatley converted only for the jokes. In fact, Seinfeld actually *confesses* as much, where else but in the confessional:

"Tell me your sins, my son," the priest says, once he explains to Seinfeld that the padded board the comedian is sitting on is a kneeler, and Seinfeld repositions himself on his knees.

"Well, I should mention that I'm a Jew."

"That's no sin."

"Oh, good. Anyway, I wanted to talk to you about Dr. Whatley. I have a suspicion that he converted to Judaism purely for the jokes."

"And this offends you as a Jewish person?" the priest asks.

"No, it offends me as a comedian."

With Whatley, identity is even more fluid and multiple, moving from Catholic to Jew, back to Catholic, and then to dentist, with him able to lay claim to each in some way.

Dyed-in-the-wool *Seinfeld* haters would probably argue that the "antidentite" jokes ultimately trivialize anti-Semitism, and that is where the self-hatred is to be found in this episode. But you could say that any treatment of anti-Semitism in any television sitcom essentially trivializes it, if you take the view that laughing about something that serious trivializes it.

DEFINING A "JEWISH VIBE"

Mehlman said the idea for the episode came to him after one his closest friends, a convert to Judaism, made a Jewish joke—a joke he said he could no longer remember. "And, even though I completely identified him as a Jew, it was the one time when it dawned on me that he was a convert, and I thought to myself, 'I wonder how long it took him to feel comfortable making a joke like that.' And then I thought, 'Wouldn't it be funny if it like took him a day.'

"So, at the start of the show, I wanted this dentist to make a joke like that, but you have to be careful that it's not offensive, yet it has to be funny."

Mehlman said that, of all the funny things in that script, the joke that describes sitting in the sauna as a "Jewish workout" is his best work. "It's not even a joke. It's just a line," he said, "but it walks this very delicate line perfectly. It's funny enough, and it takes this little poke at Jews in an area where we're not that sensitive, you know, our supposed lack of athletic prowess."

On the staying power of the stereotype about Jews as non-athletes, Mehlman said, "I mean, it's still there. I'm watching Monday Night Football the other night, and I'm going, "Who's this Jay Fiedler guy [quarterback for the Miami Dolphins]? Is he really Jewish?"

Is that self-hatred? I don't think so, but again others might read it differently.

In arguing against the charge that *Seinfeld* was filled with Jewish self-hatred, *The Jewish Journal* described the kind of Jewishness it saw at the core of the series by saying "It's a Baby Boomer Jewishness: at home in America, taken for granted, more than a little ambivalent. It's as much a part of them as family, sex and work, and just as ripe for satire. There's nothing worshipful there. You can take it or leave it. Most of us loved it."[14]

I would vote for Michael Steadman's "Baby Boomer Jewishness" in *thirtysomething* over Jerry Seinfeld's—but, again, drama is a genre more suited to multiple dimensions and nuance of character. *The Jewish*

Journal's assessment of *Seinfeld* does highlight the notion of multiple selves, which is particularly worth remembering as successive generations of Jewish characters come to reflect in whatever manner the assimilation of some of the Jewish men and women from the larger society who create them. And this becomes an increasingly important point in trying to understand the relationship between social reality and on-screen images as the culture put in place by the Jewish founders waned.

Mehlman stressed such generational differences in the characters when asked to explain what he meant by "Jewish vibe," and whether it involved, for example, a rhythm of speech, as other Hollywood writers and producers had claimed.

"I don't think there's a particular rhythm for Jews the age of Jerry and his friends," the forty-five-year-old writer said. "I think Jews are assimilated enough that it's gone. I don't think Jerry had a particularly Jewish delivery, but the parents definitely did."

Mehlman cited an episode in which Frank Costanza is informed that there might be mice in the attic of his house.

"And he gets up out of his chair and screams, 'That's it. We're moving out. I cannot live with infestation.' I mean he really goes off screaming, 'I cannot live with infestation.'

"And then, really quietly, Estelle, his wife, goes, 'Awright, that's enough, Frank.' I mean, the parents were more Jewish."

According to Mehlman, the show's "Jewish vibe" had more to do with what characters talked about than with the manner in which they said it. "I think there's something Jewish about expressing things most people don't express, you know, like George talking about his lack of self-esteem and things like that," Mehlman said.

"There's also a lot of discussion about food and tipping, which are things that Jews seem to talk a lot about. I mean, every holiday seems to revolve around what you can eat and what you can't eat, and the show talked a lot about food—tons and tons about food. And, in terms of the Jewish vibe, there's a definite New York element to it," he added.

In the end, those within the Jewish community who celebrate *Seinfeld* for what they see as a positive or enlightened construction of Jewish identity usually wind up pointing to the show's enormous popularity as evidence for their point of view. Here is the way *The Jewish Journal* argued the case: "What's so different about Seinfeld? Well, first there's the matter of scale. It's the biggest thing on the tube . . . And unlike [Milton]

Berle and [Jack] Benny, he never changed his name . . . Viewers choose shows, so the programmers believe, based on whom they'd most like to invite into their living rooms. Right now, that's Jerry Seinfeld. In effect, America has chosen a Jew as its favorite Thursday night date . . ."[15]

The ways in which viewers choose shows are far more complicated than suggested here. In fact, viewers sometimes watch characters they hate and would never want in their living rooms, like J. R. Ewing (Larry Hagman) of the 1980s hit *Dallas*. But, having cited the "favorite Thursday night date" reading, I feel obliged to also include a very different reading. This one is suggested by the manner in which Seinfeld's Jewish parents were seen by the critic for the *Washington Post*: "Jerry's parents, meanwhile, lived in a South Florida condo where the population appeared to be made up mostly of Jews who were selfish and mean-spirited. You might start to chuckle at the antics of such characters and then be struck by the thought that somewhere an anti-Semite is probably getting a big laugh out of this, too."[16]

Selfish and mean-spirited also describes the character of Seinfeld himself. In a 1993 episode, George cries out, "There's a void, Jerry. There's a void. What gives you pleasure?" Jerry replies, "Listening to you. Your misery is my pleasure." That is typical of the dark, one-upmanship humor at the heart of the series. That remark by Seinfeld has been described as "his character's philosophy on life," which is "to out order someone in a restaurant, to get the better thing, that's the true contest of life," according to Seinfeld himself.[17]

Seinfeld is consumed with having the best material possessions: best watch, car, health club membership, best fruit juice in the refrigerator, and so forth. Meanwhile, he and his self-absorbed friends produce almost nothing of use to the culture. Just these two aspects alone would make Seinfeld a masculine construction of the Jewish-American Princess under Prell's definition.

Mehlman acknowledged that the four characters at the heart of the series were "not good people." But he still believes the series "was good for Jews."

"You know, just as there's a definite New York element to the show, at the same time, if you took your ten favorite episodes of *Seinfeld*, I bet you eight of them could have taken place in any city," he said.

To me, it's not a show about Jews, but about Americans. And they happened to be Jewish, and they happened to be relate-able. And, looking back on it, with all the complaints about the gossipy rabbi or the shaky *mohel*... and the doubts somebody like Brandon Tartikoff had about how it could succeed with this real Jewish vibe, in the end, I think Seinfeld was great for Jews.

And it's kind of a funny paradox, because these were not good people. These were people, who even though they remain great friends, they screw each other at every turn. And people die, people get deported, all kinds of horrible things happen because of these characters.

And, yet, I absolutely think it was good for the Jews. I think people got familiar with Jews in a good way and also a friendly way. Here was a show with '90s people who happened to be Jewish, and everybody was like, "Hey, they're just like us. They're funny." I mean, everybody loved these characters.

I spoke to a college audience at Auburn, which is in Alabama, and they absolutely loved the show. These are the kind of people who you would have thought in the beginning, "Well, we can't put this show on because people in Auburn, Alabama, will never like it." But they loved it.

In the end, I do not think it has to be either/or—*Seinfeld* is either self-hating or totally enlightened on the matter of Jewish identity. That's not the way it usually works in commercial culture, is it?

Despite his obvious and huge self-interest in the matter, I think Mehlman's analysis will become the historical consensus on *Seinfeld*, because it is the one that best embraces the contradictions and ironies of the series and the times in which it existed, by seeing the hyphen in Jewish-American as something that connected as much as it separated at the end of the twentieth century.

Looping Back, Breaking Ground,
and Calculating Loss — *100 Centre Street,*
The Education of Max Bickford, State of Grace

This may sound surprising, but I think it happened because of McCarthy and the right-wing times. All of a sudden in the most subtle kind of guilt-by-association way, so many Jews were [considered] left wing . . . And whether it was conscious or unconscious . . . they [the network founders and executives] suddenly got very, very shy about it.

Sidney Lumet, creator of *100 Centre Street,* on the disappearance of Jewish characters from network television in the 1950s and 1960s[1]

If you're a Jewish creator, it's not a just a simple matter of being censorious, or "I don't want to do it, because I might get in trouble." For an earlier generation, there was the post–World War II feeling that anything too overtly Jewish might not be understood or embraced by anybody else . . . But, even for my generation, there's a feeling that says, "Be careful. At any moment, they can take it away from you . . . Be very careful not to put too much out there lest it give rise to anti-Semitism."

Richard Rosenstock, Hollywood producer,
on creating Jewish characters today[2]

The journey of this book concludes where it began: in New York in the 1950s with a Jewish *auteur.* Instead of Gertrude Berg on Tremont Street in the Bronx, though, this time it is director Sidney Lumet in an old, rambling, rust-belt warehouse across the East River from Manhattan on 26th Avenue in Queens.

The year of my interview with Lumet was actually 2001, but it was a 1950s time warp I found on my visit to see the making of *100 Centre*

Street, Lumet's gritty series on the Arts & Entertainment (A&E) cable channel about life in and around New York City's night court, featuring a judge named Joe Rifkind. Played by Alan Arkin, Rifkind was at the start of the twenty-first century one of the most unselfconscious and quietly complex articulations of Jewish identity in the history of television.

ON THE SET WITH LUMET

A scene was just about to start shooting as I arrived on the cluster of soundstages and sets that make up the world of *100 Centre Street*, and everything suddenly fell silent. The production assistant who was showing me around and I stopped dead in our tracks just outside a little room as a voice called "action."

Inside the darkened room, about one hundred yards from the soundstage where the actors were about to play the scene, three people sat in tall director's chairs facing a bank of TV screens, dials, buttons, knobs, and microphones. The only light in the tiny room came from the bluish glow of the screens. Seated in the center chair, leaning forward with his face less than a foot from a grouping of four screens and a microphone, was Lumet, the seventy-seven-year-old director of such acclaimed films as *Network*, *The Pawnbroker*, and *12 Angry Men*.

"Three," he called out, snapping his fingers like a jazz musician counting time in the darkened room. "One," he said a few seconds later with a finger snap. Then silence.

"Two." Snap. Silence.

"One." Snap. Silence.

"And, three." Snap. Silence.

I knew he was directing via microphone the three cameras that were shooting the action being played out on a soundstage between Arkin and Phyllis Newman, who plays Rifkind's wife, Sarah. But in twenty-five years of visiting hundreds of sets and soundstages, I had never seen or heard it done quite like this, with the unmistakable sense of meter and the finger snaps.

I closed my eyes and focused on the voice and the snaps. After a few moments, I could feel it—the rhythm that Lumet heard in his head and was imposing on the scene even as it was being filmed.

You do not talk to Sidney Lumet when he is working. But, later, I told him how transported I felt standing in the darkness listening to him direct. But I also confessed to never having seen it done that way, and I asked him to explain.

"What you saw was what we used to do in live television in the 1950s as part of the technique," Lumet said. "We weren't just filming the scene, we were also editing it. That is your editing. What you saw me doing there, that's it. That's your edited copy."

As for the finger snaps: "The reason for that is that you'd be sitting there next to the technical director, and you'd say 'take two.' Well, would the 'two' be at the beginning of the word 'two,' or at the end of the word? And then you might be doing that with five or six cameras. So, rhythmically, the thing that was always best was to just snap your fingers at the actual moment you wanted them to change cameras."

Lumet, who started directing in 1952 for CBS on such anthology series as the *Alcoa-Goodyear Playhouse* and *Omnibus*, explained the use of that technique in 2001 by saying that in part it helped save money in the post-production process, where the raw footage is generally smoothed-out, dressed-up with music, and made ready for prime-time viewing. At $1.3 million per hour, Lumet was making *100 Centre Street*, which he created, for about $600,000 less than the average hour of network drama. Editing as he filmed is one of the ways he did that—the rhythm of the piece is established as it is filmed rather than in post-production.

But there was another reason for the 1950s, live-television style of direction, Lumet said: "It allowed for a tremendous individual style of direction" that resulted in directors making more personal statements through their work. That freedom of expression is one of the reasons the era is often referred to as a golden age, according to Lumet.

While his diversity of subject matter and genre hopping in films ranging from *Murder on the Orient Express* to *Dog Day Afternoon* are remarkable, one constant to Lumet's long and distinguished career has been his exploration of Jewish identity in such feature films as *The Pawnbroker* (1965), *Bye, Bye Braverman* (1969), and *Stranger Among Us* (1992). In fact, the argument could be made that he has explored that topic as widely and wisely as any American film director.[3]

But why didn't such exploration take place on television? Why didn't Lumet get the chance to do that on television until 2001 with *100 Centre Street*? That is the question I came to ask Lumet. Why did so much great, creative, Jewish talent that was part of the television industry in the early

1950s in New York have to leave the medium to explore that aspect of their identity openly? Mel Brooks, Neil Simon, Paddy Chayefsky—the roll is far too long to call.

Some of them tried and occasionally managed to deal with Jewish identity in the earliest, most experimental years of the medium. As mentioned earlier, Chayefsky's *Holiday Song,* a *Philco Television Playhouse* presentation in 1952, told the story of a crisis of faith by a cantor on Long Island. But even here, the pattern of Jewish self-censorship was already at work, with David Susskind, then a young producer on the *Philco* series, telling Chayefsky the story was "too Jewish" and urging him "to rewrite it with the central character as a priest or minister." Which is what Chayefsky did. And that is how it would have aired, had not Fred Coe, a more senior producer on the series, urged Chayefsky to go back to the original version.[4]

The one piece of firsthand testimony that had eluded me in all the years of research for this book was an answer from Jewish artists like Lumet who were there in the earliest years of television as to why they thought Jews were made invisible onscreen, particularly in the years 1954 to 1972, when there were no leading characters. Many of the television pioneers are simply no longer alive today, but the ones who I had been able to ask always found a way not to answer.

In some cases involving former network executives, the older men simply shut down the interviews at that point—in one case, the person I was interviewing grew more and more angry at me as I laid out the chronology of Jews censoring Jews. It was as if I was asking them to talk about something that was simply not discussed. After a number of interviews with Hollywood Jews who were baby boomers like me in which we hit no such walls, I came to believe generational differences were at the core of my problem with some of the pioneers.

But Lumet did not shut down when I asked him—not at all. He paused for just a few seconds to think about it and then said, "This may sound surprising, but I think it happened because of McCarthy and the right-wing times. All of a sudden in the most subtle kind of guilt-by-association way, so many Jews were [considered] left wing. And whether . . . it was conscious or unconscious—my guess is that it was probably largely unconscious—but they [the network founders and executives] suddenly got very, very shy about it."

Lumet's mention of McCarthy reminded me of a recollection by Charlotte Brown, the executive producer of *Rhoda*, from her childhood. She shared the memory in connection with me asking how she thought her experiences growing up might have affected her work in limiting overt signifiers of Jewish identity in the pioneering CBS series from the 1970s:

"There's this old expression: Is it good for the Jews, is it bad for the Jews," Brown said, using the same expression that Marshall Herskovitz did at the start of this book to explain a sense of self-consciousness still felt among Jewish writers and producers in Hollywood today. "And I have very distinct memories as a kid growing up of watching my father read the newspaper during the McCarthy era and [him] just wincing whenever the names [of those called communists or subversives] were Jewish. And I think that at some level, however subliminal, it makes an impression on your brain.

"And I think in a way for Jewish writers—I mean, a lot has been written about I'm not going to say anti-Semitism—but that we're more sensitive to that sort of thing. And we need to be. I mean we're always aware of it."[5]

Lumet's explanation also resonated with the words of film historian Jonathan Rosenbaum's description of the McCarthy era as a time when "there became an identification in peoples' minds of things that went together: intellectuals, Jews, Russians, communists."[6]

I tried to offer a sense of those "right-wing times" at the end of chapter 2, with the HUAC hearings targeting Hollywood Jews and the Jewish moguls starting to lose their film studios, in an effort to provide context for the actions of the founders in blacklisting performers like Philip Loeb, banishing *The Goldbergs* from network TV, and establishing an unspoken policy as to those "people from New York."

Whether their actions seem understandable or not, what the founders helped create with their de-Semiticized prime-time landscape starting in the mid-1950s was a media socialization process that I believe taught Jewish viewers they were not part of the mainstream. The founders and their lieutenants were, in effect, socializing via television a generation of Jews to believe Jewish identity was not something you announced—just as the moguls had done with film.

Brown's memory of watching television as a Jewish child in the 1950s and 1960s is representative. "I grew up watching Molly Goldberg...I was such a little kid. But I knew they [the Goldbergs] were Jewish, and my parents liked the show. I guess they used to listen to it on the radio at first. It was just one of those shows that was endorsed in our house, so you watched it without question.

"But what I remember most about growing up with TV is that there were no families like my family after *The Goldbergs* went off the air. My favorite show was *Father Knows Best*, but . . . that was not my family. There just wasn't anybody like me on television. I remember when I was a little older the movie *Majorie Morningstar*, and I was supposed to believe Natalie Wood [the non-Jewish actress who played the Jewish character of Marjorie] was Jewish. But at least it was a Jewish female character. On TV, it was Lucy and Donna Reed, and there were no Jewish women."

Gary David Goldberg, the creator of *Family Ties* and *Brooklyn Bridge*, had a similar experience as a child. "I remember *The Goldbergs*. I happened to love that show and watched it in Grandma's living room," Goldberg said. "But, outside of that there were no shows I really felt connected with . . . I wasn't a huge television watcher. We would watch *Father Knows Best*, and my world had no relationship to *Father Knows Best* in a million years."[7]

Barry Levinson, the Academy Award–winning writer-director who has explored Jewish-American life as thoughtfully as anyone this side of Lumet in feature films like *Diner* and *Avalon*, points out that there were Jewish characters on television when he was growing up—but they didn't self-identify as Jews.

"You're saying there really were no leading Jewish characters on television in the '50s and '60s, right? I agree," he said.

"Historically, there has been a pattern of de-emphasizing Jewish characters. However, there were a number of Jewish performers and actors who were on shows. George Burns was Jewish, but he wasn't Jewish with Gracie Allen. Jack Benny is Jewish, but he's not Jewish in his show."[8]

Reacting to a statement from another producer, the late Danny Arnold, who said that he purposefully obscured the Jewish identity of one of his television characters in the 1970s, Barney Miller of the ABC sitcom of the same title, in part to attract a larger audience, Levinson said, "I totally disagree with the 'larger audience' comment. It's as if to say, if there's a Jewish person in the show, you're not going to get an audience. That's a bogus argument [as to why there were no overtly Jewish leading characters]. I don't think it's valid. I don't think we're not going to watch a show because a guy happens to be Jewish unless it really suddenly gets into the whole thing of Judaism or whatever and becomes a whole other issue. A Jewish detective is neither here nor there."

It is one thing to *not* see yourself on television, as was the case for Jewish viewers when it came to prime-time characters during most of the 1950s and all of the 1960s. It was during the 1960s that television became the principle storyteller of the culture, a truly national medium with shared moments like those experienced in 1963 in the wake of the assassination of President John F. Kennedy.

Sonia Manzano, a Latina who plays the Latina character, Maria, on *Sesame Street*, described her reaction to such ethnic invisibility as a child by saying, "I can remember when I was a kid in the Bronx watching hours and hours of television, and never seeing anyone who looked like me or spoke like me, and never seeing a community that looked like mine . . . I know if a child spends his childhood not seeing himself reflected in society, which is mostly on television, it will wear him down . . . If he does not see himself in the media, he does not see himself as part of the society."[9]

TRYING TO DECODE HIDDEN JEWISH IDENTITY

But for Jewish viewers, it was even more complicated in some ways than just being invisible when it came to television. As Levinson's statement indicates, there were actors and performers playing non-Jewish characters who some members of the Jewish audience knew to be Jews. In that sense, Jewish viewers watched the depiction of mainstream society in prime time from the margins, trying to decode the hidden identity of the performers much the same way that homosexual viewers did with movies and television.

Lynn Roth made the point when she said in a 1997 interview for this study, "You know what, we're still in the closet when it comes to being Jews. It's the same way as when some character is homosexual. Maybe they had a girlfriend, maybe they didn't. Maybe they were this, maybe they were that."[10]

A Jewish editor reading this book in manuscript form commented that " 'The *Dick Van Dyke Show*' is a Jewish show the way '*Mame*' is a gay musical." Sure, but the point is, why did its Jewishness have to be disguised? Of course, many Jewish viewers could read it as Jewish, but what message did they get from the fact that it needed to be disguised and decoded?

The widespread experience by Jewish viewers of trying to decode hidden Jewish identity on television is the very dynamic behind the joke of Al Franken's Jew/Not-a-Jew skit on *Saturday Night Live*. Gary David Goldberg used the same decoding game in an episode of *Brooklyn Bridge*. He said it came from his experience of television viewing as a child.

"We would really play that game, which was Jew or Not-a-Jew. There's actually a very funny moment in *Brooklyn Bridge* where they're watching the West Point Glee Club on the *[Ed] Sullivan Show* and Alan [the 13-year-old protagonist] says, 'Let's try to pick out the Jewish guys. Grandma, you take the top row. I got the middle. Natie [Alan's younger brother], you got the people on the floor,'" Goldberg said.

"And we did it all time when I was a kid: Dinah Shore, Tony Curtis. And this went on throughout my entire life with Grandma, even with Michael Fox [who starred in two series created and produced by Goldberg]. She'd go, 'He's Jewish.' I'd say, 'Grandma, he's not.' She'd say, 'Fox, it's a Jewish name.' I'm like, 'I don't care, grandma. I'm telling you he's not.' The pilot for *Brooklyn Bridge* deals with whether Gil Hodges was Jewish, remember? The reason she thought he was Jewish was because he used to throw a kiss to his wife after he hit a home run."

Goldberg says the West Point viewing event actually took place in his life. But, whether it did or not, the fact that the game is played on *Brooklyn Bridge* with the West Point Glee Club is noteworthy. West Point is, after all, about as American an institution as you can find. Looking for hidden Jewish identity among its ranks certainly seems to suggest a desire to belong to the mainstream—or, at least, the desire to see Jews as part of it. The humor is in the question of how you could possibly discern such identity given the identical gray uniforms and brush haircuts on the cadets and the dark grainy picture on the first wave of black and white television sets in American homes in the early 1950s. The wisdom within that humor is the desperate effort of Jews to see themselves on America's main stage of prime-time television during this era.

The lessons of self-censorship and hidden Jewish identity in the media were so well learned by young Jews growing up in the 1950s and 1960s that sometimes they were seen even when they weren't there. In a 1995 interview, Tartikoff, who served as entertainment president of NBC during the 1980s and then head of Paramount Pictures, was asked to name a movie that changed his life. He picked *Barefoot in the Park*, starring Robert Redford and Jane Fonda in the film based on a Neil Simon play. Tartikoff, who first saw the film in 1967, when he was eighteen years old, explained how he would have cast the film version during his years as an executive at NBC and Paramount.

"If I was producing the movie version of the stage play, I might have gone against the maxim of show business, which is, you know: 'Write Yiddish, cast British,'" Tartikoff said. "In this movie, I'm sure Neil Simon wrote it to be about neurotic Jewish people in New York City, and then, of course, they cast it very gentile with Jane Fonda and Robert Redford."[11]

Actually, while Jewish-to-gentile was often the pattern for Simon plays as they went to film, the leads for *Barefoot in the Park* when it played on Broadway were Redford and Elizabeth Ashley—both non-Jews. But, as an eighteen-year-old, Tartikoff saw the message usually sent by the mainstream media about the need to obscure or even hide Jewish identity even when it was not there.

There is another important aspect of Tartikoff's statement involving his use of the word "maxim" in terms of "the thing that was always said to Jewish writers," which was "Write Yiddish, cast British." Various forms of that expression, along with the concept of it as a rule or maxim, were heard time and time again in interviews for this study. Richard Rosenstock, the creator of *Flying Blind*, used it when talking about his arrival in Hollywood in 1978.

"When I first broke in [as a television writer], you know, they give you the rules of the business and the rules of comedy, and one of them is: write Jewish, cast gentile," Rosenstock said.

"Lowell Ganz [executive producer of *Happy Days*] told me once that one of the big changes they made in *Happy Days*—which started as a single-camera kind of muted show . . . and then moved into a multiple-camera setup which is a much more up-tempo rhythm—involved the writing. He said they wrote much more Jewish rhythms [which are faster paced in his estimation] for characters, although they would be completely embodied by supposedly incredibly WASP-y characters," Rosenstock said.[12]

Another use of the word "rule" cited earlier in the study came from network programmer Mike Dann, who used it connection with New

York, saying, "There was another rule that you couldn't have shows from New York, because everybody hated New York."[13] In chapter 3, I argued that Dann was, in fact, citing the phantom but often invoked rule against "people from New York, men with mustaches, and Jews," in his mention of New York.

What reveals itself is a kind of media socialization in which those Jews who were born during and after World War II grew up as viewers with television sending them a wall of messages suggesting that Jewish identity was something to erase, obscure, or hide in prime-time characters. Then, for those who actually went to Hollywood to work as novice writers or producers, those messages were literally stated as a rule of admission to the television industry—often by other, more experienced Jews serving as protectors.

Is this not exactly what happened with Sheldon Leonard and Carl Reiner as *The Head of the Family*, which CBS had rejected, was transformed into *The Dick Van Dyke Show* via recasting and de-ethnicizing? We also saw it in the instruction Susan Harris gave Danny Jacobson, as well as in the words of Lorne Michaels and Al Franken.

That two-step process of acculturation to the rules of no-Jews-in-prime-time worked hand in glove with all the other forces working to inhibit Jewish imagery, that we have seen in this book, forces that ranged from the Motion Picture Project in Hollywood in the 1950s—the self-described "Jewish Legion of Decency" with its Stone Reports and closed-door meetings with studio executives aimed at eliminating series like *The Goldbergs*—to the marches outside CBS's Black Rock headquarters urging cancellation of *Bridget Loves Bernie*. And, if you managed to avoid a protest, there were calls like the one Franken described from the Anti-Defamation League, or the inordinate amount of negative mail from Jewish viewers that producers say they could count on whenever Jewish issues were raised. In that regard, Carol Leifer, one of the writers on *Seinfeld*, recounted how NBC was swamped with negative mail in response to the episodes about the shaky *mohel* and the indiscreet rabbi.

"That got so much negative feedback from Jews in the audience," Leifer said. "I mean, there were so many letters about both those episodes. Then, there's the episode in which Kramer gets novocaine and sounds like he's retarded, and one, maybe two letters. I mean, nothing [in comparison]."[14]

And, always, there were the network executives themselves. If not

Paley and Sarnoff then their gatekeeper deputies who tried to avoid troublemaker shows about blacks or Jews that would invite protest.

As Silverman put it, "Who needs that grief? Who needs advertiser boycotts and the NAACP and JDL? The best thing is to just shy away from it—just don't do those kinds of ethnic shows that are going to cause trouble."[15] And so it went down through the years to Tarses and Tarikoff labeling series as "too Jewish" in the 1990s.

One of the most surprising aspects of my study is the continuity from the original Hollywood Jews in the 1920s to the men and women running network television in the 1990s despite all the change and accelerated assimilation that took place during the twentieth century for Jews in America. One of the major themes of this history is that there was a culture—in every sense of that word—of Jewish media management that held across generations despite all the acculturation and change in Jewish-American life during the last half of the twentieth century. Unless you understand that culture, you can understand almost nothing about Jewish identity on television no matter how many text-based or audience studies you undertake.

Go back to Tartikoff talking about *Barefoot in the Park* in 1995, for example. While Tartikoff was no highbrow, he did not pick *Barefoot in the Park* as a film that changed his life because he thought it was such a great film. He picked it, he said, because of the way it changed his perception of popular entertainment after seeing it for the first time as an eighteen-year-old. As he described the experience:

> In 1967, I was a movie usher working at a theater in San Francisco, the Alhambra on Polk Street. And it was a summer job right before I went to college. This movie, *Barefoot in the Park*, was the first movie that was playing my initial week at the movie theater. What you realize very quickly if you're a movie usher is—and I don't care what film it is, even if it's *Citizen Kane*—you can't watch it twenty-one times a week. And *Barefoot in the Park* is hardly *Citizen Kane*. So, what I started doing to keep my sanity, I started watching the audience watch the movie. You're now noticing where the audience is laughing where maybe you weren't. [He cites two comic scenes that involve physical, almost slapstick humor.] That wasn't my taste, but I learned from the audience . . . So I always credit my job as a movie usher and, in par-

ticular, *Barefoot in the Park* as the film that started getting me to pay attention to the audience as opposed to my own taste.

Tartikoff's sense of himself as someone in the theater yet outside the audience—somehow standing in the margin as it were and observing mainstream taste—is remarkably similar to the stance taken by Paramount founder Adolph Zukor and several other Jewish moguls in explaining their success in the entertainment industry. Compare young Tartikoff's recollection with this description of the moguls from *Jew in the Text*:

The genius of the Jewish immigrant entrepreneurs who created the economic and ideological system of Hollywood was often recognized by themselves as a patient and acute "ordinariness" of perception. For example, Adolph Zukor (a pioneer of the studio system and founder of Paramount Studios) appropriated for the title of his autobiography a "showbiz" truism, attributed elsewhere to other early film entrepreneurs—"The Public Is Never Wrong." There he is at pains to describe himself as a particularly observant member of the audience—this is a common autobiographical trope for that generation of Jewish entrepreneurs—sitting in the auditorium, watching the film and the audience at the same time, thus violating the commonplace fixation that is normally assumed to guarantee the cinematic experience. The Jewish immigrant entrepreneurs, who often started in the fashion and entertainment industries in the U.S.A., found new ways of analyzing the aspirations of the host culture.[16]

Some eighty years of accelerated assimilation separated Zukor, who was born in 1873 in a small, poor Hungarian village, and Tartikoff, who came of age in middle-class, suburban New York in the second half of the twentieth century. Zukor had no formal education, while Tartikoff earned a bachelor's degree from Yale University before moving up the corporate ladder of General Electric's NBC and then taking control of Zukor's Paramount. Along with his boss, Grant Tinker, there was no one more influential in network television in the 1980s than Tartikoff, who crafted the prime-time schedules that made NBC the top-rated and most-profitable network of the decade. This is the same Tartikoff who tried to keep *Seinfeld* from ever seeing the light of prime time as a regular series.

The biographies and attitudes toward Jewish characters of Tarses, at ABC, and Jeff Sagansky, the head of programming at CBS in the 1980s, are virtually interchangeable with Tartikoff's, except Tarses went to Williams College and Sagansky to Harvard. Like Tartikoff, Sagansky would complete another weird loop, taking over one of the motion picture studios, Sony (formerly Columbia), after leaving CBS.

"YOU CAN PUT THESE PEOPLE ON THE SCREEN?"

Given all of that, it is a wonder that any Jewish leading characters ever found their way into American living rooms via network television. But in several interviews with baby boomer producers, I also heard support for Douglas Kellner's belief that American popular culture is rife with "contradictions" and that, even in the most repressive clusters of images, there are also often ones that can be read as "emancipatory."[17]

One of the central claims of this study is that, even in a three-network universe, the lack of any leading Jewish characters for extended periods—such as existed from 1955 to 1972 and 1978 to 1987—is remarkable. To explain it, you have to investigate the production milieu and the ethnicity of the network executives buying the shows and the Hollywood producers creating and selling them.

During the years that the Jewish founders owned the networks, the nature of the industrial process greatly distorted the usual relationship between what is shown on network television screens and the larger society. Images, tensions, themes, and ideas from the larger society that traditionally find their way onto television screens as they are reworked into drama and comedy by producers living in that society were virtually absent. A more normal relationship—one in which those tensions, themes, and images find their way in some form onto the screen—only took hold starting in 1987, after the founders had sold off the networks to large corporations with no particular ethnic makeup.

The first series to embody those tensions of the larger society, as we have seen, was *thirtysomething*. Even the sitcoms of the 1990s, problematic as many were in their negative constructions of Jewish identity and idealized depictions of gentiles, were still symbolically, at least, dealing with various aspects of the process of assimilation as it was taking place for Jews in the larger society.

But the same thing had happened in film some twenty to twenty-five years earlier, as the studio system controlled by the Jewish moguls gave way to smaller independent film companies often controlled in their distribution needs, if no other way, by vast multinational corporations with no particular ethnic makeup. And so, at the very time that television was offering a landscape devoid of leading Jewish characters in the late 1960s and early 1970s, feature films were suddenly offering overtly Jewish characters, as Jewish directors and writers reacted to the ethnic concerns of the larger society in 1960s America and found their own voices in a post-mogul Hollywood that was now willing to allow Jewish expression.

Producer Richard Rosenstock's career path is representative of many of the baby-boomer Hollywood Jews I interviewed for this book. Sitting under the poster for the 1969 film *Goodbye, Columbus* in his Beverly Hills office at Castle Rock Entertainment, Rosenstock named the films that he says changed his life, *The Graduate* (1967), *Bye, Bye Braverman* (1968), *The Heartbreak Kid* (1972), each featuring Jewish stars and Jewish concerns. Rosenstock offered this portrait of the young artist discovering a new world of Jewish images and messages that contradicted what television had been telling him about Jewish identity:

> I believe television always takes its lead from other media. I don't believe it ever leads ... Me and most of my contemporaries were shaped by what movies and literature were doing at the time ... when American movies sort of found their voice with the new wave of American movies in the late '60s and early '70s that were taking root. There was an array of identity out there for us, all these Jewish writers and Jewish directors and Jewish themes in the movies. And really the breakthrough at that time was Jewish leading men. You know, there were always Jews in comedy ... But then, in the late '60s, Roth exploded, because *Portnoy* [the novel *Portnoy's Complaint*] had come out right about the same time that the film version of *Goodbye Columbus* came out. And then the doors opened, and you could go to the movies and there were suddenly all these identifiably Jewish leading men: Richard Benjamin and George Segal and Richard Dreyfuss and Dustin Hoffman. To say nothing of Woody Allen, who very possibly influenced us all more than anybody. And you say, "Oh, we can deal

with this stuff. We can deal with these themes. We can put people in these films who are like us. America isn't recoiling in mass horror. They get it." So, it was not surprising to me that eventually there would be a breakthrough in television. But I believe it followed the movies. First, with movies teaching my generation that we could deal with Jewish themes starting at the end of the 1960s . . . and then leadership of the networks changing [in the late 1980s] the way leadership of the movie studios had changed.

Rosenstock spoke lovingly and at length about each of the films that told him Jewish identity could be explored on the screen, but the actual sense of epiphany occurred at *Goodbye Columbus*, he said:

And, so, I went to see *Goodbye, Columbus*, and once I recovered from the first closeup of Ali McGraw, which thirty years later is still so iconic to me. But I watched this movie, and I just sat there stunned by it. It's not the best-made movie ever. But it woke me up. I was sitting there saying to myself, "You can do this? You can put these people on the screen? You can put their concerns on the screen, the minutiae of the class consciousness between Jews? You can do this? Yes, you can do this! You can put this whole lifestyle and milieu full of details on screen!" . . . I didn't overtly back in 1969 as a high school kid sitting in the theater say, "Boy, what I'm going to do is write television and movies like *Goodbye Columbus*," but that's where it began, and elements of it just continue to pop up in my work . . .

Seeing such films led Rosenstock to study film at New York University, and then he stumbled upon another crack in the mainly non-Jewish landscape of prime-time television. In 1977, after graduating from NYU, he and a partner starting writing and trying to sell scripts for feature films. As Rosenstock tells it, one night in 1977, while aimlessly watching television in his New York apartment, he came across a series that stopped him cold, *Busting Loose*, a short-lived series on CBS in 1977.

So, one night I'm switching channels and I come upon this odd, little, very low-profile show. I mean, it's a complete accident that I found it. It was a show about a twenty-five-year-old Jewish kid named Lenny Markowitz, who had just moved out from his overbearing, very Old World style parents into his very first apartment, where he would hang out with his friends and blah, blah, blah, blah, blah. And I'm watching this thing, and I'm thinking, "Wow, this shouldn't be hard to write. Twenty-five-year-old guy living on his own like me"... And so, we wrote a spec [a script written on speculation], sent it to them and got hired... Amazingly enough, that's my first job, and, despite this history we're talking about, it's on a show with a Jewish character in the lead played by Adam Arkin, who is also identifiably Jewish. I mean, nobody in the show says, "Hey, Lenny, you're Jewish. Hey, Lenny, you're Jewish." And I don't think Lenny ever self-identified. But Lenny was Jewish... It wasn't a very good show. It's not a show anybody remembers or particularly remembers even hearing about it. But it was on... And, yes, after it went off and *Rhoda* ended [1978], that was it for Jewish characters for a long time on network television. But it was enough for me to see that it was possible. And, yes, there still was all this resistance, network and otherwise, but there were also people trying to do it in increments.

Indicative of how much resistance to Jewish characters there still was in 1978 is the case of *Paper Chase*, a CBS spinoff of the highly successful feature film about life for first-year students at an Ivy League law school. The ensemble series, which was produced by 20th Century Fox Television for CBS, had no overtly Jewish students or professors. It was cancelled by the network after just one year in 1979.

But, in 1983, 20th Century Fox managed to interest the Showtime premium cable channel in resurrecting *Paper Chase* as its first original prime-time series. The production company made Lynn Roth an executive producer on the series, which was titled *Paper Chase: The Second Year*. She described her thoughts as she took over production of the series in 1982:

> When I took over the show, there were two things that were sorely missing from its abbreviated life on CBS: Jews and women. And obviously you look at any law school in those years, and there were plenty of women and plenty of Jews. So, I introduced a character named [Gerald] Golden, who was played by an actor named Michael Tucci... What I was trying to do was put in a character who you knew was Jewish: when you went to his house there would be a menorah there, he had some problems with anti-Semitism, in his vocabulary every so often he would use a Yiddish word. But he was an integrated Jew. He wasn't somebody who was davening in the middle

of a case or something... But I remember going to that meeting back in 1982—the times were so different back then—and saying we don't have any Jews or any women in this show, or not enough. And, if we're trying to fashion this after the Harvard or Yale Law School, we have to rectify this. We have to have some authenticity here. I think, if I had added too many, there would have been maybe some kind of objection. But everybody at the meeting knew it was such an oversight not to have any Jewish law students and professors that I was able to get it through.

And then Roth added another, Connie Lehman (Jane Kaczmarek), that same season, followed by a third in 1985 with Lainie Kazan as Rose Samuels, an older student who comes to law school after a divorce. Roth allows that some of her success in adding Jewish characters might have been the result of working with a fairly new cable channel rather than the networks. "Showtime could have easily resisted, and they didn't," she says.

But, by the time she added Samuels in 1985, all three networks had already been sold by the Jewish founders. And, even though the no-Jews culture they had established clearly lived on, with network presidents still policing against surplus visibility with the expression "too Jewish," producers would find that if they pushed Jewish identity hard enough, as Herskovitz and Zwick did in 1986 when they were negotiating a spot in ABC's prime-time lineup for *thirtysomething*, that there was no longer anyone at the very top of the network food chain who cared enough to issue an iron-clad "no."

There is still some resistance, as the culture lives on in network executives who rose through the ranks in the days of the no-Jews rules. Marshall Herskovitz gave a sense of how that resistance would surface when he said, "If tomorrow we decided that we wanted to pitch an hourlong dramatic show about an Orthodox Jewish family living in New York, I think Stu Bloomberg [then chairman of ABC Entertainment] and Jamie Tarses [then president of ABC Entertainment] and all the other Jewish people who we deal with at the networks and like very much would look at us and say, 'Please don't do that.'"

Responding to that statement, producer Jan Oxenberg, of *Relativity*, asked Herskovitz if he thought such lingering resistance was in part the product of "a residual fear" among Hollywood Jews "of the accusation that Jews control Hollywood?" Herskovitz said he did.[18]

That accusation, which is still heard in some quarters today despite the sale of the motion picture studios and television networks, hung over virtually every interview done for and word written in this study. Fear of being misread and somehow contributing to the anti-Semitism that often accompanies the accusation has been with me consciously since I started working on this study in 1991. Beyond that, I wonder if subconsciously it did not keep others and me from attempting the kind of image study and history I offer here until then—after the Jewish founders had departed the scene.

In the fall of 1992, a story I wrote about the new Jewish characters like Neil Barish and Paul Buchman in the network lineups was published in a Sunday edition of the *Baltimore Sun*. It touched briefly on the history of self-censorship of Jewish characters by Jewish producers and network executives, as well as the near-total control of the prime-time landscape that the founders enjoyed for several decades. Late that night, a message was left on my home answering machine. The voice sounded like that of an elderly woman speaking with a slight European accent. In an angry voice, she said, "You fool, how could you say such things in the newspaper? You have no idea what you have done with your stupid article, the ammunition you give our enemies. You have no idea. These are not things we discuss in public this way. You should be so, so sorry for what you have done." The voice sent shivers through me as I sat in the dark replaying the message. I came close during that sleepless night and many others the last eleven years to ending the study because of such possible readings.

But I am convinced of the need for this history and image study even at the risk of such readings. In terms of the history, it is a reminder of how important it is to study the production milieu, especially as to how that milieu can warp the more normal relationship we have come to expect between television and social reality. It also reiterates how important a role the ethnicity of those involved in production and distribution can be, while challenging the assumption that, if persons of a certain ethnic group are included in the decision-making process, then images of that ethnic group in the media will automatically be more representative.

In the case of Jews and television, what this study found were Jewish gatekeepers actively policing against surplus visibility—too much ethnicity in the minds of the gatekeepers, who used the expression "too Jewish" to explain their objections to *anything* Jewish during certain periods of time. Rather than more and representative Jewish images, what we often got were no Jewish images at all on network television.

The lesson is still relevant, despite massive changes in the media landscape. In spite of all the new channels and networks in the new millennium, a frightening consolidation of power among a handful of giant media conglomerates has the makings of an industrial milieu as tightly controlled and homogeneous as that of the Jewish founders with a two-and-then-three-network universe from the 1940s until the 1980s. The self-conscious concerns of those media conglomerates could distort the assumed relationship between on-screen images and social reality in much the same way as the psychology of the Jewish founders did with images of ethnic identity.

As for images that did find their way into our living rooms, we started with ethnicity in *The Goldbergs* and saw in Molly a character who embodied some of the tensions of the larger society in terms of gender and assimilation during the 1950s. But we also saw in Uncle David the beginnings of a pattern of the neurotic, feminized Jewish male. The most progressive, multidimensional image of Jewish masculinity was Michael Steadman in 1987. And even Ken Olin, the actor who played Steadman, thought the character a "little neurotic and whiny" compared to non-Jewish male characters in prime time.

But compared to men, Jewish women were mainly invisible. If they did exist, it was seldom as the object of desire. The interface of idealized non-Jewish women with Jewish women who are depicted as smothering mothers or self-absorbed, nonproductive, sexless, shopaholic girlfriends and mates is one of the most persistent patterns we have seen. But it is not just a matter of the gentile woman being idealized at the expense of her Jewish counterpart. What this study catalogued is a pattern of non-Jewish women having the power to literally transform the Jewish male from neurotic, ill-at-ease outsider to fully invested participant in mainstream America.

That is the dominant narrative of assimilation that network television started to tell in the late 1980s, as it began to mature in matters of Jewish identity with the founders gone and the arrival of Michael Steadman and

Dr. Joel Fleischman. And what did that maturation include in the 1990s? For one thing, a Jewish woman, Fran Fine, being transformed from neurotic, ill-at-ease outsider to fully invested participant in mainstream America through her relationship with a non-Jewish man.

AND WHAT ABOUT TODAY?

As I walked away from Lumet's world of *100 Centre Street* in the fall of 2001, I knew this would not be a book with a happy ending. Talking to Lumet and Arkin in separate interviews, it was impossible not to appreciate the care each took in creating and bringing Judge Rifkind—former police officer, night-school law graduate and dyed-in-the-wool liberal—to life. Listening to them talk so comfortably about creating Jewish identity, you could almost forget what an incredibly troubled history it had been for more than half a century.

"One of the things that I spoke to Sidney about before I took the part was Rifkind as a Jew," Arkin said.[19] "The thing in the first episode that drew me to Rifkind was the fact that he was not a typical 'New York Jew.' He was unique.

"But I said to Sidney, 'I can see the danger. He's got a very specific kind of sense of humor, and I don't want him to turn into a complaining Upper West Side guy who goes to Zabar's when he's not working and has a *New York Times* stuffed in his tweed jacket. That's the one thing I'm adamant about, Sidney. I didn't want him to turn into that kind of character.'

"So he's specific and he's complicated. He's a tough guy who's a humanist. He became a cop for reasons that were stupid, and I think he realizes that now. He became a cop because he wanted to reconcile the poor people and the 'unwashed' with the police department in New York City, and it doesn't work that way . . . But his being Jewish is just one part of all of that," Arkin said.

Later in his interview Lumet used some of the same language, describing Rifkind's Jewishness as "just a part of who he is." Lumet said one of the fundamental goals he had for the series was for it to be "unselfconscious and unexploitative" in its treatment of Jewish identity. "Well, it's my own invention and it's the way I would want it treated," he said by way of explaining the emphasis.

"When Alan said he wanted to do it, he said, 'Sidney, my only reservation is let's not make him quote-unquote Jewish.' Now, by that he didn't mean that he wanted to hide, that he wanted to make him white bread. What he didn't want was the usual cliché. I mean, on a farcical level—and, by the way, it's a terrific farce, so I'm not saying this as a putdown—but on the farcical level, he didn't want it played [as] the Nanny's mother.

"So, we were very, very careful about it. This year [the 2001–2002 season], there's an act ending [a scene ending leading to a commercial] where Rifkind's given a rather esoteric definition of two choices that a certain character in this particular episode might have. And the character says to him, 'Well, how do you know which?' And he points to his heart and he says, *tachlis*. And she looks mystified. And he says, 'Wisdom.'

"And, you're quite right, unless it came from somebody like me, one wouldn't even know that word. I'm not even talking about talking Yiddish. I'm talking about enough colloquial Jewish upbringing to know it's irony and the whole sense of what that word means . . . It's true, there was no place for any of that on television for all those years, and it is a great loss . . . And I believe you do have to go back to McCarthy to explain it."

The sense of loss is overwhelming. As I wrote the final words of this book in the spring of 2002, in addition to Judge Rifkind on A&E, there was Richard Dreyfuss's college professor, Max Bickford, in *The Education of Max Bickford* on CBS. Like Rifkind, Bickford was not only at ease with his Jewishness, he seemed to really like being Jewish. And while his Jewish identity was a healthy part of who he was, it did not totally define him in a one-dimensional way. *The Education of Max Bickford*, featuring a Jewish historian who teaches American Studies to mostly privileged students at a private college, appreciated differences among Jews in a way very few other American television series have.

"One of the aspects of being Jewish in America is that there are traditional Jews, religious Jews, cultural Jews, secular Jews. That's rarely been delineated, and I have a lot of fun doing that. I think it's important. I think it's fun to live in this character as an American Jew as I feel me, as an American Jew, really does live in this world," Dreyfuss said.[20]

"Max is a fiercely secular Jew who comes from a more traditional or religious family . . . He is more secular than his father. And he probably has some political problems with the Jewish community as in synagogues and joining temples. He was also a little more left wing than traditional

American Jewish. I think he's a very familiar character to me and many of the people I know. He is less religious and very Jewish."

While there was great promise for a rich exploration of secular Jewish identity in both characters, neither ever caught on with a large enough audience to cause passionate morning-after debates among viewers or dueling commentaries in *Tikkun* or the *New York Times* the way Michael Steadman or even Bernie Steinberg did. In fact, neither was even on the air by the summer of 2002 as the book was going to press.

The future is somewhat more promising for *State of Grace*, a gentle sitcom set in North Carolina in the mid-1960s that includes a multi-generation Jewish family just as *The Goldbergs* did. Similar in tone and concept to *Brooklyn Bridge* and *The Wonder Years*, *State of Grace* is a coming-of-age tale told in off-screen narration by forty-seven-year-old journalist Hannah Rayburn (Frances McDormand) about her adolescence and her family's move to the South when she was twelve. Her father is a self-made furniture manufacturer and Holocaust survivor. Her grandmother speaks with a Yiddish accent. Her mother is a "very modern" woman who runs a business.

But even here in 2002 the leading character can't be the Jew. That role belongs to Grace McKee, Hannah's flamboyant twelve-year-old Catholic best friend. She is the Grace named in the title and the one who is described as "fun-loving and carefree" while the Jewish females are described as "over-anxious, controlling, and fearful," in press materials distributed by ABC Family to promote the show.[21] The match between these character descriptions and the answers given by men on the differences between non-Jewish and Jewish women in the Morning Star study is eerie and depressing.

Even with that bow to the mainstream of making the non-Jewish character the lead even though a Jewish character is the one whose family serves as the narrative center of the series, Disney still keeps this critically acclaimed show on its cable channel, ABC Family, rather than on the much larger broadcast network it owns, ABC. Thus, inexplicably, *State of Grace* is marginalized at a time when the network is desperate for such family fare.

State of Grace isn't about Jewish identity today. Like *Brooklyn Bridge*, it is more about baby-boomer nostalgia and, incidentally, Jewish identity as it is fondly, if somewhat vaguely, remembered. Sociologically, such shows have more to do with grandchildren of immigrants trying to recapture—

The Rayburns are the Jewish family as it once upon a time was in a cable television drama of today, *State of Grace,* on the ABC Family channel. After moving from Chicago to set up a furniture business, the Rayburns must adjust to their new lives in 1960s North Carolina. They are (L to R): Michael Mantell as David Rayburn, Dinah Manoff as Evelyn Rayburn, Alia Shawkat as Hannah Rayburn, Jason Blicker as Uncle Heschie, and Erica Yohn as Grandma Ida. Like *Brooklyn Bridge,* this is an adolescent coming of age story. The question is why the title features the name of Hannah's non-Jewish friend, Grace, if it is primarily about Hannah and her family. Photo courtesy of ABC Family.

or at least remember—some of the ethnicity that their parents tried so hard to escape in their drive to assimilate.

The reel of more than half a century of such images with all their strange distortions, from trying to Americanize Molly in Haverville to giving George the improbable last name of Costanza, kept replaying itself in my mind as I rode the train home from that warehouse in Queens where a seventy-seven-year-old Lumet was making a series for cable in 2001 that should have been made for network television in about 1961, when he was far better suited to the incredible physical demands of producing a weekly series. But back then, people from New York like Rifkind were not allowed to exist in the world of prime time.

As troubling as the reel of weirdly refracted television images of Jewish identity is, what haunts me most is the void—all the years when there were no leading Jewish characters in prime time, a time when network television was unquestionably center ring for the representation of American life.

What did audiences make of seeing no Jews as leading men or women in this most American of media? Cultural studies can tell us how media images are used in the social construction of reality—how viewers might look at Jewish characters on television and come to conclusions about real-world Jewish identity based to some extent on what they see on the screen. But what happens in the minds of viewers when Jewish characters are not there?

It is, indeed, our great loss. And if we cannot ever redeem what a handful of incredibly powerful men who once ran the television industry did to the rest of us, we can, at least, try to understand it. In so doing, hopefully, we will come to see how the onscreen results of their actions shaped and distorted our own sense of reality and self today.

NOTES

Introduction (pp. 1–16)

1. Norman Lear, interview with author, 8 Jan. 1999.

2. Marshall Herskovitz, "Creating Jewish Characters for Television," University Satellite Seminar Series, (a panel discussion broadcast to campuses nationwide with call-in Q&A) 11 Nov. 1998, The Museum of Television & Radio, Beverly Hills, Calif.

3. Brandon Tartikoff, interview with author, 16 July 1996. See also Brandon Tartikoff and Charles Leerhsen, *The Last Great Ride* (New York: Turtle Bay Books, 1992), pp. 191–192. I used parts of the published version here, because the story is more honed than in the version he told me. Furthermore, the book version is more accessible to other researchers.

4. Al Franken, interview with author, 16 Jan. 1998. All Franken quotes are from that interview.

5. Berg told this story on 16 July 1985, opening night of "Jewish Humor on TV: Six Funny Evenings," a symposium at the Jewish Museum in New York City. The moderator was Dr. Lawrence E. Mintz of the University of Maryland Department of American Studies.

6. Lynn Hirschberg, "Network Drama at ABC; Jamie Tarses' Fall, as Scheduled," *New York Times*, 13 July 1997, part 6, p. 37.

7. Lynn Hirschberg, ". . . So What's to Become of Our Jerry?" *Vanity Fair* (May 1998), p. 243.

8. Daphne Patai, "Minority Status and the Stigma of 'Surplus Visibility,'" *Chronicle of Higher Education* (30 Oct. 1991), section A, p. 52.

9. Susan Kray, "Orientalization of an 'Almost White' Woman: A Multidisciplinary Approach to the Interlocking Effects of Race, Class, Gender, and Ethnicity in American Mass Media—The Case of the Missing Jewish Woman," in *Feminism, Multiculturalism, and the Media: Global Diversities*, ed. Angharad N. Valdavia (Thousand Oaks, Calif.: Sage, 1995), p. 225.

10. The ground for such a study had been broken by such authors as Richard Butsch, "Ralph, Fred, Archie and Homer: Why Television Keeps Re-creating the White, Male, Working-Class Buffoon," in *Gender, Race and Class in Media*, eds. Gail Dines and Jean M. Humez (Thousand Oaks: Sage, 1995) pp. 403–412; Ella Taylor, *Prime-Time Families* (Berkeley: U of California P, 1989); Todd Gitlin, *Inside Prime*

Time (New York: Praeger, 1983); and Stuart Hall, "Encoding/Decoding," in *Culture, Media, Language,* eds. Stuart Hall, et al. (London: Hutchinson, 1986), pp. 128–138. I am working within the tradition of cultural studies, with its central insight that popular culture is socially constructed and received. Cultural studies conceptualizes the process of communication by using a three-part model based on Stuart Hall's belief that there are three determinate moments in the process through which a message generates meaning: encoding, the form of the message itself, and decoding. As Taylor did with representations of family in prime-time television, I am working primarily within and between the first two segments of the model, looking at the production/distribution of shows with Jewish characters and the images within the shows themselves. I discuss reception only briefly in connection with a focus group study conducted under the auspices of the Morning Star Commission of Hadassah Southern California. My research plans also include a reception study, but since the history of Jewish images in prime time has yet to be written, I wanted to start there. A systematic overview of the images and some explanation of how they came to be that way will enable us to coherently explore the meanings they generate among various audiences. In terms of method, if nothing else, I hope media and cultural studies scholars will be reminded by my findings of the importance of production study. Despite the emphasis on reception these days, we must not ignore production. This study demonstrates the truth of the cultural studies axiom that you cannot read culture from text—you always have to examine the production milieu that mediates between culture and text. For a fuller discussion of location and method, please see my dissertation, written in the American Studies Department of the University of Maryland in 2000. *The Jews of Prime Time: Ethnicity, Self-censorship and Assimilation in Network Television, 1949–1999* (Ann Arbor: UMI, 2000) 3001430.

11. For the purposes of this study, the best source on Jewish presence is Gitlin, *Inside Prime Time,* pp. 184–185; Rick Mitz, *The Great Sitcom Yearbook* (New York: Perigree-Putnam, 1988), p. 19; and Ben Stein, *The View From Sunset Boulevard* (New York: Basic Books, 1979). In terms of control by the Big Three networks, see Robert Pekurny, "Coping With Television Production," in *Individuals in Mass Media Organizations,* eds. J. S. Ettema and D. C. Whitney (Thousand Oaks, Calif: Sage, 1982), or Bruce M. Owen and Steven S. Wildman, *Video Economics* (Cambridge Mass.: Harvard UP, 1992). Also see Butsch, "Ralph, Fred, Archie and Homer."

12. Gitlin, *Inside Prime Time,* p. 184.

13. New York: Anchor, 1988.

14. For the best descriptions of such types, see Harley Erdman, *Staging the Jew: The Performance of American Ethnicity, 1860–1920* (New Brunswick: Rutgers UP, 1997), pp. 17–40.

15. Leslie Fiedler, *Fiedler on the Roof* (Boston: David R. Godine, 1991), p. 12.

16. Alan M. Dershowitz, *The Vanishing American Jew* (Boston: Little, Brown and Company, 1997), p. 26. While the one-out-of-two estimate is much debated, it was first put forth in 1990 when a survey commissioned by the Council of Jewish Federations found that 52 percent of the Jews who had married between 1985

and 1990 had married non-Jews. See also Philip Weiss, "Letting Go," *New York* (29 Jan. 1996), pp. 24–33.

17. The one exception is Jerry Seinfeld in the NBC sitcom *Seinfeld.* I make the exception because this is the first time in the history of prime-time network television in which a character played by a Jewish actor who was portraying himself or herself was identified as Jewish. Jack Benny and George Burns, for example, played themselves in sitcoms, but neither of their personas in the sitcoms was identified as Jewish. This development—which did not occur until 1989, forty years after the arrival of television's first Jewish character—is important to understanding the change over time in the construction of Jewish identity.

18. Taylor, *Prime-Time Families*, p. 17.

19. Donald F. Roberts, interview with author, 14 Jan. 2000. Following a presentation of his latest study using leading characters, *Substance Abuse in Popular Prime Time Television* (Washington, D.C.: The White House Office of Drug Control, 2000), the Stanford University researcher summarized his reasons for using only leading characters by saying, "They have the most screen time. And the more screen time, the more chance for viewer identification. And the more identification, the more chance for affecting attitudes."

20. For a full discussion of history and method on this matter, please see my dissertation.

21. Butsch, "Ralph, Fred, Archie and Homer," p. 406.

22. Henry Bromell, interview with author, 26 July 1999.

23. Gitlin, *Inside Prime Time*, p. 14.

24. Marshall Herskovitz, "Creating Jewish Characters for Television" seminar.

25. Lynn Roth, interview with author, 7 Aug. 1997.

1. Learning to Be "More American" – *The Goldbergs* (pp. 17–47)

1. Tim Brooks and Earle Marsh, *The Complete Directory to Prime Time and Cable TV Shows 1946–Present*, 6th ed. (New York: Ballantine, 1995), p. 404. I am using show descriptions from other researchers whenever possible to minimize the charge that I am "loading the dice," as it were, characterizing shows exclusively in terms of my reading of them. Of course, there is still subjectivity involved in my selection of those descriptions, but I am, at least, making an effort to acknowledge and minimize it. And, as those who have researched this realm of television history know, there are not that many sources of such description on which to draw.

2. Gerard Jones, *Honey I'm Home: Sitcoms Selling the American Dream* (New York: Grove, 1995) p. 15.

3. Gertrude Berg, "My Imp and I," *Woman's Home Companion* (Sept. 1955), p. 14.

4. Jones, *Honey I'm Home*, p. 15.

5. Ibid., p. 40.

6. Gertrude Berg, *Molly and Me* (New York: McGraw-Hill, 1961), pp. 207–208.

There are a number of contradictions about her life and work in Berg's writings and interview comments. Rather than trying to argue with or reconcile them in print, I have tried to use only those statements that I have been able to verify through at least one other source or that are not contradicted elsewhere. I am currently at work on a biography of Berg that will offer a full assessment of the ways in which she invented and re-invented herself and Molly.

7. Albert Auster, " 'Funny, You Don't Look Jewish . . . ': The Image of Jews on Contemporary American Television," *Television Quarterly* 26 (1993): p. 65.

8. Erik Barnouw, *Tube of Plenty* (New York: Oxford UP, 1990), pp. 163–192; R. D. Heldenfels, *Television's Greatest Year: 1954* (New York: Continuum, 1994); Heldenfels, interview with the author, 22 July 2000.

9. For a more detailed analysis than what is offered in such standard broadcasting histories as Barnouw's *Tube of Plenty*, there is, for example, a series of interviews with former advertising executive and NBC and CBS programmer Michael Dann in the Oral History of Television Project at the E. S. Bird Library, Syracuse University. The interviews were conducted by Les Brown on 19 June 1996. In addition to Dann, the statement about advertising agencies controlling early network television is also supported by interviews conducted for this study with former advertising executives such as Owen Camora, who worked at the Young & Rubicam advertising agency in the 1950s, NBC in the 1960s and 1970s, and now runs his own public relations agency, representing such clients as PBS filmmaker Ken Burns. The Camora interview was on 26 Oct. 1998.

10. Berg, *Molly and Me*, pp. 207–208.

11. In addition to Berg's autobiography, this history can be documented through letters in the Gertrude Berg Collection at Syracuse University's E. S. Bird Library. They would include a 6 Dec. 1948 letter from C. M Underhill, director of programs for CBS, to Berg. Also see a 10 Feb. 1949 letter to Berg from Everard W. Meade, vice president and manager of radio-television for Young & Rubicam advertising, a 31 March 1949 letter from Howard M. Chapin, director of advertising for the General Foods Corporation, to Berg, 2nd & 10 March 1949 letter from R. C. Williams, assistant sales and advertising manager of Maxwell House Division of General Foods Corporation, to Berg. The interview with Camora for this study also supports the statement.

12. Camora interview.

13. Rick Mitz, *The Great TV Sitcom Book* (New York: Perigree-Putnam, 1988), p. 19.

14. It changed from an airshaft to a garden to Molly Goldberg speaking directly to the viewer as the family moved to a larger apartment and then a home.

15. Prior to the 1955 season, in which thirty-nine episodes were syndicated through Guild Films, episodes of *The Goldbergs* were not titled. Thus they are referenced by date unless they are from the 1955–56 season. This is the same system used by the UCLA Film and Television Archive Research and Study Center, where many of episodes cited for this study were viewed.

16. Berg, *Molly and Me*, pp. 67–134.

17. Jones, *Honey I'm Home*, p. 43.

18. Irv R. Rill, letter to Gertrude Berg, 7 July 1952, Gertrude Berg Collection, E. S. Bird Library, Syracuse University.

19. The best analysis is found in George Lipsitz, "The Meaning of Memory: Family, Class and Ethnicity in Early Network Television Programs," *Cultural Anthropology* 1:4 (1986), pp. 355–386. But it should also be noted that Lipsitz categorizes *The Goldbergs* as part of a "subgenre of ethnic, working-class situation comedies." While I certainly don't think this in any way invalidates the larger conclusions he reaches in this excellent essay, I do think the "working-class" label is worthy of reconsideration. Jake Goldberg owns his own business. He and Sammy are always in shirt and tie. Gertrude Berg, in the quote cited early in this chapter, says, "I write about middle-class Jewish people." In short, I believe that the Goldbergs are middle class and not working class in the same way that Chester Riley's family or Ralph and Alice Kramden were in *The Life of Riley* and *The Honeymooners*, respectively. The working-class designation lends itself more neatly to Marxist critique, but it is not representative of what is in the texts, though there is room for disagreement on what working class or middle class is.

20. Alex McNeil, *Total Television: The Comprehensive Guide to Programming from 1948 to the Present*, 4th ed. (New York: Penguin, 1996), p. 332.

21. Jones, *Honey I'm Home*, p. 43.

22. Berg, *Molly and Me*, p. 167.

23. Unlike many sitcoms, though, in which the actions of the characters only make matters worse, Molly's actions are almost always for the better and solve problems that rarely dissolve on their own or through some miraculous happening.

24. Maurice Berger, "The Mouse That Never Roars: Jewish Masculinity on American Television," *Too Jewish? Challenging Traditional Identities*, ed. Norman L. Kleeblatt (New Brunswick: Rutgers UP, 1996) pp. 93–107.

25. Robert C. Allen and Douglas Gomery, *Film History: Theory and Practice* (New York: Knopf, 1985), p. 185.

26. Berg, *Molly and Me*, pp. 168–169.

27. Ibid., pp. 202–203.

28. Berg, "My Imp and I," p. 14.

29. R. R. Kaufman, letter to Gertrude Berg, 31 Aug. 1955, Gertrude Berg Collection, E. S. Bird Library, Syracuse University.

30. Stone numbered each report, and I include that number and year with specific citations. The Stone Reports are part of the Motion Pictures Project Collection at YIVO Institute for Jewish Study in New York City.

31. Stone Reports #20 (1950).

32. Stone Reports #26 (1951).

33. David Marc, lecture at the Jewish Museum, New York City, 21 Oct. 1990.

34. Berg, *Molly and Me*, p. 168.

35. The 1955 episode from Guild Films is housed at UCLA Film and Television Archive at the University of California, Los Angeles.

36. Gertrude Berg, "My Favorite Recipes," *TV Guide* (7 Aug. 1953), pp. 7–8.

37. There is one major exception: "Molly's Fish," one of the last episodes of *The Goldbergs* in 1955 and one of the most profound half hours of television during the decade. It involves a national supermarket chain expressing an interest in Molly's recipe for gefilte fish. For a close reading of the episode that shows how Molly served as a site for managing contradictions within 1950s' American culture, see my dissertation, *The Jews of Prime Time: Ethnicity, Self-censorship and Assimilation in Network Television, 1949–1999,* (Ann Arbor: UMI, 2000), 3001430, pp. 76–81. "Molly's Fish" is in the UCLA collection.

38. Harley Erdman, *Staging the Jew: The Performance of an American Ethnicity, 1860–1920.* (New Brunswick Rutgers UP, 1997), p. 36. Erdman offers an excellent analysis of the effeminacy of Jewish male characters onstage in nineteenth-century America, particularly in connection with the sheeny type. For the fullest discussion of Jewish male sexuality in connection with "deviancy," see Sander Gilman's *The Jew's Body* (New York: Routledge, 1991) and *Jewish Self-Hatred: Anti-Semitism and the Hidden Language of the Jews* (Baltimore: Johns Hopkins UP, 1986).

39. Berg, *Molly and Me*, p. 179.

40. Berger, "The Mouse That Never Roars," p. 96.

41. Judith Butler, "Imitation and Gender Insubordination" in *Inside/Out: Lesbian Theories, Gay Theories,* ed. Diana Fuss (London: Routledge, 1991), pp. 15–29.

42. Brooks and March, *Complete Directory to Prime Time*, p. 543.

43. This stereotype is best described in Riv-Ellen Prell's "Why Jewish Princesses Don't Sweat: Desire and Consumption in Postwar American Jewish Culture," in *Too Jewish? Challenging Traditional Identities,* pp. 74–92.

44. Berg, *Molly and Me*, p. 168.

45. For a fuller explanation of Jewish identity being constructed in terms of the body, see Gilman, *The Jew's Body.* For the same construction of the feminine body, see Prell, "Why Jewish Princesses Don't Sweat."

46. Beyond the gender dynamics, it is worth noting that this is 1955, and Jake and Molly are not in separate beds. They are together in a king-sized bed, and their bodies are touching—something that was not supposed to have happened in prime-time television until a decade later.

47. These connections will be developed and explained fully as the shows are dealt with in later chapters.

48. Berg, *Molly and Me*, pp. 167–168.

49. McNeil, *Total Television*, p. 1143.

50. Ibid., p. 1040.

51. Stephen Birmingham, *"The Rest of Us": The Rise of America's Eastern European Jews* (Syracuse: Syracuse UP, 1999), p. 347.

52. As quoted in the *Long Island Press* (22 April 1951). The newspaper and periodical articles quoted in the rest of the chapter can all be found in the Berg Collection at Syracuse University. All are from box no. 2, folder no. 39, titled "General Scrapbook." It is a scrapbook Berg herself kept of articles about Loeb's blacklisting. The clippings are originals with the newspaper or periodical masthead

and date attached, but not page numbers. While the library labels it "General Scrapbook," Berg's label, "Loeb," can still be seen on the cover.

53. *Variety* (11 June 1951).

54. Actually, the decisions by General Foods and CBS were made in April of 1951, but not reported in the industry press until June.

55. *Billboard* (26 May 1951).

56. *Billboard* (7 April 1951).

57. *New York Times* (8 Jan. 1952).

58. John Crosby, "The Goldbergs Return," *New York Herald Tribune* (10 Feb. 1952).

59. *Billboard* (2 Feb. 1952).

60. Milton Heimlich, letter to Gertrude Berg, 10 June 1952, Gertrude Berg Collection. E. S. Bird Library, Syracuse University.

61. John McKinney, letter to Gertrude Berg, 14 July 1952, Gertrude Berg Collection, E. S. Bird Library, Syracuse University.

62. In the Baltimore-Washington market, for example, the Gilbert Sandler Advertising Agency represented the show for such sponsors as Pariser Bakery of Baltimore. In the Berg Collection at Syracuse are letters from Beryl Zerivitz, owner of the bakery, and Sandler himself.

63. Obituary, *New York Post* (2 Sept. 1955).

64. Quoted in Mitz, *The Great TV Sitcom Book*, p. 22.

65. Quoted in Morris Freedman, "From the American Scene: The Real Molly Goldberg," *Commentary* (April 1956), pp. 359–364.

2. "Write Yiddish, Cast British" –
From Dick Van Dyke to Mrs. G (pp. 48–77)

1. Michael Dann, interview with Les Brown, Oral History of Television Project, 19 June 1996, E. S. Bird Library, Syracuse University.

2. One possible exception to the scholarly consensus that there were no series with leading Jewish characters during these eighteen years is *Mrs. G. Goes to College*, on CBS in 1961. It starred none other than Gertrude Berg and will be explored at the end of this chapter in connection with the larger themes of Jewish identity that it contains.

3. David Marc, lecture, The Jewish Museum, 21 Oct. 1990, New York City.

4. In *Comic Visions* (2nd ed., Oxford: Blackwell, 1997), Marc says, "With the end of *The Goldbergs* in 1955, only families of northern European descent were left on the sitcom (with the exception of course of Ricky Ricardo)," (p. 36).

5. Alex McNeil, *Total Television: The Comprehensive Guide to Programming from 1948 to the Present*, 4th ed. (New York: Penguin, 1996), p. 509.

6. Tim Brooks and Earle Marsh, *The Complete Directory to Prime Time and Cable TV Shows 1946–Present*, 6th ed. (New York: Ballantine, 1995), p. 240.

7. Marc, *Comic Visions*, p. 70.

8. Ginny Weissman and Steven Coyne Sanders, *The Dick Van Dyke Show*, 2nd

ed. (New York: St. Martin's, 1993), p. 2; Marc, p. 76. These parallels were first reported by Weissman and Sanders; Marc cites them as his source in his discussion of Reiner as *auteur*.

9. Weissman and Sanders, *Dick Van Dyke*, p. 2.

10. Ibid., pp. 3–6.

11. Ibid., p. 2.

12. Ibid., p. 6.

13. As quoted in Todd Gitlin, *Inside Prime Time* (New York: Praeger, 1983), p. 185.

14. Harry Stein, "Reiner's pilot asks: 'Whose sitcom is it anyway?' " *TV Guide*, 2 Jan. 1993, p. 35. In the column, Stein explains the pilot for *Head of the Family* not being picked up by CBS by saying, "Simply put, Reiner was deemed 'too ethnic'—read 'Jewish'—to portray the lead. The quote from Reiner is his direct response to that statement by Stein.

15. Brandon Tartikoff, American Movie Classics interview, 17 Feb. 1995.

16. David Marc, lecture, The Jewish Museum.

17. Richard Butsch, "Ralph, Fred, Archie, and Homer: Why Television Keeps Recreating the White Male Working-Class Buffoon," in *Gender, Race and Class in Media*, eds. Gail Dines and Jean M. Humez (Thousand Oaks, Calif.: Sage, 1995), p. 404.

18. Quoted in Grant Tinker and Bud Rukeyser, *Tinker in Television: From General Sarnoff to General Electric* (New York: Simon & Schuster, 1994), p. 90.

19. Allan Burns, interview with author, 18 Nov. 1997.

20. In addition to *Tinker in Television*, pp. 90–91, the story has been told in Horace Newcomb and Robert S. Alley, *The Producer's Medium: Conversations with Creators of American Television* (New York: Oxford, 1983), p. 198. It was told again by Burns in my interview, as well as during a press conference on January 16, 1991, held at the Ritz-Carlton Hotel in Marina Del Ray in connection with the *Mary Tyler Moore Reunion* on CBS in February of that year. Also in attendance and elaborating on the story were Jim Brooks, Ed Asner, Ed Weinberger, and Mary Tyler Moore. In this telling, after Burns quoted the CBS research executive who said, "Americans would not tolerate divorce, people from New York, people with mustaches and Jews on television," Brooks cracked, "That's what's wrong with TV today." Moore asked, "Who said that?" And Burns replied, "Some Jewish guy with a mustache who's divorced." Indicative of how self-censorship still affects the telling of history as it regards Jews and television, some authors are still laundering the story to exclude any mention of New Yorkers and Jews, such as Steven D. Stark in his 1997 book *Glued to the Set* (New York: Dell), p. 224.

21. Burns, interview with author.

22. Jay Eliasburg, interview with author, 13 March 1999.

23. Fred Silverman, interview with author, 23 Aug. 1997.

24. David Poltrack, interview with author, 14 Oct. 1997.

25. Neither former executive will go on the record with those statements,

however. One said, "I say this only on background for the sake of historians to know." Another said, "I say this only for your guidance in trying to sift through all the lies and bullshit you are going to hear when you start getting to the truth on this." This is not surprising. As documented in Lewis J. Paper's *Empire: William S. Paley and the Making of CBS*, (New York: St. Martin's, 1987), CBS executives who dared to talk about Paley were regularly threatened with the loss of pension. Authors such as David Halberstam, who wrote about Paley's ambivalence about his Jewishness, were threatened with lawsuits. Halberstam, Bedell-Smith, and Paper—the three principal biographers—all had to go off the record with certain key sources to tell the Paley story due to the extent to which Paley went in controlling his image and the historical record connected to it. This is the only instance in which I go off the record in this study, and I think it is warranted.

26. Michael Dann, interview with Les Brown, Oral History of Television Project.

27. Stephen J. Whitfield, *In Search of American Jewish Culture* (Hanover N.H.: University Press of New England, 1999), pp. 25–26, 59–65.

28. Dann, interview with Les Brown, Oral History of Television Project.

29. Paper, *Empire*, pp. 194–195.

30. Quoted in Sally Bedell Smith, *In All His Glory* (New York: Simon and Schuster, 1990), p. 14.

31. Dann, interview with Les Brown, Oral History of Television Project.

32. Smith, *In All His Glory*, p. 466.

33. Neal Gabler, Arts & Entertainment channel press conference, 19 Jan. 1998, Ritz-Carlton Hotel, Pasadena, California.

34. David Halberstam, *The Powers That Be* (New York: Dell, 1980), p. 50.

35. Smith, *In All His Glory*, pp. 19–20 and 115.

36. Halberstam, *The Powers That Be*, pp. 49–50 offers one version of Paley's reaction to Metz describing him as a "Russian Jew." The original statement by Metz appears on p. 14 of his *CBS* (Chicago: Playboy 1975). Whereas Halberstam is technically right in saying the letter of "correction" from CBS said Paley is an "American Jew," the actual letter says, "Mr. Paley is not 'a Russian Jew.' He is a native American . . .

37. Smith, *In All His Glory*, p. 45.

38. Ibid.

39. Ibid., p. 320.

40. Paper, *Empire*, pp. 4–6.

41. Smith, *In All His Glory*, p. 348, and Paper, *Empire*, p. 194.

42. Smith, *In All His Glory*, p. 510.

43. Paper, *Empire*, p. 299.

44. Smith, *In All His Glory*, p. 511.

45. Paper, *Empire*, p. 7.

46. Quoted in Les Brown, *The Business Behind the Box* (New York: Harcourt, 1971), p. 216.

47. Smith, *In All His Glory*, p. 146.

48. Neal Gabler, *An Empire of Their Own: How the Jews Invented Hollywood* (New York: Anchor, 1988), p. 2.

49. Stephen Birmingham, *The Rest of Us: The Rise of America's Eastern European Jews* (Syracuse: Syracuse UP, 1999), pp. 350–351.

50. Brown, *Business Behind the Box*, pp. 215–216.

51. Carl Dreher, *Sarnoff: An American Success Story* (New York: Quadrangle, 1977), pp. 225–226.

52. Leonard Goldenson, *Beating the Odds* (New York: Scribner's, 1991), pp. 236–237.

53. Goldenson, *Beating the Odds*, pp. 322–323.

54. Jeffrey Shandler, *While America Watches: Televising the Holocaust* (New York: Oxford UP, 1999), pp. 46–47.

55. Holly Cowan Shulman, interview with author, 23 Aug. 1997.

56. Neal Gabler, interview on *Hollywoodism: Jews, Movies, and the American Dream*, Arts & Entertainment cable channel, 24 March 1998.

57. This is Gabler's figure. According to Alvah Bessie, one of those subpoenaed, thirteen were Jews. Bessie's version can be found in his 1965 book *An Inquisition in Eden*.

58. Gabler, *An Empire of Their Own*, p. 366.

59. Ibid., pp. 366–367.

60. Quoted in *Hollywoodism* (see note 56).

61. Marshall Herskovitz, "Creating Jewish Characters for Television" University Satellite Seminar Series, 11 Nov. 1998, The Museum of Television and Radio, Beverly Hills, Calif.

62. Arts & Entertainment channel press conference, 19 Jan. 1998, Ritz-Carlton Hotel, Pasadena, Calif.

63. Michael Elkin, "Jews behind the Camera Change Portrayal of Jews on TV Screen," *Long Island Jewish World* (30 Aug.–6 Sept. 1985), p. 16. Elkin's Smolar Award–winning series is a landmark in seeing the connection between the Jewish founders and the lack of Jews onscreen. As for critics counting fifty years of the kind of token appearances Wincelberg describes in Elkin's series and coming to the wrongheaded conclusion that Jewish identity has been widely and richly explored on network TV, see Jonathan M. Pearl and Judith Pearl, *The Chosen Image* (Jefferson, N.C.: McFarland, 1999). In only doing such tree counting, the Pearls fail to see the fence encircling the forest. While a series like *Barney Miller* might deal with Jewish characters in one or two episodes, the larger issue of why Miller's ethnicity is masked is not explored. *Barney Miller* and network resistance to signaling Jewish identity in the lead character is discussed here in chapter 3.

64. Rick Mitz, *The Great TV Sitcom Book* (New York: Perigree-Putnam, 1988), p. 22.

65. The series was essentially remade during the 1997–98 season on CBS as *Pearl*, starring Rhea Perlman as the freshman and Malcolm McDowell as the professor. For the record, Perlman and the producers denied having ever heard

of *Mrs G. Goes to College* or *The Gertude Berg Show* when I asked them about it during a CBS press conference in July 1997.

66. Zalman King, interview with author, 20 July 1998.

67. Gitlin, *Inside Prime Time*, p. 186.

3. Prime-Time Intermarriage I – *Bridget Loves Bernie* (pp. 78–103)

1. Leonard Davis, letter to *The New York Times* (1 Oct. 1972), part 2, p. 19.

2. Albin Krebs, "Bridget Loves Bernie Attacked by Jewish groups," *New York Times* (7 Feb. 1973), part 1, p. 79.

3. "The Team Behind Archie Bunker & Co.," *Time* (25 Sept. 1972), pp. 50–51.

4. Geoffrey Cowan, *See No Evil: The Backstage Battle Over Sex and Violence in Television* (New York: Touchstone, 1978), pp. 50–51. This view was also expressed by filmmaker Barry Levinson, who was then a writer in the television industry. This author's interview with Levinson took place on 20 Oct. 1997.

5. David Marc, *Comic Visions*, 2nd ed. (Oxford: Blackwell, 1997), p. 146.

6. Leonard Goldenson, *Beating the Odds* (New York: Scribner's, 1991), p. 322.

7. Ibid., p. 323.

8. A fuller discussion of the psychology of the suppliers and buyers of network programs will be undertaken in chapter 8.

9. Cowan, *See No Evil*, pp. 23–28.

10. Ibid., p. 240.

11. Sally Bedell Smith, *In All His Glory* (New York: Simon and Schuster, 1990), p. 494.

12. Richard Butsch, "Ralph, Fred, Archie and Homer: Why Television Keeps Recreating the White Male Working-Class Buffoon," *Gender, Race and Class in Media*, eds. Gail Dines and Jean M. Humez (Thousand Oaks Calif.: Sage, 1995), pp. 403–412.

13. Cowan, *See No Evil*, p. 236.

14. Smith, *In All His Glory*, p. 494.

15. John J. O'Connor, "Two CBS Series Show Half-Hour Potential," *New York Times* (15 Sept. 1972), part 1, p. 75.

16. Fred Silverman, interview with author, 13 Aug. 1997.

17. M. Mautner, letter to the *New York Times* (21 Jan. 1973), part 2, p. 29.

18. Maurice Berger, "The Mouse That Never Roars: Jewish Masculinity on American Television," in *Too Jewish? Challenging Traditional Identities*, ed. Norman L. Kleeblatt (New Brunswick: Rutgers UP, 1996), p. 203.

19. The use of minor-key violin music to signal Jewish identity onscreen has been noticed elsewhere by other researchers. See Jeffrey Shandler, *While America Watches: Televising The Holocaust* (New York: Oxford UP 1999) pp. 145 and 146. See also Mark Slobin, "The Music of Jewish Film: A Research Report," *Jewish Folklore and Ethnology Report* 16:1 (1994), p. 45. Further discussion can also be found in Slobin's *Tenement Songs: The Popular Music of Jewish Immigrants* (Urbana: U of Illinois P, 1982), pp. 182–197.

20. Edward B. Fiske, "Some Jews Are Mad at Bernie," *New York Times* (11 Feb. 1973), part 4, p. 8.

21. Joseph Greenblum, "Does Hollywood Still Glorify Intermarriage?" *American Jewish History* (December 1995), p. 451.

22. Leonard Davis, letter to the *New York Times* (1 Oct. 1972), part 2, p. 19.

23. M. Mautner, letter to the *New York Times* (21 Jan. 1973), part 2, p. 29.

24. James F. Clarity, "Notes On People," *New York Times* (19 Jan. 1973), part 2, p. 39.

25. Meredith Baxter, interview with author, 21 March 1995.

26. Clarity, "Notes On People," p. 29.

27. Fiske, "Some Jews," p. 8.

28. Krebs, "Bridget Loves Bernie Attacked," p. 79.

29. Fiske, "Some Jews," p. 8.

30. Krebs, "Bridget Loves Bernie Attacked," p. 79.

31. Ibid.

32. Cowan, *See No Evil*, p. 60. On March 9, 1973, three days before the anti–Vietnam War play *Sticks and Bones* was supposed to air, Wood announced he was postponing it. He later acknowledged that it was Paley who made the decision out of fear of angering conservative affiliate station managers. Wood said he merely fronted for Paley, as was often the case at that point in CBS's history.

33. Alex McNeil, *Total Television: A Comprehensive Guide to Programming from 1948 to the Present*, 4th ed. (New York: Penguin, 1996), p. 119.

34. Kathyrn C. Montgomery, *Target Prime Time: Advocacy Groups and the Struggle Over Entertainment Television* (New York: Oxford UP, 1989), pp. 27–50.

35. Baxter, interview with author.

36. Judy Klemesrud, "Birney and His 'Irish' Rose," *New York Times* (29 Oct. 1972), part 2, p. 21.

37. Harley Erdman, *Staging the Jew* (New Brunswick: Rutgers UP, 1997), p. 120.

38. In fact, the Motion Picture Project was formed in response to the images of Jews in Bing Crosby's feature film version of *Abie's Irish Rose*. The Stone Reports #20 (1950) Motion Pictures Project Collection at YIVO Institute for Jewish Study, New York.

39. For more on *Bridget Loves Bernie*, see Greenblum, "Does Hollywood Still Glorify Intermarriage?" pp. 445–451. The "three issues" model is found on pp. 446–447. Greenblum's statement about *Bridget Loves Bernie* "reverting to the melting pot model" is found on p. 451, as is Greenblum's "greater cognizance" statement, Greenblum and I have discussed the article and the issue of intermarriage and *Bridget Loves Bernie* on several occasions.

40. Alan M. Dershowitz, *The Vanishing American Jew* (Boston: Little, Brown and Company, 1997), pp. 25–27. While the one-out-of-two estimate is much debated, it was first put forth in 1990 when a survey commissioned by the Council of Jewish Federations found that 52 percent of the Jews who had married between 1985 and 1990 had married non-Jews. See also Philip Weiss, "Letting Go," *New York* (29 Jan. 1996), pp. 24–33.

41. Silverman, interview with author.

42. Weiss, "Letting Go," p. 28; Dershowitz, *Vanishing American Jew*, p. 26.

43. Allan Burns, interview with author, 18 Nov. 1997. Burns, one of the creators and executive producers of the series, said they "shied away" from dealing with her as a Jew.

44. Sally Bedell, *Up the Tube: Prime-Time TV in the Silverman Years* (New York: Viking, 1981), p. 117.

45. Gitlin, *Inside Prime Time* (New York: Prager, 1983), p. 186.

46. Ibid., p. 186.

4. The Dramas – *thirtysomething* and *Northern Exposure* (pp. 104–139)

1. Ken Olin, interview with author, 30 Sept. 1997.

2. Marshall Herskovitz, et al., thirtysomething: *Stories by the Writers of* thirtysomething (New York: Pocket Books, 1991), p. 246.

3. Terry Barr, "Stars, Light and Finding the Way Home: Jewish Characters in Contemporary Film and Television," *Studies in Popular Culture* 15:2 (1993), pp. 88–89.

4. Olin, interview with author.

5. Marshall Herskovitz, interview with author, 28 July 1999.

6. For a full discussion of the stereotype and an analysis that links it to a deeper constructions of Jewish women as non-productive members of society, see Riv-Ellen Prell "Why Jewish Princesses Don't Sweat: Desire and Consumption in Postwar American Culture," *Too Jewish?: Challenging Traditional Identities*, ed. Norman L. Kleeblatt (New Brunswick: Rutgers UP, 1996), pp. 74–92. To see the stereotype discussed in terms of misogyny, self-hatred, and anti-Semitism, see Evelyn Torton Beck, "From 'Kike' to 'JAP': How Misogyny, Anti-Semitism and Racism Construct the 'Jewish American Princess,'" *Race, Class and Gender: An Anthology*, eds. Margaret L. Anderson and Patricia Hill Collins, 3rd ed. (Belmont, Wash.: Wadsworth, 1998), pp. 430–436.

7. Tim Brooks and Earle Marsh, *The Complete Directory to Prime Time Network Television and Cable TV Shows: 1946–Present*, 6th ed., (New York: Ballantine, 1995), p. 1033.

8. Jay Rosen, "*thirtysomething*," *Tikkun* 4:4 (1989), p. 29.

9. Michael Lerner, "*thirtysomething* and Judaism," *Tikkun* 5:6 (1990), p. 6.

10. Ibid.

11. Marshall Herskovitz, "Creating Jewish Characters for Television," University Satellite Seminar Series, 11 Nov. 1998, The Museum of Television & Radio, Beverly Hills, Calif.

12. Ibid.

13. In *Marty*, Paddy Chayefsky had to change the ethnicity of his Bronx butcher, Marty, from Jewish to Italian to get it produced for television on May 24, 1953, on the *Goodyear TV Playhouse*, which aired on NBC.

14. Olin, interview with author.

15. Quoted in John J. O'Connor, "They're Funny, Lovable, Heroic—and Jewish," *New York Times* (15 July 1990), part 3, p. 30.

16. Robert J. Thompson, *Television's Second Golden Age* (New York: Continuum, 1996), pp. 166–167.

17. Lois K. Solomon, "Farewell, Fleischman," *Baltimore Jewish Times* (3 Feb. 1995), p. 49.

18. Jeff Melvoin, "Creating Jewish Characters for Television," University Satellite Seminar Series, 11 Nov. 1998, The Museum of Television & Radio, Beverly Hills, Calif.

19. Joseph Campbell, *The Hero with a Thousand Faces,* 2nd ed. (Princeton, N.J.: Princeton UP, 1968), pp. 36–37. This is where Campbell describes the "monomyth" with its three stages of separation, initiation-battle, and return for the hero's journey. As I describe later in this chapter, all three elements are seen in Fleischman's final episode.

20. Solomon, "Farewell, Fleischman," p. 46.

21. Jan Oxenberg, "Creating Jewish Characters for Television," University Satellite Seminar Series, 11 Nov. 1998, The Museum of Television & Radio, Beverly Hills, Calif.

22. Thompson, *Television's Second Golden Age*, p. 127.

23. Solomon, "Farewell, Fleischman," p. 46.

24. Melvoin, Museum of Television & Radio interview.

25. Quoted Charlotte Baum, Paula Hyman, and Sonya Michel, *The Jewish Woman in America* (New York: Dial, 1976), pp. 249–250.

5. Intermarriage II (Shiksa Goddesses Transforming Jewish Guys) – *Anything But Love, Flying Blind, Mad About You, Brooklyn Bridge*, and More (pp. 140–171)

1. Jennifer Grey, "Loose Talk" column, *Baltimore Jewish Times* (26 March 1999), p. 8.

2. Lynn Roth, interview with author, 7 Aug. 1997.

3. Lynn Hirschberg, "Network Drama at ABC; Jamie Tarses' Fall, as Scheduled," *New York Times* (13 July 1997), part 6, p. 3.

4. Peter Mehlman, interview with author, 11 Dec. 2001.

5. Tim Brooks and Earle Marsh, *The Complete Directory to Prime Time Network and Cable TV Shows 1946–Present*, 6th ed. (New York: Ballantine, 1995), p. 187.

6. Ibid.

7. Alex McNeil, *Total Television: A Comprehensive Guide to Programming from 1948 to the Present,* 4th ed. (New York: Penguin, 1996), p. 521.

8. Richard Rosenstock, interview with author, 13 Jan. 2000. All quotes from Rosenstock in the book are from this interview.

9. The poster—and, indeed, posters in general—are very important to Rosenstock, by his own admission, in terms of their revealing of authorial intent.

The poster from *Flying Blind* that I describe is mounted on the wall in his office at the Castle Rock Entertainment production company in Beverly Hills. During the interview, he sat under a poster for the movie *Goodbye, Columbus*, often referring to it.

10. Brooks and Marsh, *Complete Directory*, pp. 362–363. They did not meet at a party. They met at a restaurant—he is on a lunch break from the office when she rushes in, fleeing from an enraged lover. Noting this negligence is important in terms of the larger matter of how unreliable in some ways even our primary reference works on television are. Like every other television researcher, I have used Brooks and Marsh for years. But, in going back and viewing epsiodes, I have found a number of such inaccuracies in several series. I think it points to a larger problem about the kind of historical record that has been kept when it comes to television.

11. David Zurawik, "Cultural Shift: Prime-time Hits with Jewish Stars as One of the Latest TV Trends," *Baltimore Sun* (1 Nov. 1992), part L, p. 1. All Jacobson quotes are from the interview for this story.

12. Quoted in Naomi Pfefferman, "Owing It All to Jerry," *The Jewish Journal*, (15 May 1998). Available at http://www.jewishjournal.com/elongold.5.15.8.html.

13. A reminder that I am using show descriptions from researchers other than myself whenever possible to minimize the charge that I am "loading the dice," as it were.

14. Brooks and Marsh, *Complete Directory*, p. 612.

15. Naomi Pfefferman, "Bob and Judd," *The Jewish Journal*, (12 Sept. 1997). Available at http://www.jewishjournal.com/upfro.9.12.7.html.

16. Rob Long, interview with author, 13 Jan. 1998.

17. *Lateline* press release from NBC, 10 Feb. 1998.

18. *Lateline* press conference, 16 Jan. 1998, Ritz-Carlton-Huntington Hotel, Pasadena, Calif.

19. Al Franken, interview with author, 16 Jan. 1998. All other Franken quotes come from the interview.

20. I use one of Leo Rosten's definitions. There are other meanings of the word, according to Rosten. *Baleboosteh* can also mean "an excellent homemaker," for example. But "bossy woman" is the meaning closest to the sense in which Franken was using the word.

21. Gary David Goldberg, interview with author, 6 Nov. 1997. All other Goldberg quotes come from the interview.

22. For a much fuller discussion of Jewish masculinity with close readings of several episodes, particularly one involving Sophie's cousin, Jacob (Joel Grey), a Holocaust survivor, please see my dissertation. The New World/Old World dynamic is shown as being central to masculinity as well, with Alan's grandfather at one pole and Brooklyn Dodgers' first baseman Gil Hodges at the other.

23. Sylvia Barach Fishman, "I of the Beholder," Working Paper Series, No. 1 (Waltham: The Hadassah Research Institute on Jewish Women, May 1998), p. 11.

24. Ibid., p. 1.

25. Morning Star Commission, "First-Ever Study of Media Portrayals of Jewish Women Including 'Fran' and 'Dharma' Indicates Surprising Outcome." Available at <*http://www.morningstar.org/firstever.html*>. This includes the Kirscher quote. For the fullest description of the methodology and results, see Barbara Goldberg's "Jewish Women: The Mirror and the Media," unpublished manuscript prepared for Hadassah Southern Califronia, The Morning Star Commission, January 1998, Job #1597. Copy available at the International Research Institute on Jewish Women at Brandeis University, Waltham, Mass.

6. Intermarriage III (Some Jewish Women Get Gentile Guys) – *Rhoda, The Nanny, Dharma & Greg, Friends, Will & Grace* (pp. 172–200)

1. Allan Burns, interview with author, 18 Nov. 1997.

2. Fran Drescher, interview with author, 4 Feb. 1998.

3. For a consensus view, see Joyce Antler, "Epilogue: Jewish Women on Television: Too Jewish or Not Enough?" *Talking Back: Images of Jewish Women in American Popular Culture*, Joyce Antler, ed. (Hanover: University Press of New England, 1998), pp. 243–248.

4. Gerard Jones, *Honey, I'm Home: Sitcoms Selling the American Dream* (New York: Grove, 1992), p. 196.

5. Burns, interview with author.

6. Quoted in Peggy Herz, *All About Rhoda* (New York: Scholastic, 1975), p. 7. All other quotes by Burns in the chapter are from my interview with him.

7. Herz, *All About Rhoda*, p. 8.

8. Ibid., p. 9.

9. Ibid., p. 9.

10. Sharon Pomerantz, "Letter From New York: Rhoda Revisited," *Hadassah* (March 1995), pp. 11–13.

11. Grant Tinker and Bud Rukeyser, *Tinker in Television: From General Sarnoff to General Electric* (New York: Simon and Schuster, 1994), pp. 93–94.

12. Ibid., p. 94.

13. Charlotte Baum, Paula Hyman, and Sonya Michel, *The Jewish Woman in America* (New York: Dial, 1976), pp. 236–237.

14. Charlotte Brown, interview with author, 1 Dec. 1997.

15. Antler, "Jewish Women on Television," *Talking Back*, p. 243.

16. Riv-Ellen Prell, "Cinderellas Who (Almost) Never Become Princess: Subversive Representations of Jewish Women in Postwar Popular Novels." In Antler, *Talking Back*, p. 124.

17. Antler, *Talking Back*, p. 131.

18. Ibid., p. 138.

19. Rick Mitz, *The Great TV Sitcom Book* (New York: Perigree-Putnam, 1988), p. 287.

20. Silverman, interview with author, 13 Aug. 1997.

21. For example, Antler's "Jewish Women on Television: Too Jewish or Not

Enough?" essay in *Talking Back* tells us Rhoda "was soon cancelled" after the wedding episode. But, in fact, the wedding episode was only the eighth in the show's history. The series ran for another four and a half seasons and more than one hundred episodes after it, finishing in the Top 25 highest-rated series on network TV for three of those seasons. That is not "soon cancelled" by any calculation.

22. Riv-Elen Prell, "Why Jewish Princesses Don't Sweat: Desire and Consumption in Postwar American Jewish Culture," in *Too Jewish? Challenging Traditional Jewish Identities*, ed. Norman L. Kleeblatt (New Brunswick: Rutgers UP, 1996), pp. 74–92.

23. The construction of heterosexuality as "healthy" sexuality is the prime-time network norm, not necessarily mine.

24. Many of Drescher's favorite Fran lines from the show, such as the one cited, are collected in *The Wit and Wisdom of The Nanny: Fran's Guide to Life, Love and Shopping* (New York: Avon, 1995). The author is listed as Nan E. Fine.

25. Fran Drescher, *Enter Whining* (New York: Regan, 1996), pp. 152–153.

26. Again, for the fullest of such depictions in terms of body parts, see Sander L. Gilman's *The Jew's Body* (New York and London: Routledge, 1991).

27. For a similar reading of this text, see Antler, "Jewish Women on Television," *Talking Back*, pp. 246–247.

28. Drescher, interview with author, 4 Feb. 1998.

29. Sylvia Barack Fishman, "I of the Beholder: Jews and Gender in Film and Popular Culture," Working Paper Series, No. 1 (Waltham: The Hadassah Research Institute on Jewish Women, Brandeis University, May 1998). Fishman, in turn, is echoing Riv-Ellen Prell's "Rage and Representation: Jewish Gender Stereotypes in American Culture," *Uncertain Terms: Negotiating Gender in American Culture*, Faye Ginsburg and Anna Lowenhaupt Tsing, eds. (Boston: Beacon Press, 1990), pp. 248–267. Also see Paula Hyman, *Gender and Assimilation in Modern Jewish History: The Roles and Representations of Women* (Seattle: U of Washington P, 1995).

30. Drescher, interview with author.

31. Drescher herself claims authorship of the character and the sitcom in "Intimate Portrait: Fran Drescher," Lifetime cable channel, 16 Feb. 1998.

32. Fishman, "I of the Beholder," p. 5. In turn, she is citing the pioneering work of Sander Gilman in *The Jew's Body* (New York and London: Routledge, 1991).

33. Maurice Berger, "The Mouse that Never Roars: Jewish Masculinity on American Television," *Too Jewish: Challenging Traditional Identities*, Norman Kleeblatt, ed. (New Brunswick: Rutgers UP, 1996), pp. 97–98.

34. Gertrude Berg, *Me and Molly* (New York: McGraw-Hill, 1961), pp. 236–237.

35. Drescher, *Enter Whining*, p. 200.

36. Tim Brooks and Earle Marsh, *The Complete Directory to Prime Time Network and Cable TV Shows 1946–Present*, 6th ed. (New York: Ballantine, 1995), p. 838.

37. Drescher, *Enter Whining*, pp. 123–124.

38. Norman Lear, interview with author, 8 Jan. 1999.

39. Nora Lee Mandel, "Who's Jewish on 'Friends,'" *Lilith* 21 (Summer 1996), p. 6.

40. Antler, "Jewish Women on Television," *Talking Back*, p. 250.

41. Charlotte Brown, interview with author, 18 Nov. 1997.

42. Chuck Lorre, interview with author, 3 May 1998.

43. Barbara Goldberg, "Jewish Women: The Mirror and the Media," unpublished manuscript prepared for Hadassah Southern California, The Morning Star Commission, January 1998.

44. Quotes from Mutchnick, Kohan, and Messing are all from an NBC press conference, 18 July 2000, Ritz-Carlton Huntington Hotel, Pasadena, Calif.

7. A "Too-Jewish"/Not-Jewish-Enough
Jew for the '90s – *Seinfeld* (pp. 201–217)

1. Peter Mehlman, interview with author, 11 Dec. 2001

2. Tom Shales, "So Long, 'Seinfeld.' Let Me Show You to the Door," *Washington Post* (16 April 1998), p. B1.

3. Peter Ephross and Rebecca Segall, "Critics call show 'self-hating': Was 'Seinfeld' good for Jews?" *Jewish Bulletin of Northern California* (8 May 1998). Available at http://jewishsf.com/bk980508/1sein.? htm.

4. J. J. Goldberg, "Seining Off," *The Jewish Journal* (15 May 1998). This article is available in the archives at www.jewishjournal.com.

5. All Mehlman quotes come from interview with author.

6. Nikki Finke, "Brandon Tartikoff's Last Words," *Esquire* (November 1997), p. 67.

7. Lynn Hirschberg, ". . . So What's to Become of Our Jerry?" *Vanity Fair* (May 1998), p. 243.

8. Ibid.

9. Allan Burns, interview with author, 18 Nov. 1997.

10. Estelle Harris, NBC telephone press conference, 7 Oct. 1997.

11. Jonathan M. Pearl and Judith Pearl, *The Chosen Image* (Jefferson, N.C.: McFarland, 1999), p. 31.

12. Ephross and Segall, "Critics call show 'self-hating.'"

13. Werner Sollors, *Beyond Ethnicity: Consent and Descent in American Culture* (New York: Oxford UP, 1986) pp. 5–6.

14. Goldberg, "Seining Off."

15. Ibid.

16. Shales, "So Long, 'Seinfeld,'" p. B1.

17. Jerry Seinfeld, interview with Jane Pauley, NBC *Today*, 26 Oct. 1993.

8. Looping Back, Breaking Ground, and Calculating Loss — *100 Centre Street, The Education of Max Bickford, State of Grace* (pp. 218–241)

1. Sidney Lumet, interview with author, 31 Oct. 2001. All Lumet quotes are from that interview.

2. Richard Rosenstock, interview with author, 13 Jan. 2000.

3. See, for example, Sylvia Barack Fishman, "I of the Beholder: Jews and Gender in Film and Popular Culture," Working Paper Series #1, The Hadassah Research Institute (Waltham, Brandeis University). Fishman uses Lumet's *Stranger* as one of her brackets for looking at "seventy-plus years (1927–1998) of American commercial films about Jews." Her other bracket: *The Jazz Singer*. Her critique shows the richness of Lumet's understanding of both Jewish identity and the cinematic depiction of it.

4. John Kampner, *The Man in the Shadows: Fred Coe and the Golden Age of Television* (New Brunswick: Rutgers University Press, 1997), pp. 62–63; Paddy Chayefsky, *Television Plays* (New York: Touchstone, 1971), p. 132. See also Jeffrey Shandler, *While America Watches: Televising the Holocaust* (New York, Oxford UP, 1999), p. 48.

5. Charlotte Brown, interview with author, 1 Dec. 1997. All Brown quotes come from that interview.

6. Jonathan Rosenbaum, *Hollywoodism: Jews, Movies, and the American Dream*, Arts & Entertainment (A&E) cable channel documentary, 24 March 1998.

7. Gary David Goldberg, interview with author, 6 Nov. 1997. All Goldberg quotes come from that interview.

8. Barry Levinson, interview with author, 20 Oct. 1997. All Levinson quotes come from that interview.

9. "White House Conference on Children and Public Television," 14 Aug. 1995, Washington, D.C. I am purposefully going outside the ethnic group to avoid charges of Jewish producers or actors "whining"—a charge often leveled against the Jewish characters of *thirtysomething* when they discussed such matters.

10. Lynn Roth, interview with author, 7 Aug. 1997. All Roth quotes come from that interview.

11. Brandon Tartikoff, American Movie Classics interview, 17 Feb. 1995.

12. Richard Rosenstock, interview with author, 13 Jan. 2000. All Rosenstock quotes come from that interview.

13. Michael Dann, interview with Les Brown, "Oral History of Television Project," 19 June 1996, E. S. Bird Library, Syracuse University.

14. Carol Leifer, interviewed as part of "Creating Jewish Characters for Television," University Satellite Seminar Series, 11 Nov. 1998, Museum of Television & Radio, Beverly Hills, Calif.

15. Fred Silverman, interview with author, 13 Aug. 1997.

16. Barry Curtis and Claire Pajaczkowka, "Assimilation, Entertainment and the Hollywood Solution," *The Jew in the Text: Modernity and the Construction of Jewish Identity*, eds. Linda Nochlin and Tamar Garb (London: Thames and Hudson, 1995), pp. 238–252.

17. Douglas Kellner, "TV Ideology and Emancipatory Popular Culture," *Socialist Review* 9 (1979), pp. 13–53. Kellner was using the term to describe ideology that was in opposition to or questioned that of the dominant culture. In the case of American network television, he was speaking specifically about capitalism.

18. The exchange took place during the "Creating Jewish Characters for Television" seminar.

19. Alan Arkin, interview with author, 22 Oct. 2001.

20. Richard Dreyfuss, CBS telephone press conference, 20 Feb. 2002.

21. ABC Family channel, "Character Descriptions," *State of Grace* press package, 23 Jan. 2002.

INDEX

Page numbers in *italic* represent illustrations.

Guild Films, 28, 32, 44
Gunty, Morty, 52
Gwynne, Fred, 51

Hadassah Southern California, 169, 197
Halberstam, David, 63–65, 66–67, 251nn.25&36
Hall, Stuart, 244n.10
Hansen, Marcus Lee, 139
Happy Days, 226
Hardwicke, Sir Cedric, 194
Harper, Valerie: on *The Mary Tyler Moore Show,* 173, 174, 175; on *Rhoda, 180,* 182; as ugly duckling character, 35. See also *Rhoda*
Harris, Estelle, 206
Harris, Mel, 105, *106*
Harris, Robert H., 39
Harris, Susan, 155, 227
Haynes, Lloyd, 51
Head of the Family, 51–54, 114, 227, 250n.14
Heartbreak Kid, The (film), 80, 231
Heimlich, Milton, 44
Herskovitz, Marshall: on lingering resistance to Jewish characters, 234–35; *Relativity,* 135; on self-censorship, 1, 15, 222; on television as Jewish medium, 105; *thirtysomething,* 9, 73, 107, 109, 117, 123, 168, 234
Herz, Peggy, 174–75
Heyges, Robert, 102
Hiken, Nat, 51
Hiller and Diller, 6, 143
Hill Street Blues, 102, 123, 124
Hirsch, Judd, 158, 160, 190
Hoffman, Dustin, 80, 231
Holiday Song (Chayefsky), 74, 221
Hollywood film industry. *See* Film industry
Hollywood's Image of the Jew (Friedman), 7
Holocaust, the, 34, 71, 74, 91, 208

Holocaust: The Story of the Family Weiss, The, 74
Horn, Alan, 205
Horton, Peter, 105
House Un-American Activities Committee (HUAC), 71–72, 222
Hughes, Langston, 25
Hunt, Helen, 154, 185, 195

I Love Lucy, 23, 26, 31, 50
Inside Prime Time (Gitlin), 8, 14
Intermarriage: on *Bridget Loves Bernie,* 78–79, 83–100; in films, 98; increase in rate of, 12, 99, 100, 244n.16, 254n.40; by Jewish characters, 11–12; Jewish men marrying non-Jewish women, 140–71; Jewish men transformed by shiksa goddesses, 12–13, 153–54; Jewish women marrying non-Jewish men, 172–200; and Jewish women's perceptions of themselves, 170; in *Northern Exposure,* 135; in *Relativity,* 135–36; in *thirtysomething,* 105, 116–17, 119, 123
I Spy, 51
It's a Wonderful Life (film), 117

Jacobson, Danny, 155, 156, 227
Jacobson, Peter, 190, 192
Jerry Lewis Show, The, 70
Jew in American Cinema, The (Erens), 7
Jewish characters: absence of clearly identified Jewish character, 1954–72, 7, 9, 47, 48–51, 62, 69, 71, 73–74, 218, 221, 223–24, 230, 235, 241; alleged CBS research on, 9, 58–61, 77, 174; crypto-Jews, 195; images seen as "too Jewish," 4–11, 16, 236; Jewish network control and, 6–8, 20, 49–50, 74, 80, 107–8, 205, 228, 230; leading characters starting to appear, 9–10, 230–37; no-

Jews rule lives on, 234–35; in popular culture of 1960s and 1970s, 80; quota on in 1960s, 74. *See also* Jewish female characters; Jewish male characters

Jewish Defense League (JDL), 146, 228

Jewish female characters: as absent by early 1990s, 140–41, 236; Dharma Finkelstein as only positive image of Jewish women on television, 197; grotesque bodies attributed to, 183–84; intermarriage by, 11, 12, 172–200; the Jewish-American Princess, 10, 26, 35, 36, 113, 183, 185, 188, 216, 255n.6; Jewish identity projected onto women in films, 191; Jewish mother stereotype, 24, 26, 31–32, 173, 177, 178, 188, 189–90, 193; Molly Goldberg, 20–32; negative characteristics in *The Nanny*, 170–71; Rosalie of *The Goldbergs*, 35–38; in *State of Grace*, 239; types of, 10, 26

Jewish identity: Baby Boomer Jewishness, 214–15; the body in, 35, 45, 174, 183–84, 189, 193; in *Brooklyn Bridge*, 165–66; decoding, 224–30; extended kinship marking, 92; food as defining, 31–32, 54, 75, 90, 147, 188–89, 215; in *The Goldbergs*, 45; Jewishness as both religion and ethnicity, 98, 122, 148, 190, 207, 210, 213; lack of athletic prowess associated with, 210, 214; loudness associated with, 86; *Mad About You* and, 155–56; in *The Marshall Chronicles*, 148–49; minor-key music signaling, 84, 91, 127, 159, 253n.19; *The Nanny* emphasizing, 172, 185; in *Northern Exposure*, 127–31; physical cowardice attributed to, 129; recovering in wake of parents' as-

similation, 138–39; *Rhoda* not emphasizing, 172, 179, 181; *Saturday Night Live* "Jew/Not-a-Jew game show," 2–3, 12, 225; in *Seinfeld*, 170–71, 206–9; social class marking, 88–89, 157–58, 186, 190–91; in *thirtysomething*, 9, 114, 121–23. *See also* Jewish characters

Jewish Journal, The, 214–16

Jewish male characters: Buddy Sorrell of *The Dick Van Dyke Show*, 54–57; in female authored series, 191–93; the feminized Jewish male, 32, 136, 143, 193; gentile women as superior to, 155; intermarriage by, 11–12, 98–99, 140–71; Jake of *The Goldbergs*, 39–42; *Menasha the Magnificent*, 35; the obnoxious Jew, 158–60; the pushy Jew, 120, 158; Sammy of *The Goldbergs*, 38–39; Steadman of *thirtysomething*, 123–24, 236; the Tough Jew, 102, 124; types of, 10; Uncle David of *The Goldbergs*, 5, 32–35, 192, 235; Uncle Stanley of *The Nanny*, 190, 194

Jewish Woman in America, The (Baum), 178

Jews: Big Three networks run by, 7, 68–69; de-ethnicization of, 30; in film industry, 8, 15, 30, 62–63, 67–68, 229; German versus Russian, 64–65, 76; the Holocaust, 34, 71, 74, 91, 208; Jewishness seen as pathological, 192; Jewish women's perceptions of themselves, 170; left-wing politics attributed to, 73, 221, 222; New York seen as synonymous with, 61, 133–34, 150, 215; responsibilities as a Jew, 137; seen as too powerful in the media, 8, 68–69, 73; shtetl Jews in humor of, 209; as suppliers of television programs, 8, 62; third generation American, 139; varieties of Ameri-

Jews (*continued*)
    can, 238. *See also* Anti-Semitism;
    Assimilation; Jewish characters;
    Jewish identity; Self-censorship
Julia, 51

Kaczmarek, Jane, 234
Kalcheim, Harry, 52, 53
Kaplan, Gabriel, 101
Katz, Oscar, 53
Kaufman, R. R., 28, 30
Kavner, Julie, *180,* 181
Kazan, Lainie, 234
Kelley, David E., 136, 138, 206
Kellner, Douglas, 230, 262n.17
Kennedy, Joseph, 52
King, Alan, 118, 158
King, Zalman, 76–77
Kirscher, Sarah, 170
Kohan, David, 199
Kudrow, Lisa, 196

Laemmle, Carl, 62
Lafferty, Perry, 82
L.A. Law, 32, 136, 143
Lanning, Nile, 146
Lardner, Ring, Jr., 72
Lateline, 1, 161–62
Lawford, Peter, 52
Lawson, Leigh, 194
Lear, Norman, 1, 70, 80, 81, 195
Leave It to Beaver, 48, 51
Leifer, Carol, 208, 227, 261
Leonard, Sheldon, 53, 227
Leoni, Tea, 151, *152*
Lerner, Michael, 118, 120–21, 122
Levinson, Barry, 223, 224, 253n.4
Lewis, Jenny, 163
Lewis, Jerry, 70
Lewis, Richard, 6, 141, *142,* 143
Liebman, Ron, 196
Linden, Hal, 101
Lipsitz, George, 247n.19

Loeb, Philip, 39, 41, 42–45, 69, 71,
    72, 222
Loews Corporation, 7, 107
Long, Rob, 160
Lord, Marjorie, 51
Lorre, Chuck, 197
Louis-Dreyfus, Julia, *203,* 206
Love and War, 140, 156–58, 159
Ludwin, Rick, 204–5, 206
Lumet, Sidney, 218–21, 237–38, 241
Lynn, Meredith Scott, 147

Mad About You, 154–56; gentile
    woman transforming Jewish man
    in, 12, 153; Jewish female charac-
    ters in, 185; Jewish identity not
    discussed on, 155–56; Jewish man/
    gentile woman pattern in, 140,
    141, 195; *Love and War* compared
    with, 158; message about Jewish
    women in, 38; "The Penis" epi-
    sode, 156
*Make Room for Daddy (The Danny Tho-
    mas Show),* 50–51
Male characters. *See* Jewish male
    characters
Mama, 19
Manoff, Dinah, *240*
Mantell, Michael, *240*
Manzano, Sonia, 224
Marc, David, 48–49, 50
Marjorie Morningstar (Wouk), 183, 223
Marsh, Tim, 35, 257n.10
Marshall, Penny, 2, 3
Marshall Chronicles, The, 146–50
Marty (Chayefsky), 255n.13
Mary Tyler Moore Show, The: and al-
    leged CBS research about Jews on
    television, 58–62; and *Bridget Loves
    Bernie,* 78, 83; "Christmas and the
    Hard Luck Kid" episode, 176–77;
    initial audience response to Rhoda,
    176; in "new look" CBS, 82; pilot
    episode of, 173–74; Rhoda Mor-

genstern, 35, 38, 113, 114, 141, 173–78; "Some of My Best Friends Are Rhoda" episode, 205–6; "Support Your Local Mother" episode, 177

M*A*S*H, 52, 72, 82, 95

Mason, Jackie, 144, *145*, 146, 150

Maude, 82, 96

Mayer, Louis B., 15, 62

Mayron, Melanie, 112

McCarthy era, 218, 221, 222

McDonald, Norm, 3, 4

McDormand, Frances, 239

McGraw, Ali, 147, 232

Meade, Kidder, 64, 66, 67

Me and Molly (Berg), 18, 27

Mehlman, Peter: on *Anything But Love*, 143–44; "The Hamptons" episode of *Seinfeld*, 202, 208; on Jewish vibe, 215; on *Seinfeld* as good for Jews, 201, 216–17; on *Seinfeld* as not easy on Jews, 202; on Seinfeld's Jewishness, 206–7; "The Yada Yada" episode of *Seinfeld*, 209, 214

Melting pot model, 99

Melvoin, Jeff, 127, 137–38, 139, 206

Men. *See* Jewish male characters

Menasha the Magnificent, 35, 154

Messing, Debra, 197, 199

Metz, Robert, 64

Meyer, Bess, 158

Michaels, Lorne, 4, 14, 227

Miniseries, 74

Mintz, Eli, 32

Mitchell, John H., 94, 95

Molly. See Goldbergs, The

Moore, Mary Tyler: in *The Dick Van Dyke Show*, 53. *See also Mary Tyler Moore Show, The*

Moore, Tom, 70

Morgan, Gary, 52

Morning Star Commission, 169–71, 239, 258n.25

Morrow, Rob, 104, 125, *126*, 134

Mostel, Zero, 45

Motion picture industry. *See* Film industry

Motion Picture Project, 29, 227

Mrs. G Goes to College (*The Gertrude Berg Show*), 74–75, 162, 194, 195, 252n.65

MTM, 176, 177

Murphy Brown, 32

Mutchnick, Max, 199

Myles, Sylvia, 52

Nanny, The, 185–95; bacon sandwich in the temple on, 190; on bodily characteristics of Jews, 189; "The Cantor" episode, 190; engagement ring episode, 189–90; female authorship of, 173, 191–92; food in, 188–89; Fran's healthy sexual appetite, 185; Fran's idea of work, 186, 188; Fran's twins, 185–86, 195; gentile male idolized in, 191; Jewish-American princess in, 35, 185, 188; Jewish identity emphasized in, 172, 185; Jewish woman wanting non-Jewish partner in, 10, 12, 173, 186, 192, 194–95, 237; as landmark series, 173; mother Sylvia, 188, 189–90; negative attributes of Jewish women depicted in, 170–71; social class in, 186, 190–91; as "too Jewish" and "too New York," 60, 77; Uncle Stanley character, 190, 194; "The Wedding" episode, 186, 189, 186, 190–91; *Will & Grace* compared with, 197

Nat "King" Cole Show, The, 51

NBC: *Bay City Blues*, 123; as founded by a Jew, 7, 49; *Friends*, 195; General Electric buys, 7, 107; and *The Goldbergs*, 17, 18–19, 43–44, 205; *L.A. Law*, 136; *Lateline*, 1, 161; *The Nat "King" Cole Show*, 51; *Saturday*

NBC (*continued*)
Night Live, 2, 3; *Seinfeld*, 201, 202, 204, 227; *Will & Grace*, 195
Necchi sewing machines, 44
Newhart, Bob, 82, 83, 158, 160
Newman, Phyllis, 219
New York: alleged CBS research on audience reaction to, 9, 58, 60, 61, 77, 227; Jews associated with, 61, 133–34, 150, 215; *The Marshall Chronicles* set in, 150; *Northern Exposure*'s Fleischman as New Yorker, 132–35; *100 Centre Street* set in, 219; Rhoda Morgenstern as "too New Yorky," 176; *Seinfeld* set in, 204, 216
Northern Exposure, 125–39; allowing the lead to be Jewish, 14, 104–5; assimilation narrative in, 9, 132, 135; *Brooklyn Bridge* compared with, 169; Fleischman as New Yorker, 132–35; Jewish identity explored in, 127–31; Jewishness emphasized in, 125; "Joel Misses New York" episode, 132; "Kaddish for Uncle Manny" episode, 127–31; *Love and War* compared with, 158; *thirtysomething* opening door for, 104; "Yom Kippur" episode, 125, 127, 132

O'Connor, Carroll, 80
O'Connor, John, 83
Olin, Ken, 104, 105, *106*, 108, 109, 123–24, 235
100 Centre Street, 10–11, 218–19, 220, 237–38
Oxenberg, Jan, 135, 136, 234–35

Pace, Judy, 76
Paley, Barbara (Babe) Cushing, 65, 66
Paley, Sam, 64, 65
Paley, William: and *All in the Family*, 81, 82; ambivalence about his Jewish identity, 49, 62, 63–67, 70, 73; and *Amos 'n' Andy*, 18; and the blacklist, 45, 69–70, 71; and *Bridget Loves Bernie*, 95, 100; controlling his image, 66, 251n.25; *Fiddler on the Roof* turned down by, 19, 64, 66, 206; as founder of CBS, 6, 7; as gatekeeper, 6, 50; and *The Goldbergs*, 19, 20; Loews Corporation buys CBS, 7, 107; as not wanting Jewish characters on CBS, 60–61; power of, 48, 61–71; Wood fronting for, 95, 254n.32
Paper, Lewis J., 61–62, 251n.25
Paper Chase, 233
Paper Chase: The Second Year, 233–34
Parker, Corey, 140, *152*
Pawnbroker, The (film), 219, 220
Pearl, 252n.65
Pearl, Jonathan M., 252n.63
Pearl, Judith, 252n.63
Peerce, Larry, 148
Pepsodent toothpaste, 18
Perlman, Rhea, 252n.65
Philco Television Playhouse, 74, 221
Picket Fences, 136–38, 206
Pickles, Christina, 196
Poltrack, David, 60, 77
Portnoy's Complaint (Roth), 149, 173, 231
Powers That Be, The (Halberstam), 67
Prell, Riv-Ellen, 183–84, 216
Prime-Time Families (Taylor), 12
Princesses, 194
Production. *See* Television production

Rankin, John, 71
RCA (Radio Corporation of America), 43–44
Red Channels (book), 42, 43, 72
Redgrave, Lynn, 144, *145*
Reiner, Carl, 51–54, 69, 114, 227, 250n.14
Reiner, Rob, 52, 81, 204
Reinhold, Judge, 208
Reiser, Paul, 140, 154, 155, 156, 199